The C...
Book of
Healing

The Complete Book of

Healing

A spiritual guide to healing
yourself and others

Tara Ward

This edition published in 2017 by Arcturus Publishing Limited
26/27 Bickels Yard, 151–153 Bermondsey Street,
London SE1 3HA

AD000242UK

Printed in the UK

CONTENTS

INTRODUCTION

What does the word 'healing' mean to you? Many people view healing as a purely physical experience. For instance, if you have a cold, the symptoms of sore throat, runny nose and cough will eventually work their way through your system and you will eventually end up 'healed'. You feel secure in the knowledge that all these physical actions add up to the way illness and healing works. Major diseases such as cancer or heart disease could be viewed in much the same way, although they may also require certain orthodox medical treatment to assist the healing process. Even so, they remain just physical problems that require physical solutions to sort them out. In this context, healing itself is seen fundamentally as a physical act.

And what of mental and emotional problems? Whilst we cannot actually 'see' them, we know they are real experiences. For instance, few would deny that the depression or stress which can be triggered by the loss of a loved one, a divorce or the break-up of a relationship is a real emotion. We do not deny its existence simply because we can not see it. Such an emotion can also seem to have a physical dimension. People often describe sadness as an empty well inside the stomach, or unrequited love as a sharp pain in the heart area. Mental confusion can appear as a headache or a feeling of the brain about to explode. The fact we can not see this taking place inside our body does not stop us experiencing the sensation. Again, we can treat these problems physically by using time as a healer or by taking medication, reinforcing the notion of healing as a physical process.

In many other instances, however, physical healing techniques are not effective. Cancer and heart disease are not always cured by medication and treatment; an emotionally distressed person taking anti-depressant drugs will not always end up cured of his problems; time does not always make the break-up of a relationship or the loss of a loved one more bearable.

Yet in recent years, we have taken giant leaps forward. Never before have so many medications and treatments been available to so many people. We now know so much more about the human body and can manipulate it in incredibly complex ways with far-reaching consequences. Our living conditions are constantly becoming more hygienic and sanitised. In these areas of life we have undoubtedly progressed.

Then why are so many diseases on the increase, especially in Western societies? Where have AIDS and an ever-increasing number of antibiotic-resistant infections sprung from? Why is mental illness affecting more people every year? Why are particular forms of cancer killing more people than ever before?

Given these unwelcome developments, we have to acknowledge that orthodox medicine is not always coping as effectively as we would like. So, in the cases where orthodox medical treatment fails to provide the answer, where else can we turn?

We can go back into the past to see how healing has worked for thousands of years, long before pharmaceutical companies came into being and subsequently became so powerful and numerous. Thousands of years ago people relied on what is called 'spiritual healing'. The best way to realise that spiritual healing is a vital, invaluable life force is to understand the effect it has had on people through the ages.

Let's take a brief look at the origins of spiritual healing, its effect on people and how it is regarded today.

The first healers
We can find proof of spiritual healing going back 15,000 years to the cavemen. Caves in central and western France show a remarkable array of painted hands, depicting healing images. Shamanic traditions, which are as old as mankind, acknowledged all of the individual: the physical, mental, emotional and spiritual. Their concept of health was based on people being in harmony with their surroundings, accepting the influence of what we would call 'nature' in man's make-up. In other words, it was believed that a person's well-being was affected by a range of factors involving the world beyond – from the sun and moon to the weather and geographical

location. Yet in the 20th century in the West we have 'discovered' – and been surprised by – Seasonal Affective Disorder or SAD syndrome (illness from lack of sunlight), that the female menstrual cycle is influenced by the moon and tides and that living squashed together in massive concrete high-rises is actually creating a hostile society. Why are we having to relearn truths that were intuitively understood by our 'primitive' ancestors?

In Indian and Chinese cultures spiritual healing has been practised for over 5000 years and knowledge of it continues to be handed down to each new generation. Whilst their techniques might be different, both cultures are at one in their appreciation of the ways in which healing enhances everyday life. Even today, they do not question the relevance of healing. They know it works.

The Indians draw on the yogic tradition for their concept of the individual. According to this, each of us has two basic systems of internal and external functions (roughly, the physical is seen as the external system, and the emotional and mental are grouped together as the internal system). Spiritual healing is what draws the two systems together and creates perfect health. Each person is viewed as being made of disparate forms of energy which have to be pulled together and harmonised. Life is a journey towards completeness.

The Chinese see health as uninterrupted energy flowing freely through the body via numerous meridians or currents. They use acupuncture (needles painlessly inserted into specific areas of the body) to release blockages and aid health. Conversely, by placing needles in other areas, they can actually stop the flow of energy and thus anaesthetise the body for an operation without resorting to conventional means. Their general philosophy is that man is part of nature and that everything within the universe is also found within man, including negative and positive energy flows.

In order to understand how these concepts worked in practice, we need look no further than Greek philosophy, which contains fascinating references to spiritual healing. One of the most illuminating is from no less a person than the father of modern medicine, Hippocrates. Here is a rough translation from a passage he wrote around the 5th century BC:

'It is believed by experienced doctors that the heat which
oozes out of the hand, on being applied to the sick, is highly
salutary . . . It has often appeared, while I have been soothing
my patients, as if there was a singular property in my hands
to pull and draw away from the affected parts aches and
diverse impurities, by laying my hand upon the place, and by
extending my fingers towards it. Thus it is known to some of
the learned that health may be implanted in the sick by
certain gestures, and by contact, as some diseases may be
communicated from one to another.'

The phenomenon which Hippocrates was describing was already
widely accepted by his fellow Greeks, and had been for many
years. Five hundred years earlier the Greek healer Aesculepius
had been well respected for the work he did during his lifetime.
Later, the increasing shift towards a scientific approach to medicine
would bring warnings of the perils of moving too far from the old
ways. Plato would chastise physicians for being too materialistic
and for dealing with the body as though it were separate from the
soul. For Plato, such an approach was a great error.

There are also plenty of indications in Egyptian history that
spiritual healing was accepted and widely used to promote health.
In fact, the earliest documented healer is an Egyptian physician,
Imhotep (2980–2900BC), who lived in Memphis. He was a healer
to King Zoser and was also known as a sage, astrologer and architect.
His skill was such that within a hundred years of his death he had
become revered as a kind of demigod. By 525BC his status had
risen to that of a full deity and a temple in his name became
crowded with the sick who slept and prayed there as part of their
healing process.

The best known spiritual healer in Western society is, of
course, Jesus. His healing abilities are documented in numerous
religious texts. No one was excluded from his healing: lepers,
cripples, he gave to all who asked, whether by laying on of
hands, anointing with his saliva or just using the power of his
mind to heal. Whatever form your religious belief takes, his
example remains a powerful advertisement for spiritual healing.

So what happened to push this once widely accepted and used form of healing to the fringes? Firstly, it must be acknowledged that this decline is largely a Western phenomenon. The majority of cultures elsewhere in the world continue to use spiritual healing as a normal part of everyday life. Here in the West a number of influences slowly crept in which shifted the balance of spiritual healing.

The early Church fathers initially spread the power of healing. However, the more laymen practised this art, the more the Church felt its power slipping away. Over the years, this precipitated a swift back-pedalling of attitude, such that by the Middle Ages spiritual healing was virtually regarded as a form of witchcraft and its practise was covert and considered dangerous.

To redress the balance of power, various kings were deemed to have the 'royal touch': a euphemism for healing powers. Subjects would line up for a single touch from their king which would pronounce them free from illness. Statistics do not reveal the efficacy of the 'royal touch', perhaps indicating that royal status does not automatically guarantee healing abilities.

It is only relatively recently, as people have become increasingly aware of escalating illness and human dissatisfaction, that the recognition of a need for spiritual well-being has resurfaced in Western society. It is ironic that it has taken deep unrest and unhappiness to bring about this change.

Far from being a New Age gimmick with no basis in reality, spiritual healing has been well documented over thousands of years. If we suspect the objectivity or truthfulness of our ancestors, then we can examine the first-hand accounts of the effects of many powerful modern-day healers. Of course, there are also a few charlatans who call themselves healers, just as there are rogue doctors in the world of orthodox medicine. Charlatanism exists in every corner of life. We need to be vigilant. However, we can look with confidence at the endeavours of many modern-day spiritual healers. If you are interested in reading about them and their work, look for the following names in your library or local bookshop: Harry Edwards, Maurice Tester, Godfrey Mowatt, Matthew Manning, Betty Shine, Edgar Cayce, Barbara Ann Brennan, Deepak Chopra, Echo Bodine, Ethel Lombardi, Rita Benor.

What it means to be a healer

The next question must logically be, what does it take to become a spiritual healer? Some may see the ability to heal spiritually as the domain of a chosen few. It is regarded as something that 'other people' do. You might admire or revere it in others but firmly believe you do not have the ability to do it yourself. You might even be uncertain as to what it really involves, but whatever it is, you will be certain you cannot do it! Some of you may have your doubts but still be curious as to how you might be able to help yourself and others. A few of you may have an in-built sense that you want to try it because it feels right in some vague, intangible way.

Whatever stage you are at personally, this book is to show you that everyone can heal. Everyone. It is not some special gift that only a chosen few are born with. It is true that some people find learning the healing process easier than others, but that does not necessarily make them the most effective. Some people learn to drive a car quite effortlessly. It does not necessarily follow that they make the best drivers. Someone who has worked hard and really put their heart and soul into learning to drive safely and efficiently may end up being the better driver.

Whilst spiritual healing works on many levels and can become extremely complex and demanding, it can also be very effective on a basic level. Learning how to work with the basics of healing does not have to be a long, arduous process. Unlike the orthodox medical profession who need to train for four years or more to become a doctor or dentist, simple spiritual healing can be taught relatively easily. In fact, you will already have experienced some form of spiritual healing yourself and will also have healed yourself and other people at some level.

Let's look at when this might have been. Can you ever remember as a child falling over and hurting yourself and then running to someone for comfort? Can you remember being hugged or the hurt area gently being touched and kissed? Do you have a memory of waking up in the middle of the night when you were little after having a bad dream and either having someone come in to soothe you or crawling in to their bed for some warmth? Perhaps you may have been at the giving end of this exchange as well. Have you ever felt deeply distressed and reached out to an animal for comfort, burrowing your face in its warm fur? (Animals can be a powerful source of healing through the special, unconditional love they give out; this will be discussed in detail later.)

As an adult, have you gone to see a friend to discuss a troubling situation and left their company feeling calmer and much relieved? After a rough day at work have you found that an understanding smile from someone you love can release that tight knot in your stomach or ease a headache? Conversely, are there people you avoid when you feel stressed because you know they will make you feel worse? Do you have certain rituals that you follow if you need to make yourself feel better? It might be a walk along a beach or a stroll through some woods. You might read a book or watch a comedy programme which makes you laugh. An increasing number of people are turning to various forms of meditation. There is also meditation that can be coupled to a physical activity such as tai chi or yoga.

If you have experienced any of the above, you already know what spiritual healing feels like. Of course, these are the most basic examples. Healing works on so many other, deeper levels as well but it can help to know that simple healing is a starting point from which you can expand.

You should also know at this point that expanding your horizons to encompass deeper levels of spiritual healing has limitless possibilities. Many believe the power of spiritual healing has no boundaries. Boundaries only come when a person's mind puts up barriers. In this book, you are going to work at constantly knocking down some of the barriers which you will have unconsciously created over the years. Let's look at why some of these barriers have appeared.

First, many people have trouble defining the word 'healing'. A simple explanation would be to describe it as feeling better. Yet there are levels of 'feeling better'. Imagine you have contracted a nasty flu virus. For several days you feel dreadful and then one morning you wake up feeling less achy, less congested. You feel better, so have you been healed? But you still feel slightly fuzzy-headed and sluggish. A week later, your head has cleared and your body feels as though it belongs to you again. You decide you are healed. However, you might notice you are less effective at work than usual for the next week or so. Perhaps your appetite has not fully returned. You may feel more tired than usual at the end of each day and need more sleep. Perhaps you feel more emotional or irritated than usual. So at which point are you fully healed? You may not even be aware of it yourself. Also, healing can be relative to someone else's experience. If you have had flu for a week and are slowly recovering when a friend then comes down with it, your friend will view your condition as perfectly healthy. Someone who has never caught a flu virus would consider your state as being very unwell.

It is important to acknowledge these different stages of healing because they reveal how we view our own health. How healthy do you think you personally are? What do you call 'being healthy'? Some people spend their entire lives never knowing true health simply because they have never experienced complete health since no one has taught them what it actually means and how to achieve it. As you read through the upcoming chapters, particularly those in Part One, you will have the opportunity to discover for yourself just how healthy all of you really is: physically, emotionally, mentally and spiritually!

Why do we all have such differing views on what health really means? A large part of the answer to that question lies in upbringing and the way we were taught to view health. Let's do a small experiment.

When you were a child and developed a cold, what was your reaction to this and how did others around you deal with the situation? Consider some of the following options:

A   You ignored it and hoped it would go away.
B   You were tearful and clingy, feeling upset if no one paid you attention.
C   You were tucked up in bed and told not to move.
D   You were told not to be so silly and to go to school.
E   You were whisked off to the doctor.
F   You were given some medication and told you would be better the next day.
G   You were cuddled and kissed and made to feel special.
H   You were given a smack and told to pull yourself together.

I   You have no memory of having a cold.
J   You have very little memory of any of your childhood.

Possibly you experienced some of the above, depending on how you and those around you felt at the time. Maybe you feel very differently now and have come to understand what getting a cold meant to you at the time. (Yes! We can actually make ourselves ill on occasions because we know it will create a particular result. This is explained in detail later.) How you were handled and how you reacted to being ill as a child will reflect how you feel about healing now and how the actual process of being healed affects you.

For instance, if you react consistently as per A, you are quite likely to be the sort of person who keeps your emotions to yourself. You hate to admit weakness and vulnerability and would much rather suffer in silence. Your stoical qualities may be appreciated by many, but they also indicate a tendency not to let people get close to you. This is not wrong or bad, it simply means there are certain areas in your life which could benefit from healing.

If you respond frequently as per E, you may have a tendency to rely heavily on orthodox medicine. You will go to your doctor frequently and believe he has all the answers. You probably keep a store of headache tablets, cough syrups and other medicines in your cabinet. You believe that being unwell at times is quite a normal part of life and that everyone goes through stages of regular illness. Again, you are not wrong to think this way, but you might benefit from considering other possibilities.

So you can see that our upbringing can distort our view of spiritual healing. What else may have affected us?

We often have difficulty understanding something when we cannot physically see it. We have agreed we can accept that humans fall prey to physical, mental and emotional difficulties in life, so it is not difficult to acknowledge these as separate parts of our make-up. However, some people regard the concept of a spiritual part of us as a strange no-man's-land of the unseen and unknown. What we cannot see and do not understand tends to frighten us. Ignorance breeds fear.

You have to take one step beyond that fear and start learning. As you come to grasp the significance of your spiritual nature, it ceases to be a strange phenomenon. In fact, the more you understand, the more you start to have that rather odd feeling of 'déjà vu' (when you feel you have experienced something before without knowing why). This is perfectly natural, because all you are doing with spiritual work is rediscovering what is already deep inside you. It is part of you, even now as you are reading this; you simply have to acquire the tools which will allow you to delve into it.

You may already know that humans use very little of their physical brain – some doctors believe as little as 15 per cent. No one fully understands what the remainder of the brain does. We know we need it but not what we can do with it! It may help you to think of spiritual enlightenment as using a little bit more of your brain.

You will no doubt agree that there are instances in our lives when we need healing (whether it be physical, emotional and/ or mental) and nothing orthodox, medical or commonplace seems to help. If you have not experienced this yourself, try to recall someone else you know who has. It can be deeply frustrating to go through a series of orthodox medical treatments and find none of them works. Eventually, after exhausting all avenues, you give up and resign yourself to being stuck with whatever difficulty has arisen. You might be convinced that you were born a certain way and cannot change it.

For those of you who may still be struggling to believe in the spiritual, try using the following stepping stone to help you bridge the gap between your physical/mental/emotional spheres and your spiritual nature. Consider this possibility. There is indeed something else you can try but no one has told you about it before now. This unknown dimension, called spiritual healing, might just help you. This is your stepping stone. To help you embrace the spiritual you can regard this dimension as basically no more than another kind of doctor.

True, you cannot see this doctor or have verbal conversations with him or her across a surgery or hospital bed. The spiritual doctor will not give you tablets or potions to cure you. But you will get something tangible from this doctor. You know the warm, glowing feeling that can come over you when someone gives you a loving smile? You cannot physically feel the smile and no exchange of medication has taken place, has it? Yet you know something has happened to you. Some exchange of something has made you feel better. Well, that is what spiritual healing is. That sensation that initially you cannot quite explain, that suddenly makes you feel a bit better. Although you may feel nothing physical happens in that moment of a smile being exchanged, it is in fact a physical experience because energies are being exchanged in a very subtle way. These energies relate to the energy currents which the Chinese have worked with in acupuncture for thousands of years. They will be discussed in great detail in this book to enable you to understand that energy is not just about the physical energy which we see and use, it is also about how we interact with everything around us. How we interact determines how healthy we may be.

So, acknowledging the spiritual side of yourself can be likened to registering with a new doctor! The wonderful benefits of this are that your spiritual doctor is completely free of charge and can be called upon at any time, 24 hours a day, forever. It is a constant source of love and healing. It has infinite possibilities. Let's do a quick visualization game to see if you can expand your thoughts on this concept of perfect healing.

The spiritual surgery

Read through the exercise below first and when you feel reasonably familiar with its contents, find a quiet spot where no one will disturb you for a few minutes. Close or lock a door if necessary. Close your eyes and take a few comfortable, deep breaths. When you feel nicely relaxed, slowly work your way through the exercise.

Close your eyes. Imagine a clean, white door in front of you which is closed. You can see it leads into a building but you don't know what is inside. Go up to the white handle, open the door and walk inside.

Inside is an enormous bright, white room which is scrupulously clean. All around you are rows and rows of shelves, filled with medications of every imaginable size, shape and form: bottles of pills, capsules, liquids, salves, bandages. Everything looks brand new, shiny and bright as if it is has only just been placed there. Notice there are endless cabinets everywhere with labels on detailing items with names you do not recognize.

When you look up, there does not seem to be a ceiling on the room – the walls seem to extend upwards into infinity. Look in front of you and realise you are in a room that goes on forever. It stretches into infinity, filled with unimaginable potions and medications that stretch further than you can see.

As you stand in the midst of this wondrous place, you realize all these medications belong to your spiritual doctor, who will dispense them for you at any time, as you need them. The possibilities for healing in this sanctuary are endless, just as the walls and ceiling and medicines are endless. Everything you will ever need to heal anything can be found in this amazing, limitless building. Take a moment to consider the immeasurably powerful healing which can take place with all these tools at your disposal.

When you feel you have seen all you want to see, make your way back to that bright, white door. If you have wandered quite far into the surgery, it does not matter, because at all times the door is lit up, bright and white. You can see it no matter where you are. Go back to the door, open it and walk out of the surgery.

Now take a minute to remember where you are, whether at home or in an office and which room you are in. Remember you are reading a book. Take a few deep, comfortable breaths and then when you feel ready, open your eyes.

How did that feel? If you are naturally a visual person, you may have found it easy to see everything around you. Otherwise, you may have just had a sensation of space and possibility, or have had a few thoughts about what is available rather than seeing it. You may even have smelt the medication rather than seen it! It doesn't matter what experience you had, because all visualizations and meditations are deeply personal and applicable only to you. You need never compare what other people have seen and felt, because they will have been following their own personal progress, which may not coincide with yours.

It is a fact that people naturally fall into different categories of awareness. Some people are visual and always find it easy to picture things in their mind's eye. Others like to listen and prefer to use their awareness through hearing what is said. Yet others sense and feel what is present rather than seeing or hearing. Through the exercises in this book, you will discover the way you automatically respond. Everyone is individual and should work with what is right for them. If you have trouble seeing anything during exercises, do not struggle with it. Instead, just enjoy either the things you may hear or what you may feel.

Don't worry if your spiritual surgery was small and you couldn't see it expanding; it really isn't important at this stage. You are only starting your voyage of discovery into spiritual healing. Some pieces of information will strike you as more important and helpful than others, and you may have breakthroughs and insights at some times and not others.

This mirrors the healing process. Two people can have identical problems and yet each will heal at a very different rate. The method of healing used can also vary. One particular healing technique may work wonders on one person but leave another completely unchanged. This is an important aspect of spiritual healing: the ability to recognize each person as a unique individual and treat their needs accordingly. It takes great sensitivity coupled with unconditional love to be effective.

It is also important to acknowledge at this early stage that although we may have these somewhat separate levels of physical, emotional, mental and spiritual health, they are all inter-connected. In other words, humans are made up of all four of these elements, which exist in a particular and very important relationship to one another. They are inter-dependent and to achieve whole health, or holistic health, we need to become aware of all four areas and work with each, separately and as a whole, to make them function fully. Only by working with all of us can we heal each and every part of us.

One final, very important word before we start looking specifically at healing and how it works.

Nothing contained in this book implies that you should ignore orthodox medical care. If you are taking a particular form of medication, for example, under no circumstances should you discontinue it without prior consultation with your doctor. Spiritual healing can work effectively and harmoniously in conjunction with orthodox medicine.

It is unlikely that any form of spiritual healing recommended in these pages could be construed as harmful by your doctor. By all means, discuss it with him or her. At worst, what you say may be dismissed or treated with scepticism; at best, you may receive encouragement and support.

At this stage in your development, you should regard spiritual healing as a complementary addition to your life, not a concept which should take over and replace orthodox healing methods. Remember your body has probably spent most of its life being dealt with in a conventional fashion. Any changes should be gradual and take place with the support of your own doctor. Fortunately, a large, constantly increasing number of conventional, medical practices are leaning towards spiritual concepts and embracing alternative methods of healing. It is an exciting prospect that as our medical knowledge rapidly expands, people's spiritual needs are also being addressed.

PART ONE:

HEALING YOURSELF

Now you are gaining an understanding that spiritual healing can be a kind of new doctor for you, you are probably wondering how this can ever work. This form of healing will not be conventional in the sense that there will be no consultations, no physical treatment as such. So what will you be working with and how can it possibly be effective?

You have to start thinking of human beings in a slightly different way. This does not mean that you should ignore what you already know. You can still acknowledge everything you understand about the human body and how it works physically, about how we react emotionally and mentally. All of that is still important for health. Next we are going to add a little more to create the full picture

HEALING AS ENERGY

Every human being is a ball of energy. This energy is not just the physical kind we use to get through each day. It's more than that. Apart from having our own energy, we are also giving out and receiving different types of energy all the time. Some energies are helpful and encouraging; others can make us unwell.

The simplest way to understand human energy is to compare it to an experience you have already had. Earlier we touched on the effect that someone giving you a loving smile can have. That is an exchange of energy. There is also the less enjoyable experience of being in someone's company for a while and ending up feeling exhausted and drained. Some people can leave us feeling as though we have just done ten rounds in the boxing ring. Physically, as well as emotionally and mentally, you feel wiped out. Most people have experienced this at some time. You may even be able to immediately identify one particular person who has this effect on you every time you see them. Do you have a slight feeling of dread when you know a meeting with them is coming up? It does not mean you do not like them or appreciate their good qualities on other levels, but you might wish they were less tiring personalities.

An exchange of energy is also taking place in this instance. This person is actually tapping into your energy field and drawing your energy into themselves. In other words, you are being used as a recharging unit for their batteries! The more sensitive and naturally giving you are as a person, the more difficult it will be for you not to let this happen, unless you take steps to prevent it. Later in the book exercises are provided to show you how to protect yourself in these circumstances. It does not mean you have to withdraw your friendship, it just means you handle your own energy slightly differently and refuse to give quite so much of it away.

As humans we do not just react with other humans, we also exchange energies with animals, plants and endless other forms of energy and life. Take, for example, an occasion when you may have been working extremely hard and realised that you must have a break. What do humans often choose to do? To go away somewhere by the sea or other stretch of water, to lie in the sun, to take walks in the woods or enjoy some beautiful change of scenery, whether it be mountainous or flat. We often use the expression 'I need to recharge my batteries'. All you mean is that your own energy field is depleted and you need to take in some more energy.

Different places have extraordinarily different atmospheres and energies, and individuals respond better to certain areas than others. Some people find a wild, raging sea invigorating and energising, while others find it frightening and simply shut down. Some people love to climb mountains; others find them unfriendly and threatening. You might choose a gentle stroll by a still lake; your friend might want to stand under a gushing waterfall! The reason we all like different things is because we are unconsciously responding to what we know we need. Just as humans have different energies so do different geographical locations and physical features have different energies too. A basic study of feng shui, the art of living harmoniously within a given area, shows how these energies can be used to our advantage. So, if you can accept that something is happening on different levels with these forms of energy and that spiritual healing is connected to these activities, the next step is to gain an understanding of human energy and how it works.

Human energy is often called the human aura. To easily distinguish human energy from other forms during this book, we will call the human energy field the 'aura'. The most helpful way to start your new relationship with the aura would be to see it. This is not as daunting as it sounds. However, some people find it easier than others. The people who can see auras are not necessarily smarter or more talented than the people who can not, nor does it mean they have the ability to work well with auras or that they will make good spiritual healers. All it means is that they see auras.

Looking at the human aura
Try the experiment below one day when you are with a willing friend or relative who does not mind sitting still for a few minutes.

Make sure you choose someone with whom you feel comfortable and who is receptive to the possibility of the aura. It will help you if they encourage and respect your attempts, rather than ridiculing you. Like all new experiences, this exercise may feel strange initially.

Ask your friend to sit in front of a plain background, preferably a very dark or very light colour. Now shine a reasonably bright light at them but have the rest of the room dark. Ask them to relax; let them close their eyes if they prefer. Now sit comfortably yourself, at least 6 feet away from them, and take a few deep breaths. There is no contest here for you to do well and it doesn't matter if you see nothing.

When you feel comfortable, start gazing at the top of your friend's head. You don't need to stare intently because the more relaxed you are, the more likely you are to see something. It might help if you imagine that you are looking at a 3D picture. If you soften your focus and relax your eyes, it becomes easier to see. Don't worry if you see nothing.

After a few minutes, you may notice a hazy sort of glow around your friend's head, which may look like the top of a candle flame. This glow is usually very fuzzy and radiates outwards, gradually fading into the background. Sometimes the aura seems to shimmer and pulsate. Alternatively you may see it as a solid colour, perhaps a golden yellow or white. You might might even see different colours.

If you do see something, continue to breathe comfortably and keep studying what you see. How far out does it extend from the head? Is it brighter in some parts and more intense? Is there an even glow around the head or are there gaps? Do your friend's shoulders give off any sort of glow? Study it for as long as you like. If it suddenly disappears, that is fine too.

When you feel ready, close your eyes and let the image disappear. Wait a few minutes before you get up and turn

*on other lights, then share with your friend what you
experienced. Ask them if they would like to try to see your
aura and offer to sit in the light. Don't worry if their experience
is completely different from yours. There are no set rules.*

You might find this exercise quite exciting or it might leave you
feeling deflated. Whatever you see, it is right for you. There are
many healers who never actually see auras in any shape or colour.
They work entirely on instinctual feelings and with what they sense,
rather than with what they see. You may see nothing for a long time
and then suddenly, when you no longer care about seeing auras
(because you are already working with them anyway), you may
suddenly start seeing them all the time! It can then get to the stage
when you wish they would go away for a while because it becomes
off-putting seeing colours and shapes around people all the time.
It simply does not matter how you work with the aura as long as
you can acknowledge its existence in the first place.

If you do not feel comfortable asking a person to help you with
this exercise, you can always substitute a plant or a patient animal.
All living forms have energy fields. It would be interesting for you to
compare plants, animals and human auras when you have the time,
particularly if you are someone who sees auras with very little effort.

Feeling a human aura

It would also help you to try the experiment below. Again, you
can use a plant or animal instead if you do not feel happy about
asking a friend to help you.

*Ask your friend to stand in the middle of a room. The lighting
does not matter for this exercise. What is important is that
your friend keeps their eyes open, so they do not end up feeling
dizzy or off-balance. Explain that you want to feel the space
around them but you won't touch them. Ask them to let you
know immediately if they feel uncomfortable or if they want
you to move further away. Keep asking them how they feel
during this exercise and be sensitive to their response.*

Now you're going to try to feel their aura. Start by standing several feet away from them. Now hold your arms out in front of you and see if you can feel around their energy field. Don't get too close to begin with. The more sensitive you are, the further away you will be able to feel their energy. If you get too close, they may feel threatened or nervous. Avoid letting your hands linger over their heart area or the top of their head. These are especially sensitive areas, as you will discover later.

Slowly, move your hands closer in to their body. At what point do you feel something? What does it feel like? Keep concentrating and, as you slowly move around their body, notice where the sensations change. Are there areas which feel warmer or colder than others? Are there areas you feel you should move away from? Notice if you have any sudden sensations or emotions which you weren't expecting. Don't forget to feel the area around their legs and feet too, and notice if that feels different.

When you feel you have thoroughly explored around their aura, move well away from them and let them know you have finished. Thank them for being willing to help with your experiment. Again, offer them the opportunity to feel your aura if they wish.

It can be very useful to reverse the process, because it is only when you experience someone else approaching your aura that you realise how unnerving it can be. Even if you know someone well, there is an awkward moment when you wish they would not stand quite so close. Notice when you start to feel encroached upon and how far back they need to stand for you to feel safe. Remember that when you subsequently feel someone else's aura.

Hand energies
If both the above exercises still seem too daunting to try, but you really want to experience the human aura, here is a simple exercise to enable you to check your own energy. You can do this quite quickly and easily on your own.

Start off with your hands held out a little in front of you, about 18 inches apart, palms facing each other. Cup your fingers very slightly. Now slowly move your hands in towards each other, palm to palm. The more slowly you do this, the more opportunity you give yourself to feel the energies properly.

As soon as you feel something, stop. What does it feel like? A slight pressure? A little tingle? A sort of buzzy sensation? Move your hands slowly apart again. When does the sensation stop? Move them together again. Feel the sensation grow stronger still.

Now pat that energy into a big ball. Try to condense it even more. Depending on your sensitivity, you might feel a strong repelling sensation at this point, as if your hands can't move further together. When you have 'played' for long enough, move your hands further apart again and feel the energy disperse. Give your hands and arms a good shake when you finish.

That was you feeling your own hand energies. Hands have a lot of energy coming from them. They are an extremely active part of the body and both receive and give out a great deal of energy during each day. In this exercise you tapped into a small amount of their potency. They represent a tiny percentage of your whole aura, with which you will start to develop a much stronger relationship.

Your relationship with your own aura will become an extremely personal, private experience which you do not have to share unless you feel it is appropriate to do so. Working with spiritual energy is a very delicate exercise. You are tapping into parts of you that require sensitivity and gentleness. You may feel vulnerable at such times. That is fine. If you do, work by yourself initially and make sure you are not interrupted. Through working with yourself initially, you can gain the necessary sensitivity and understanding which will enable you to work better when healing others.

Working with auras is how you will effect spiritual healing. The aura is your blueprint, if you like, with which you will work to move and/or unblock energies to create holistic health. Do not worry if this idea seems odd. You may need to understand more about the aura before you can accept how important it is.

The aura explained

At this stage you should begin to believe the human aura exists. Whether you saw it or felt it or simply sensed it was there, you are ready to acknowledge that it exists. But what exactly is the human aura? If it is indeed a blueprint for spiritual healing, what does it contain? The amazing answer is that it contains all of you. This is why the aura is so powerful, so sensitive, and needs to be treated with the utmost respect and consideration. It is all of you in energy form. Let us delve further into that statement.

The aura is not in fact just that one fuzzy glow you might have been able to see around your friend's head. The aura actually consists of seven different layers that expand outwards from the body. Each layer contains its own catalogue of information about you, with each layer becoming finer and lighter in vibration. The finer the layer, the more difficult it is to see. However, the fact you cannot see the outer layers does not mean they do not exist.

The analogy of an electric fan is a useful illustration of this point. Picture the wings of the fan when the machine is turned to a low setting. You can see the wings as they revolve slowly. If you turn the setting to medium speed the wings move faster and start to become blurred. You know they are still there but they are not as easy to see. Now envisage the setting turned to 'high' – the wings move so quickly they are invisible to the eye. Again, you know the wings are there, but the speed of their movement prohibits a clear sight of them. The levels of the human aura work in this way. The finer the layer of the aura, the faster its vibrational frequency and the more difficult it is to see it. You can tune your eyes to gradually see the finer layers of the aura. It takes practice and time, however, and you may decide it is not necessary for you to see them in order to work with them.

The aura is often called the 'subtle body', which seems rather appropriate. It is not as noticeable as your physical body to most human eyes, but it is there. Now let us look at what each layer contains as far as information is concerned. If you turn to the picture on page 33, this may help.

Layers of the aura

The first layer is the layer nearest the body. It is the densest and therefore the easiest to see. If you saw anything in the human aura exercise, it probably related to the first layer. This first layer is known as the physical blueprint of our life. What that means is that it relates to our physical body and how we react to practical, earthly matters. So, if you love physical exercise and live very much on a practical, day-to-day basis, this layer of your aura will be strong.

The second layer is called our emotional blueprint. This is where we store how we feel about things emotionally, especially in relation to our self. So it is not so much about how we deal with others. It is to do with self-love and self-expression and how happy we feel with our own company. It would show whether we bottle up our emotions or release them freely.

The third layer is the mental blueprint. This concerns how agile we are in our minds and how rationally we think. Philosophers and writers often have strong third layers as they spend a great deal of time thinking through equations or ideas. Do you often have negative thoughts about yourself and other people? These negative images would show up as energy blocks within your third layer.

The fourth layer is about love. It means how you love yourself and others around you. It is about relationships at all levels and how you deal with them: family, friends, colleagues. Even animals and your feelings for inanimate objects are contained here. Your ability to both give out and receive love will be shown within this layer. As love is a complex issue for most of us, this layer is where the vibrations start to change and become finer, lighter and brighter. It also becomes more difficult to define using human language.

The fifth layer is called your blueprint for divine will. This does not mean personal goals and aims; it is about completely unselfish acts that relate to looking at the universe in a much wider context. It is to do with knowing where you fit into the universe as a whole and generally broadening your horizons. Until you expand your thought processes, it is hard to understand how divine will relates to you personally.

The sixth layer is about unconditional love. This does not mean loving yourself or others to whom you are close. This is love in a

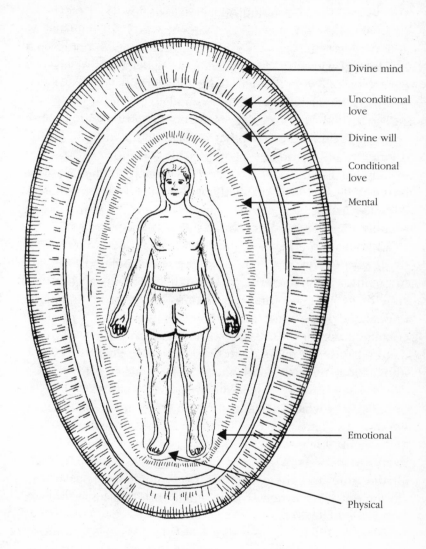

Divine mind

Unconditional love

Divine will

Conditional love

Mental

Emotional

Physical

The seven levels of the human aura.

larger, universal context where you love and appreciate all around you, irrespective of your individual relationships with people and material things. You may know someone who has committed an abhorrent act. The sixth layer is about your ability to understand and to deal with that situation without condemning. Again, you have to expand your thoughts to be able to deal with this sphere, because it requires universal understanding on a large scale.

The seventh and final layer is the finest, lightest and brightest of all. It is called the blueprint for bliss and a fusion with the divine mind. Don't worry if this sounds impossibly incomprehensible. There is so much to learn about the first three layers of the aura that you need not concentrate on something as complex as the seventh until a later stage. It is enough to acknowledge that it exists without trying to understand it.

So you can see that our aura is indeed a blueprint for all of us. It says everything there is to say about our individuality, from physical characteristics, through emotional and mental spheres to higher spiritual aspirations. Are you beginning to understand how spiritual healing can work? If all of us is contained within these layers of energy and we can learn to manipulate these energies in a constructive, positive way by unblocking, releasing and encouraging their free flow, then can you see how we can create complete health?

Looking at what is contained within the aura also shows why we must be extremely careful and gentle both with ourselves and others. When we let people into our aura, we are letting them into all of us. We do not necessarily want to be vulnerable all the time and there are occasions when protection and closing down are extremely important. This is discussed later in detail (see page 208).

Although it is not essential, it will help if you can memorise the seven layers of the aura and have a rough idea of what is contained in each. Spend a few minutes recapping on the auric levels and then have a look at the statements below. Can you guess which level of the aura might be strongest for each person?

1. *An enthusiastic athlete running a marathon*
2. *A compassionate nurse tending a patient*
3. *A scientist working on his latest experiment*
4. *An actor arguing passionately about a scene*
5 *A young spiritualist contemplating their purpose in life*
6. *A guru meditating upon universal laws*
7. *A priest hearing confession from a paedophile*

The answers are as follows:
1. *First – Physical*
2. *Fourth – Loving Relationships*
3. *Third – Mental*
4. *Second – Emotional*
5. *Fifth – Divine Will*
6. *Seventh – Bliss/Divine Mind*
7. *Sixth – Unconditional Love/Universal Understanding*

These scenarios are all about people in particular situations. It is important for you to realise that our auras are not static and constant in appearance. They change continuously according to what we are doing, how we are feeling and outside influences. For instance, on a crowded train or bus, we tend to close our auras tightly into our body and withdraw. Feeling dissatisfied or doing a job you dislike can cause the auras to become blocked, leading to energy imbalances. When we are doing a job we enjoy, the opposite tends to happen and our auras are energised, expanding and opening fully. Any strong emotion creates enormous energy changes.

Let us now take the characters above and change their action. Which part of their aura might now be stronger and brighter?

1. *An athlete concentrating on a complicated mathematical problem*
2. *A nurse having a blazing row with her partner*
3. *A scientist nursing their sick pet through the night*
4. *An actor meditating on his intended spiritual path*

  5. *A young spiritualist making love*
  6. *A guru working hard on his exercise machine*
  7. *A priest writing a difficult sermon*

The answers therefore become:
  1. *Third – Mental*
  2. *Second – Emotional*
  3. *Fourth – Loving*
  4. *Fifth – Divine Will*
  5. *First – Physical*
  6. *First – Physical*
  7. *Third – Mental*

One can conclude that it is important to have some variety in life, in order to keep all the auric levels fully active! This is what holistic health means: enjoying all of you. It is important to accept this, because as you move into the realms of spiritual healing, it is not intended that you ignore all the other aspects of you. In other words, concentrating solely on your aura and discovering the different aspects of spiritual healing will not nurture the other parts of you. You have to continue eating, you need to have some form of exercise, you want to continue your interaction, emotional and mental, with other people. Balance becomes the key word in healing yourself; it is not always easy to accomplish.

Imbalances in the aura will show up in different ways. Sometimes they manifest as a blockage where energy cannot flow. Sometimes it will be seen as a smudgy, dark area which pulses discordantly. On other occasions, you will actually see or sense a complete hole or rip in the aura, showing that energy is leaking out or unwanted influences are creeping into the aura. It is most common to talk of energy blockages.

So, if we know that our energies can become unbalanced and we want to use tools to re-balance them, what are those tools? Two major tools which we are going to use throughout this book are other forms of energy.

Grounding energy

The first kind, which is called grounding energy, we have already touched on. When we were discussing geographical locations and the benefits of the sun and bodies of water, we were discussing this form of physical energy. Grounding energy is useful if we feel that we are going around with our head in the clouds, not really focusing on day-to-day reality and appreciating what we have around us. This energy is invaluable to help balance us, particularly if we have spent a lot of time working on spiritual healing and light vibrational energies. You can literally feel slightly disconnected from our planet after a period of time. We then draw this grounding energy up into us and let it help balance our auric energies. The method we use for doing this is discussed in the next chapter.

Another name for grounding energy is Mother Nature. We think of Mother Nature as being so many different things: the trees, the grass, the animals, the plant-life. Taken on a deeper level, it could be said to be the primitive force of consciousness which allows nature to take its own course, irrespective of man's involvement. For instance, we are learning that we cannot control the forces of Nature without creating disastrous results, a fact that we are having to relearn and that our ancient ancestors always knew. Shamanic and other societies which use spiritual healing as the backbone of their existence know they have to live in harmony with all of nature and to respect and revere its great strength. They would see any attempt to control nature as an evil force. One could also describe Nature as part of the universal laws of existence.

To further help your appreciation of this, spend as much time as you can observing nature for the next few months. Go for a walk in a park or some quiet woods. Just sit on the ground for a while and observe the minute insect life going on around you. Watch the birds flying and imagine what it feels like for them. Start noticing plants and trees and how different and beautiful they all are. Observe all the different colours of nature and how intricate and beautifully patterned they are. Sit and observe a body of water: the sea, a stream or lake and notice what thoughts and emotions crop up. If you have the time, read up on a subject relating to nature which you would not normally consider. For instance, did you know that ants live and work in a highly intricate, structured society? Their behaviour is instinctive, not taught, so where does their primitive consciousness come from? If you do not do so already, start watching some of the superb televised documentaries on wildlife which can make us appreciate the complexity and beauty of nature. The more you discover about nature, the more you realise how we as humans have lost appreciation of this vital aspect of existence. Grounding energy is all part of this wonderful force.

When we work with grounding energy we draw it up from the ground, which is where all the energies of our planet are stored. Have you ever thought about what is contained in the core of our planet? Most of us never stop to consider that there must be something below the surface of the earth. What is it?

The scientific reality is that our planet Earth is approximately 8,000 miles in diameter. However, the actual land mass is only 22 miles thick (except under the ocean, where it is only 4 miles thick). Beneath that, what is there? Molten lava: incredibly hot, thick molten lava, which scientists estimate could be as hot as 6,000 degrees Celsius at the core. That is as hot as the surface of the sun. Is it not strange to think of that incredible powerhouse of heat and energy being such a short distance under our feet? It's hard to grasp just how powerful that focused heat could be and how much energy is contained within its core.

Cosmic energy

The second form of energy which we use in spiritual healing is cosmic energy. Unlike grounding energy, which is Earth-related, cosmic energy deals with a very different realm. It comes from above, from our infinite universe. It is also infinite in supply and perfect in structure, a pure, undiluted 'perfect' energy. Cosmic energy bears no relation to earthly matters and is of what could be called 'heavenly' extraction.

Cosmic energy may mean different things to different people. One of the greatest joys and benefits of spiritual healing is that it crosses all religious barriers. You do not even need to have any religious beliefs to practise it. All you need is a belief in and a respect for a higher source of perfect energy, love and power which emanates from the universe above.

This source of power has been given many different names over the centuries: God, Buddha, Allah, Great White Spirit. It does not matter what you call it. You can discover your own name for it which feels right: Supreme Being, Universal Energy or Creator of All. Whatever name you choose, the power and purity of cosmic energy is undisputed. Its strength remains ever-constant and infinite in supply. Creating your own name can help strengthen your relationship with cosmic energy. If you are still uncertain whether you believe in this energy, do not worry at this stage. The next chapter will discuss ways in which you can work with this energy and prove its existence for yourself.

You might find it helpful to know that all these forms of energy have been acknowledged and discussed through time for thousands of years. Again we are not talking about new phenomena. These energies have had a number of different names: prana, ch'i, odic force, monads, magnetic fluids, maya, mana, bioplasma, orgone, iliaster, yin and yang, num, kia. The name is not significant. The important issue is that these energies have been accepted, studied and respected for a very long time. If you want to read more about people who have studied life forces, look for books written by or about the following people: Wilhelm von Reichenbach, Walter J. Kilner, Semyon and Valentina Kirlian, Dr Hans Jening, Frans Mesmer, Wilhelm Reich, Barbara Brennan, George de la Warr, Maxwell Cade.

To move forward with the information you have been given in this chapter, you will need to spend some time thinking about and working towards an acknowledgement of the forces or energies we have discussed. You have already read about how observing and appreciating nature can help your relationship with grounding energy. Try to do this as often as you can and reflect on how time spent this way makes you feel.

As far as cosmic energy is concerned, you might want to take some quiet moments to reflect upon your beliefs about the universe and our reasons for being here on Earth. Do you believe there is some universal, all-powerful influence which is guiding and protecting us? How do you see this force? Do you believe we as humans are all part of that force? What else is out there in the universe? Are you aware that recent research has indicated there may be as many as 125 billion galaxies in our universe? (Earth is in the galaxy of the Milky Way which comprises approximately 100 billion stars. Our universe may therefore contain well over 10 thousand billion billion stars.) What is infinity to you? If you hold particular religious beliefs, spend a little more time than usual in prayer and ask for guidance and support in this new area of your life. Notice what thoughts or inspirations come through as a result of this gently reflective time.

As far as your own aura is concerned, you can start to become aware of it on a regular, daily basis. How does it feel when you wake up in the morning? Does it feel expanded outwards or pressed closely into you? How does it feel when you step into the shower or bath? If you play some music does your aura feel different? Notice how your aura interacts with others as well. Can you feel it rush outwards on a pleasurable experience and pull inwards when you feel threatened or wary? What happens when you feel very angry or very happy? Observe your aura in all aspects of your life and you will start to regard it as your friend: indeed, as your ever-present shadow.

Now you are beginning to understand about these three energies, how can you get them all to work harmoniously together and to persuade both cosmic and grounding energy to interact and positively influence your own aura? The key to this lies with the energy centres in your own body, known as chakras. The next chapter explains what these are and how they work for you.

THE CHAKRAS

The word 'chakra' is as old as humans themselves, although it is quite possible you have never heard it before. In fact, the origin of the word can be found in Indian Sanskrit and means 'wheel'. It is a useful analogy because the chakra centres are wheel-like in shape and movement. Once you take their movement into 3D imagery, they then become more cone-like. If you look at the diagram on page 42 you will see this more clearly.

First, what are chakras? They are basically funnels through which we receive cosmic energy and grounding energy and through which we interrelate with everything around us. We do not just receive through these funnels; we also give out through them. Chakras are found within each level of our aura and therefore affect every part of our being. When we are balanced and enjoying perfect health, all our chakras are flowing evenly and openly, all connecting with each other and pulsating together to create a unique glowing aura that resonates fully with everything and everyone. Many people never know this state of health because they do not understand the blocks, rips and tears which have occurred in their subtle body or aura over the course of time. Spiritual healing is all about learning to work with these chakras and learning how to heal the areas which may not be functioning fully at present.

So let us start exploring the chakras. First, it should be said that as these ancient energy systems have been acknowledged and studied for thousands of years, we are dealing with a much-researched concept. Many years ago the chakras were treated with a deep reverence and respected as a highly complex, almost mystical, phenomenon. The true significance and purpose of the chakras were treated as profound secrets that would only be handed down by the wise men of the day to their honoured students. Fasting and meditation were

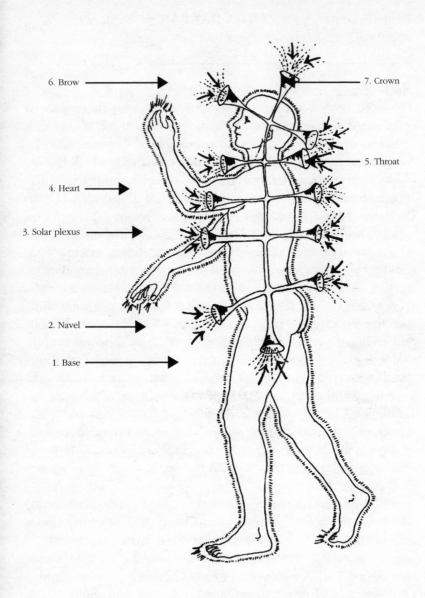

6. Brow

7. Crown

5. Throat

4. Heart

3. Solar plexus

2. Navel

1. Base

The seven chakras.

common methods through which sages could contact a higher consciousness and thus gain greater insights. Lifetimes were spent solely concentrating on the chakras.

The difficulty with trying to bring the knowledge of chakras into everyday Western society is twofold. First, because the understanding of these energies is having to be relearned, you run the risk of finding much of the information confusing and you may mistrust what you read. Words such as cosmic, vibrational energies, chakras and higher consciousness can sound vaguely worrying initially! So you have to be accepting and be prepared to look beyond the words and study the concepts with an open mind.

Secondly, trying to westernise these ancient concepts can tend to trivialise them and their significance. You can liken this to trying to explain any deep emotion that touches your very core. Whatever language you use, the words cannot quite capture the essence of what you really experienced. If you have ever tried to explain the moment of holding your just-born child in your arms or some profound spiritual experience, you will know that mere words are inadequate. Insights with the chakras come into this realm.

We have to accept the use of simpler terms and find some way of describing at least the early stages of working with the chakras.

There are seven major chakras and 21 minor chakras. There are also a great number of even smaller chakras. During the course of this book, we will be looking at the seven major chakras, although passing reference will also be made to the others.

A major chakra is described as a point where 21 lines of energy cross the body. A minor chakra is where 14 lines cross each other. Do you remember the discussion of acupuncture, where Chinese doctors insert needles into the body to make contact with lines of energy, in order either to release or aid energy flows? These enter the body from many different angles and criss-cross it in a highly complex pattern. It is believed that in each of us there are more than 72,000 meridian crossing points.

The chakra is often likened to the lotus flower, with each chakra being assigned a different number of petals according to their meaning. One of the reasons a lotus flower is believed to have been chosen is because this extraordinarily beautiful flower grows in the dirtiest and muddiest of waters. It symbolises how the beauty of the spiritual can transcend harsh physical reality when necessary. This idea becomes more relevant later.

If you look at the illustration on page 42 again, you will see roughly where the seven chakras are located. The first is at the base of the spine, the second is just below the navel, the third is just below the breastbone and slightly to the left, the fourth is at the heart, the fifth is at the throat, the sixth is at the brow and the seventh is located at the top of the crown of the head. You will notice that the second through to sixth chakras all have two openings, front and back. The first chakra has only one opening, downwards to the ground, and the seventh chakra has just one, which opens upwards to the sky. Have a close look at the diagram to make sure you have taken in this information.

Some people say the narrow tip of the funnel just touches the physical body at this point. Others see the chakras as being a couple of inches away from the physical body. When we start exercises to improve awareness of these energy centres, you can decide for yourself if the chakras feel as though they are connected to your body or if they feel just outside of it. Different people have different sensations or awareness about this, depending on their individual sensitivity.

You will also notice that each chakra opening forms its own line of energy which then connects to all the other chakras.This is important for you to realise. The chakras are not separate entities but all part of a whole energy system. Each chakra only works fully when the other chakras are also fully engaged. They are all part of a whole, hence again the term 'holistic health'.

When a chakra is open, a vortex of energy swirls into the cone-like funnel and is absorbed into the body. The more open we are to a situation or experience, meaning the more involved or passionate we are about a particular scenario, the more open the chakra will be. However, bear in mind that for the chakra to be a large gaping hole is as much of a dysfunction as a closed chakra. When people use the expression of being 'too open and vulnerable', what they really mean is that the chakras are too open and too much energy is either being taken into the body or being released from it. Awareness of the chakras enables you to adjust these imbalances. We also give out varying degrees of energy through these same centres.

In the previous chapter, we saw that there are seven levels to the aura. The seven chakras relate directly to the seven layers of the aura. This does not mean that the first chakra is in the first level of the aura, the second chakra is in the second, and so on. Each chakra is in each of the seven layers of the aura. Thus the first chakra has seven counterparts radiating outwards from the body through the seven layers. If you imagine seven ice-cream cone bases nestled one inside the other, it will give you a rough image of what is happening.

If you are feeling as though everything is suddenly getting very complicated, don't worry. Although it's good for you to have an inkling of how complex our energies are, this does not mean you have to understand them fully. After all, you can have a good relationship with your physical body and nurture it without necessarily understanding how every aspect of it works.

At this point we need to look at each chakra individually to give you an understanding of the basic functions of each. This will be helpful when you practise healing on yourself and others, enabling you to be aware of which chakra is being affected by the dysfunction you are treating. This will apply whether the imbalance is physical, emotional, mental or spiritual in origin.

Apart from each chakra having a different location within the subtle body, each also relates to different parts of the physical body and to a different aspect of your life. Each has a colour associated to it and an action as well.

Base chakra

This is the first chakra, which has only one opening, downwards to the ground, and is located at the base of the spine. The base chakra relates very much to the physical, earthly part of you. It is sometimes called the root chakra, an apt description because it reveals whether you are well grounded. It also demonstrates your will for life. So if you enjoy all of your physical, day-to-day life, if you have a strong will to live and feel well-grounded in the present, appreciating your strong physical energy and vitality, then this base chakra will be functioning well. The base chakra is connected to the spinal column, the adrenals (endocrine organs which produce hormones) and the kidneys. The words which relate to this 'I am' and also 'I am becoming'. Its associated colour is red.

Navel chakra

This second chakra has two openings, front and back, and is located just below the navel. Sometimes called the sacral chakra, it is all about your emotions, sensuality and sexuality, and how you enjoy sharing sexual intimacy. These are difficult areas for many people. This navel chakra is a hot-bed of emotion and therefore needs to be treated with great sensitivity and respect. The sexual act, in its complete form, signifies a unity and a divine coming together spiritually. It is the means through which one can let go of one's own ego and fuse with something far greater and more meaningful. However, sexual intimacy is not always possible for a variety of reasons, and if your situation prohibits it, this does not mean you are an incomplete or dysfunctional person. You can benefit from healing in this area and by looking deeper into the power of letting go of your own ego and fusing with others on a deeper, more spiritual level. This chakra also relates to your emotional relationships with people and your enjoyment of them. So, if you enjoy relating to people, if you have a fulfilling sexual relationship, if you appreciate sensuality, if you are aware of your sexual strength and drive and enjoy its presence, then you are likely to have a fully functioning navel chakra. If you over-indulge sexually, then this chakra will be enlarged and lead to imbalances. Notice this chakra also relates to sensuality, the appreciation of sexual beauty, not just the act itself. Physically, the navel chakra is related to the reproductive system known as the gonads (ovaries in women, testes in men) and affects our immune system. The words relating to this chakra are 'I feel emotionally'. The colour which symbolises this chakra is orange. Remember, the navel chakra must be handled with particular compassion and awareness.

Solar plexus chakra

This third chakra is just below and slightly to the left of your ribcage. It has two openings, front and back. Your mental capacities and your sense of how you belong in the world are connected to this chakra. It relates to your will and how you see your destiny in relation to the universe as a whole. Although this is very much your mental sphere it is also connected to your emotions, as so many mental attitudes are derived from your emotions. So this chakra is also about how much we take care of ourselves and our self-esteem. It is a chakra which healers use when giving healing; this will be discussed during Part Two. If this chakra is functioning fully, you will have a great sense of belonging and you will have an expressive emotional life which creates mental satisfaction and fulfilment rather than worry. This chakra's physical connections are to the organs within the solar plexus area: the stomach, liver, gall bladder, pancreas, spleen and nervous system. The related words are 'I think'. The associated colour is yellow.

Heart chakra

This fourth chakra is located at the heart itself and opens both front and back. It is at this chakra that the vibrational frequencies start to change, to become lighter, finer and higher. This chakra is often considered a hinge between the physical and spiritual. Whilst the first three chakras are very much based in the real world (physical, emotional and mental), this is where we start to spiral higher into the more spiritual realms of our being. This chakra is all about love. It is about our interpretation of love and how we relate lovingly in our relationships with others; 'others' includes everybody and everything: family, friends, fellow human beings and all creatures on Earth. It is not discriminatory and the more love we give, the more open this chakra will be. This love is about unconditional, free-flowing energy that acknowledges all people and situations as deserving of love and compassion.

This centre also deals with how connected we are to other people. The expression 'tugging on the heart strings' literally means energy which is still connected between people. A break-up of a deep relationship does not necessarily mean the energies between the two people are severed. Sometimes you have to consciously cut heart ties to be able to let go of somebody. (This is a form of healing we will discuss in detail later.) This chakra is used a great deal by healers because love is a very powerful healing force. So, if you have a strong capacity for loving others and are not judgmental or discriminatory in expressing love, if you feel connected with love to everyone and everything, this chakra will flow freely. Its physical association is to the heart, circulatory system, upper back, thymus (a gland near the throat whose function is not clear) and vagus nerve (cranial nerve which affects the larynx, heart, oesophagus and most abdominal organs). The words relating to the heart chakra are 'I love humanly'. The colour associated with this chakra is green (grass-green as opposed to dark or lime green).

Throat chakra

The fifth chakra is located at the throat and it also has two openings, both front and back. This is about taking responsibility for everything in life and behaving truthfully with everyone, by speaking that higher, spiritual truth and living by it. As the energies spin at a finer, higher vibration, so we have to concentrate more to take in these concepts. This is also about your ability to take in and digest information. It is about how you see your professional life and the degree of fulfilment you are experiencing within it. This centre can store the fear of failure which prevents us from moving forward at times in life. We can also store blame here for others not giving us opportunities we wanted. If you have reached the stage in life where you no longer blame others for your own difficulties, if you have reached fulfilment in your professional life, if you go out and create what you want rather than relying on others, and live with truth and integrity, this chakra will be functioning well. Physically, the throat chakra is connected to the thyroid (gland-secreting hormones which regulate body growth and metabolism), bronchii (passages leading into the lungs), lungs and alimentary canal (the digestive passage which extends from mouth to anus). The related words are 'I will'. The associated colour is blue (sky-blue as opposed to dark blue).

Brow chakra

This sixth chakra is located at the brow, in the middle of the forehead. Again, this chakra opens both front and back. We are climbing yet higher into more spiritual concepts now – the brow chakra is often called 'the third eye'. This is our ability to 'see' things which normal human vision can not, to see life in a much larger context than just our earthly existence. This type of 'seeing' involves our ability to understand the concept and then move forward with this understanding into new territory. If your spiritual concepts are fully formulated and you can 'see' universal truth and understand where you fit into that plan and then carry out your work accordingly, your brow chakra will be functioning well. This chakra's physical associations are with the lower brain, left eye, ears, nose, nervous system and pituitary (gland secreting hormones which influence body growth and other endocrine activities). The words connected with the brow chakra are 'I love universally'. The colour is purple.

Crown chakra

This last, seventh, chakra is located at the top of the head, right in the middle, at the crown. Like the base chakra, the crown chakra has only one opening, which is pointing upwards to the sky. This chakra vibrates at the highest vibrational frequency of all the chakras and accordingly it deals with the highest of spiritual relationships: complete connection with the perfect spiritual energy of the Divine. (You may translate this into your own word, such as God, Buddha, Allah, Great Spirit etc.) Not surprisingly, the crown chakra is the most difficult to explain using earthly words. Perfection, the true divine, supreme bliss – all these words are much over-used and mis-used in our language. Again, it might help you to think of extraordinarily emotional moments which were beyond your ability to explain. If your crown chakra is open, then your earthly personality will have fused with all spiritual knowledge, you will experience a state of bliss generally unknown to normal human experience and you will 'know' divine law without question or confusion. Do not worry that this may sound unintelligible at this stage. Just keep opening your mind to the possibility of everything without trying to grasp the specifics. It does become easier with time! The crown chakra relates physically to the upper brain and right eye. The associated words are 'I know'. The colour is pure white.

How does all that new knowledge feel to you? Confusing? Exciting? Or nonsensical? These chakras really are the gateway to all forms of spiritual healing and the better your relationship becomes with your own chakras, the more you will be able to tune in and to understand others, thereby helping them as powerfully as possible. We will be exploring exercises which will afford you the opportunity to work personally with your chakras and to give you the chance to discover yourself in a new light.

It is important that you realise that all seven chakras are of equal significance and that no one chakra is better or more powerful than the others. Sometimes by calling the crown chakra the highest vibrational frequency, you can mistakenly think it must be the 'best' one, and worth more than the others! All seven need to be fully functioning for you to enjoy complete health. You will need to look at all of them individually in yourself before you learn which chakras need more healing than others.

So let us now take a look at what happens if all the chakras are open and functioning fully:

- *You enjoy all of your physical, day-to-day life, you have a strong will to live and feel well-grounded in the present, appreciating your strong physical energy and vitality.*
- *You enjoy relating to people, you have a fulfilling sexual relationship/you appreciate sensuality, you are aware of your sexual strength and drive and enjoy its presence.*
- *You have a great sense of belonging, you have an expressive emotional life which creates mental satisfaction and fulfilment rather than worry.*
- *You have a strong capacity for loving others and are not judgmental or discriminatory in that expression, you feel connected with unconditional love to everyone and everything.*
- *You have reached the stage in life where you no longer blame others for your own difficulties in life, you have reached*

fulfilment in your professional life, you go out and create what you want rather than relying on others, and live with truth and integrity.

- *Your spiritual concepts are fully formulated and you can 'see' universal truth and understand where you fit into that plan and then carry out your work accordingly.*
- *Your earthly personality has fused with all spiritual knowledge, you experience a state of bliss generally unknown to normal human experience and you 'know' divine law without question or confusion.*

Does this not sound a pretty comprehensive guide for living life to the full? This is what is meant by holistic health. It is enjoying and appreciating every single facet of physical, emotional, mental and spiritual health and resonating freely and fully with everyone and everything around you. Of course, the process to accomplishing this may take a little while, but it is not the 'curing' of something in spiritual healing which is important, it is the process through which you cure and what you learn which will change your energy and enable you to enjoy every aspect of your life more fully.

Now we are going to start straight away to look at our relationship with our chakras. This does not have to be an in-depth experience; we can start gently and gradually work deeper into the power of each chakra, as and when you feel ready to look at it.

As chakras can feel so intangible to begin with and you can initially doubt their existence and wonder if you are simply imagining them, we are going to start off by combining the experiences of trying to feel the chakra's presence with an actual physical exercise which will help the individual chakra to open.

Discovering your chakras

It is best for this exercise if you can find the time to work through all your chakras, so you need to find at least half an hour during which you will not be interrupted. You need to be by yourself, and there be no possibility of somebody bursting in and disturbing you. Any sudden interruption can badly jar the energies and leave you feeling very unbalanced. You need to wear loose, comfortable clothing and preferably not to have just eaten a heavy meal. You also should be alcohol- and drug-free as both these substances impair the ability to work with the chakras. If you feel you need some spiritual help, try putting on some soft, relaxing music, dim the lights, or even light a candle (making sure it cannot burn anything around it) and perhaps light some incense or burn some essential oils. Anything that feels right for you is fine.

If at any time during the exercises, you feel uncomfortable or upset, close your chakra and let the sensation wash away from you. Imagine you are standing under a wonderful, warm shower and let the feeling literally drain away into the ground with the water. Do this constantly if you feel uncertain about what is happening. Remember this is not intended as a deep exercise. You are exploring the physical sensations of your chakras, not working in-depth with them at this stage.

If you feel yourself going too deeply inside the chakra's energy, it is up to you to pull yourself back and save that exploration for another day. You are in control of all these exercises and it is only you who can regulate what is happening. Remember that the chakras are part of you, not a separate entity and it is your energy and your thought processes which control them, no one else's.

If for some reason, you cannot do any of the physical exercises listed, that is fine. Just continue to concentrate on the particular area with your mind. It is probably most relaxing to sit during your chakra awareness. So once you have completed the physical exercise section of each chakra, then sit in a comfortable, upright chair to continue the exercise.

As you work through the chakras you might want to refer back to the chakra illustration on page 42 and also look at the descriptions of the chakras on pages 45–49. Try to give yourself enough time so you don't have to rush this experience, and remember to work through all seven chakras at one sitting.

Base chakra awareness
Start by sitting on your heels on the floor. Put your hands palm-down on your thighs. As you take a deep breath in,

roll your spine into the pelvis area. As you breathe out, roll your spine back out again. Continue this gentle movement for up to a minute, if it is comfortable. Do not strain, and if the movement feels uncomfortable, stop. When you are ready, sit in your comfortable chair. You might find it easier to concentrate if you close your eyes.

Now think about the base of your spine, remembering that this chakra opens downwards to the ground. It has only one cone or one opening. The interesting fact about this chakra is that it is always open. It opens further during healing work, but it is not possible to close it down completely. Just as we need to breathe to live, so our base chakra always has some degree of movement. Try to tune in to that part of your body, just below your spine or tailbone. Trying to visualise the colour red may help you. Can you feel any energy down there? It's not an area we tend to concentrate on much, unless we have lower back pain. Does it feel tense right now? If your buttocks feel tense in the chair, try to gradually relax or soften them, feeling them become heavier. Take a few deep comfortable breaths – often when we concentrate on a physical area in our body, we forget to breathe. Keep concentrating on that area of your body.

You might feel something beginning to happen. This sensation of chakra movement is different for everyone. Sometimes it feels rather like a butterfly flicking its delicate wings against your skin. Sometimes it is more like a warm or cool draught. Others describe it as a whirring sensation. Some people see it as a flower opening, perhaps even a lotus flower, its petals slowly opening to embrace the light. Other images are of a wheel starting to spin, or a door or drawbridge opening, or even a gift being unwrapped. Some people have absolutely no physical sensation or mental image at all, but they still know the chakra has opened. You might be the sort of person who hears a whirring or vibrating sound as your chakra opens. You will discover what is right for you in time. As you feel the chakra opening, notice if you can feel energy coming into your body or if you seem to be expelling some of your own. If you are struggling to feel any sensation at all, try repeating the physical exercise again gently, and then repeat the thought process.

At this stage, don't do further work on this chakra. Don't go into the energy and start exploring that yet, because you have more work to do before you are ready to deal with what you may find. Instead, imagine that the chakra is slowly closing again. It won't stop completely, remember, because this chakra is always open to some degree. Imagine the petals of the flower closing, or feeling the whirring sensation slow

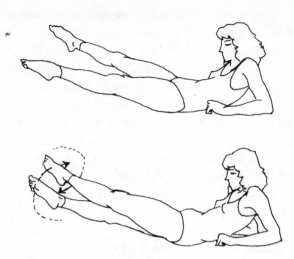

down, or imagine the butterfly moving away. Use whatever image or sensation is right for you. When you are ready, try the second physical exercise.

Navel chakra awareness

You could try either of two physical exercises for this chakra. Try one or both, depending upon how you feel.

First, you can sit cross-legged on the floor, holding onto your ankles (see illustration opposite). As you breathe in, tilt your spine forward and lift your chest; then flex the top of your pelvis back. Breathe out and move the spine backwards and the pelvis forwards. Repeat the movement a few times, then stop.

Secondly, you could lie on your back and prop yourself up with your elbows (see above). Lift both legs about 12 inches off the floor. Breathe out and open your legs. Breathe in and cross legs at the knees but keep your legs straight. Do this several times. Now raise your legs a little higher and repeat the whole process. Then start lowering your legs in the same fashion. (This exercise conveniently doubles as a good toner for the stomach muscles!) Return to your chair. If you feel a

little breathless, wait until your breathing is comfortable again
before you continue.

Now close your eyes and concentrate on the area just below
your navel. This is a chakra which opens both front and back.
Most people find it easier to envisage the front opening and
forget about the back. Try to concentrate on both. It may help

you to increase the sensations, knowing this experience is
taking place in two areas. Visualise the colour orange. Now
imagine the wheels turning or the cones spinning, or whatever
analogy you want to use. Call upon your tickling butterfly or
create the gentle draught. What does the energy feel like coming
into this chakra? Is it stronger coming in from the front or
back? Are you giving out a lot in this area or does it feel
contained within you? Again, don't delve further. Remember
to treat this chakra with particular gentleness. Enjoy the
sensation of the chakra opening and its movement and then
let it gently close again. When you feel ready, move on.

Solar plexus chakra awareness

Sit crossed legs on the floor. Hold onto your shoulders with
your hands: fingers in front, thumbs in back. Keep your
spine straight as you breathe in and turn to the left. Then
exhale and turn to the right. Keep your breathing as deep
as possible. Repeat and then reverse direction. Now sit on
your heels and do it all again. Return to your chair.

This chakra isn't quite in the same line as the others. It isn't directly above the navel or below the heart. Feel where your ribcage ends below your chest, and then concentrate on the area just to the left of that. Again, this chakra opens front and back, so try to concentrate on both areas. This is a

Bear grip

powerful area of both emotional and mental energies, so be gentle. Visualise the colour yellow. What does it feel like as the chakra starts opening? If you have a spinning or whirring sensation, which way is it moving – clockwise or counter-clockwise? Can you feel energy moving into the chakra or does it feel as though you are releasing energy? Is it coming in a rush or a trickle? If you feel anything unpleasant, just wash it through and let it disperse. When you have explored the physical sensation of your solar plexus chakra, gently close the chakra again. Remember to close both the front and back. When you feel ready, move on.

Heart chakra awareness
Sit with your legs crossed and grip your fingers in front of you in what is called the bear grip (see inset above). Hold your hands up at the heart centre in the middle of your chest. Now move your elbows in a seesaw motion as you breathe deeply and comfortably. Do this for several breaths and then breathe in, breathe out and pull on your hands. Relax a moment and then repeat the exercise sitting on your heels. Now return to your chair.

Close your eyes and concentrate on the middle of your chest, at your heart centre. Are you suddenly aware of your heart beating? Visualise the colour green, soft grass-green. This chakra opens both front and back, so remember to consider both. Can you feel the chakra opening? If you are a naturally loving, compassionate person, this chakra may feel quite strong for

you. If the sensation is rather over-whelming, do not be afraid to wash the emotions away. Don't let yourself go into the energy, just observe what the chakra feels like as it opens. Is it the same sensation as the others? Remember the vibrational frequencies start to change at this chakra; it is often called a 'hinge' between two worlds. Can you feel any difference? Can you feel energy coming into you? It should manifest as a very warm, loving sensation. Let that trickle through into all of your body, if you like. Let the loving feeling nurture all of you. You may have a sudden sensation of well-being. Enjoy it. When you feel ready, gently close the heart chakra. Make sure it is properly closed, both front and back, before you move on.

Throat chakra awareness

Sit on the floor with your legs crossed and hold your knees firmly. Keep your elbows straight. Breathe in, flex the spine forward. Breathe out, flex the spine back. Repeat and then relax. Now shrug the shoulders up as you breathe in and flex forward. Shrug the shoulders down and breathe out as you flex back. Breathe in and hold your breath for a few seconds as you hold your shoulders up. Relax. Then repeat sitting on your heels. Return to your chair.

Close your eyes and bring your concentration to your throat area, near the hollow of your throat. Visualise the colour blue – soft sky blue – and remember this chakra opens front and

back. Do you suddenly have the urge to swallow? Can you feel a gentle pulsing in your throat? Feel the chakra slowly open and notice if the energies feel different yet again. You are moving onto higher frequencies now and the energy starts to feel lighter and brighter. How different is the sensation between the back and the front openings? The chakra might seem to manifest itself in a different image now. Notice whatever is happening without becoming involved in it. Enjoy the different sensations. Is there much energy coming into your throat? Does it feel warm or cool? Are you releasing any energy yourself? Slowly close the throat chakra. Close it front and back and notice what sensations come with the closing of the chakra. Sit for a minute before you continue.

Brow chakra awareness
Sit cross legged on the floor and lock your fingers into a bear grip (see illustration on page 57), this time at throat level. Take a deep breath in and hold it as you squeeze in your

abdomen and buttocks and imagine the energy pushing up
through your body. Then as you exhale, bring your hands
up over your head, still in the bear grip. Do this once and
then repeat it, sitting on your heels. If you feel dizzy at any
time, stop. Then return to your chair.

Now think about the area in the middle of your brow, between
your eyes. How does it feel? Is there a slight pulse in your
forehead? Remember to acknowledge the back of this chakra,

as well as the front. Visualise the colour purple. If you feel very
little with this chakra opening, that is fine. The vibrations are
becoming so light and so fine that you need to develop quite a
sensitivity before you can feel them. It doesn't matter if at this
stage you can simply acknowledge its presence and know where
the chakra is, even if you don't feel any movement. See if you
can feel energy coming into your brow area. Then let the chakra
close again, front and back. Notice if any other images come
into your mind or if the energies feel different. Sit for a moment
before you continue.

Crown chakra awareness

Sit on the floor with your legs crossed. Stretch your arms above your head and lock your fingers, with the two index fingers pointing upwards. Breathe in and pull the navel in. Breathe out and let the navel relax. Breathe in and out for a few seconds. Then breathe in and squeeze first your buttocks and then your stomach muscles, feeling the energy as it whooshes up from the base of your spine to the top of your head. Hold your breath for a few seconds. Then release your breath but keep all the muscles taut. Then relax the muscles. Rest. If you feel dizzy, stop. If you feel fine, you can repeat the above sitting on your heels. Then sit back in your comfortable chair.

Now concentrate on the area at the very top and middle of your head. Does it feel warm or cool? Focus hard on this part of the head. The chakra opens upwards to the sky. Does it feel as though the chakra is moving already? Here is another secret: just as the base chakra is always open, so the crown chakra never closes down completely. It is always open and receiving and expelling energy in different forms. Does it feel open enough? Does it feel too open? Which way is the chakra spinning? How much energy are you giving out through the top of your head? Visualise the colour white. Now imagine the beautiful, pure cosmic energy flowing down from above and entering you through the crown chakra. Feel it washing through and over all of you. Enjoy the cleansing, revitalising sensation. Feel cleansed, purified and energised. When you feel ready, slowly focus on your crown chakra and see it slowing down in frequency. This chakra won't close completely but make sure it's not too open before you finish. Now sit still for several minutes, with your eyes closed, before you get up. Feel that your feet are resting firmly on the floor and that you feel solid and heavy. Wait until you can feel the heaviness of both your feet before you get up.

Were you surprised by how different each chakra felt? Were some easier to sense than others? Did you feel sure that you actually do not possess all the chakras; you might be one or two short? Did some feel uncomfortable and others feel lovely? Did you struggle with the chakras on the back of your body? Everyone will have experienced the chakras differently. Here are some feelings, images and/or sounds you could expect to experience:

- *light tickling*
- *heat or coolness*
- *slight pressure*
- *whirring sensation/noise*
- *beautiful but unknown scent in the nostrils*
- *turning of a wheel*
- *faint humming or buzzing sound*
- *petals of a flower opening*
- *door or drawbridge opening*
- *something being unwrapped*
- *a flash of colour*
- *sensation of something being there but not sure what*
- *knowing without understanding why you know*
- *absolutely nothing*

If you fall into the last category, it really does not matter and it will not stop you from healing yourself or others. All it takes is a belief in spiritual energy for it to work. You do not have to feel anything or see anything. Many healers do not. Try not to compare yourself with the experiences of others. However, do keep working on yourself and your chakras and continue to improve your relationship.

A variety of circumstances could be preventing you from working as well as you would like. One major reason could be your ability to relax and breathe deeply. The next chapter is going to look at why this is vital in healing work and how, with just a small amount of practice and application, you can learn to relax and breathe deeply.

LEARNING TO RELAX

Most people think they know how to relax. It seems that it is a natural function, particularly at the end of a hard day at work. You just unwind, don't you? You might read a book or watch television or have a stiff drink, and then you slowly relax. There might still be some tension in your neck and shoulders, of course, but that does not count because everyone has that problem. You find your brain is still whirling around, too, and that it refuses to shut off because all sorts of problems and unfinished projects keep coming into your head and you keep remembering things you have to do, but then everyone experiences that. You cannot say that you feel contented and at peace with the world because there are a lot of issues in your life that you have not yet looked at. One day you will, of course – everyone is like that. And when someone is demanding too much of you, you snap, and then you feel cross because you were trying to relax – but then that is the same for everyone. You are not tired because you get enough sleep. It might be a restless sort of sleep and you wake up often and you vaguely remember a lot of odd dreams and you get up feeling tired – but then, so do lots of people. You are fine, really. You are quite relaxed.

In fact, you almost certainly aren't relaxed. You probably never experience complete relaxation because you do not know what it is. It is part of holistic health. It is the place you find deep inside yourself, where you know everything is as it should be. It does not matter that there are problems, sadnesses, unfinished tasks, disappointments, irritations and large responsibilities in your life, because *everything is exactly as it should be right now*. That is what true relaxation means: when you acknowledge there may be a lot more to accomplish and a number of difficult obstacles ahead *but none of these matter because your life is exactly the way it should be. Everything is perfect just as it is.* Creating this space is not easy but once you find it you will forever be able to acknowledge the difference between thinking you are relaxed and being truly relaxed.

The more you practise true relaxation, the easier it becomes to switch into that altered state and to reap the benefits of living in an environment when you can truly accept what is around you. You may not like it at times, or enjoy it but you can accept it. This is what we want to strive towards in this chapter. By learning this art of relaxation, you will also be performing all sorts of healing acts on your own system: physically, emotionally, mentally and spiritually.

The breathing system

We start this journey by understanding our own breathing system. The basics are simple: we breathe air in, it passes through and nurtures our body and we breathe the surplus out again. Yet this act in which we take part, day-in, day-out, relentlessly, whether consciously or unconsciously, is our very source of relaxation and, ultimately, spiritual perfection. Our breath contains all the knowledge we will ever need. By breathing deeply and rhythmically and fully communicating with this life force, we can reap the benefits of immeasurable good health.

Most of us barely breathe. We do not use the full power of our lungs. We do not use our diaphragm muscle properly and it is therefore weak and does not serve us as well as it could. You need to understand how the breathing apparatus works in order to appreciate it fully and bring about improvements in your breathing technique.

Take a look at the illustration opposite. This shows what happens every time we take in a breath of air. We take air in through our nose and/or mouth. It is better to breathe through the nose, because it has tiny rough particles inside which help to filter the pollution out of the air we are taking in. It also warms the air as it goes through the nose in preparation for its onward journey. If we breathe cold air through our mouth, it actually hurts as it goes further into our body. The nose has not warmed it. Unless you have a cold or sinus problems, try to develop the

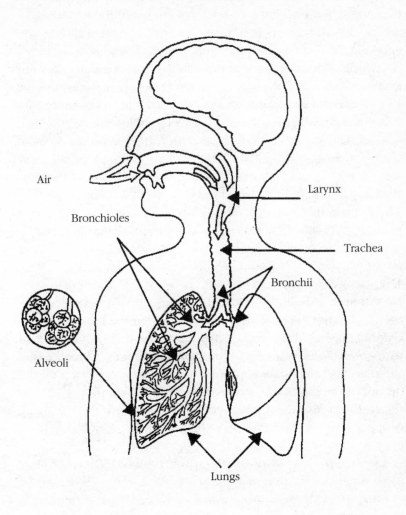

The breathing system.

habit of breathing through your nose. (There are exceptions to this rule when practising certain specific breathing techniques.)

The air then travels down the passage called the trachea and splits into two tubes called the bronchii, which lead into our lungs. Each lung contains a series of bronchioles, which are basically just smaller tubes that branch off from the two main bronchii. All the bronchioles eventually end in individual clusters of miniature sacs called alveoli. We have over half a billion of these tiny sacs in each lung. When we breathe deeply and to our full capacity, all these miniature air sacs are inflated. Many of us never inflate all these sacs. In other words, we never breathe fully. Many people use less than a third of their lung capacity throughout their entire life. These miniature sacs therefore lose their elasticity and stop working properly. The reason for this lies in a large, flat muscle called the diaphragm, which lies just below our lungs.

Diaphragm awareness

Now take a look at the two illustrations opposite. These show the diaphragm in two different states. When we breathe in, the diaphragm should assume a shape rather like a long, flat pancake as it encourages the lungs to fully inflate. When we breathe out, the diaphragm should then push up into an arc, forcing all the air out of the lungs and enabling them to deflate properly. Most of us do not use this muscle properly. Complete the following quick test to see how well your diaphragm is working.

Stand in front of a full-length mirror. Breathe out and bring your hands around your ribcage, with your fingertips just touching each other. Now take a deep breath in. Have your fingertips moved a few inches apart? If they haven't, you are doing what is called shallow breathing. Your diaphragm is not working to its full capacity. You are probably also lifting your shoulders as you breathe. Try again, and this time try to be conscious of taking air further down into your lungs. Are your shoulders still rising? Breathe out and then breathe in again and try to keep your shoulders feeling comfortable and heavy, trying not to let them rise. Again, think about the air going deep into your lungs. Was that a little better? Now imagine that every breath you take in is actually sucking air right down into your stomach. Feel the nourishing breath literally filling the whole of your stomach. Keep your shoulders down. Did your fingertips move further apart this time? With practice, you will be able to breathe deeply without effort, at last allowing your diaphragm to do its job properly.

If you start to feel dizzy as you breathe deeply, stop. Try the exercise again later, this time working with your breath for a shorter period of time. We will work further with the breath and

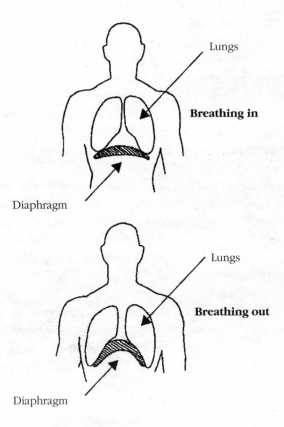

The diaphragm in operation:
Top, when we inhale; bottom, when we exhale

the diaphragm throughout this book. Why is it so important? A wonderful old yogic proverb sums it all up:

> **Life is in the breath; therefore he who only half-breathes half lives.**

This concept of all of us being accessed through our breath is not new. Ancient yogis knew breathing was the way to accomplish any state of heightened awareness. Anyone who practices yoga or tai chi or who meditates will already be used to working with their breathing.

Breathing into stillness

To achieve true relaxation we have to work with our breath to obtain a state of stillness within ourselves. We cannot be still without having an appreciation of our breathing and its beautiful, rhythmic simplicity, which is quite perfect. This degree of stillness is not gained over night, but the more you work with your breathing, the easier it will feel. When you have half an hour of quiet time for yourself, try the following exercise.

Sit quietly in your comfortable, upright chair. Wear loose clothing, preferably nothing on your feet, and make sure you have not had alcoholic drinks or drugs in the last 12 hours. Don't use music for this exercise, and ensure your environment is as quiet as possible. Close your eyes and breathe comfortably for a minute or two.

Now start to concentrate on your breathing. In fact, you want only your breath to be in your thoughts. This will be difficult at first. You are trying to still your mind. A good trick to help you in the beginning is just to concentrate on the words 'in' and 'out' as you inhale and exhale. This will help to quieten your mind. Breathe in. Say 'in' silently to yourself. Breathe out. Say 'out' silently. Continue this process for as long as you can. If you feel sleepy, tell yourself you will not sleep. Then go back to the words 'in' and 'out'.

The first time you try this exercise, every thought imaginable will start crowding into your mind. The more you try to stop thinking, the more you will want to think! Don't get irritated with yourself. Simply acknowledge the thought, let it go and then return to concentrating on those two words, again and again.

If problems persist in coming into your mind, know that you cannot solve them during this period of quietness. Resolve to let them go until you have finished the exercise. You can own them again quickly enough afterwards. Every time a thought comes in, gently let it go. Keep returning to your breath, however many times your mind wanders.

You may also find every part of you starts itching and feels uncomfortable. You will want to wriggle in the chair, rub your nose or do a hundred other things. Try to let these sensations go, too. Your mind has created them and you can erase them. Keep going back to the words 'in' and 'out'.

After a while, a change will come over you. You and your breathing will become as one. You will stop fidgeting. You won't be aware of the noises you were aware of initially. Your body will feel pleasantly comfortable and heavy without being sleepy. By concentrating solely on your breathing, you will become one with a greater force, a greater spiritual understanding. When this happens, it is unmistakable and extremely powerful.

You will probably immediately think how extraordinary it and wonderful it all feels. At that point you then lose the stillness and come back to reality with a thump! All the everyday thoughts crowd in on you again and you can feel quite deflated. It really isn't important if this happens. All that matters is that you had a brief moment of that unquestionably wonderful 'other' state which made you feel truly relaxed. Once you have experienced it, you can always find it again. Always.

When it is time to come back to reality, focus your thoughts on your feet, which should be resting flat on the ground or floor. (Preferably you should be barefoot.) Concentrate on how heavy your feet feel, how secure and solid they are, resting on the ground. You may feel the energy suddenly whoosh back through your legs, into your feet. Notice how heavy your buttocks feel resting in the chair. Your shoulders feel nice and heavy. Wriggle your fingers and toes, then give your hands and feet a gentle shake. Open your eyes and concentrate on an object in front of you. Remember which day of the week it is, the date, what you have to do for the rest of the day. Give yourself several minutes to reorientate your thoughts and physical body. Don't stand up until you feel centred and comfortable. If you do, you will feel dizzy. Take three more deep breaths before you rise.

You will need to come back to this exercise time and again. It becomes most powerful when it is practised daily. You need only spend ten minutes on it initially, but it is best practised alone. Deep levels of relaxation are achieved best in solitude. If you spend ten minutes a day discovering your stillness, you will soon find that you will be able to tap into this lovely space of peace and contentment at will. If you can spend longer, you will find that you can go deeper into spiritual fulfilment. Whatever level you work to, always take time to centre yourself afterwards.

You can use your breath to help you in other ways on a day-to-day basis. You can appreciate your breath and work with it when you are on a crowded train or bus or sitting at your office desk, feeling frustrated. You can use it to calm down if you feel yourself about to explode with anger. Pain and sadness can also be relieved through the breath. As you will start to appreciate, the breath is the means through which we access all spiritual healing. This applies whether you are healing someone else or yourself. Let's look at how your breathing can help you in everyday circumstances.

First of all, what actually happens with your energies when you have a strong emotion? If you suddenly feel angry, where does the energy rush to? (Often it is the navel to ribcage area where everyone stores a lot of emotion.) If you have the urge to dissolve into tears over a broken relationship, where is the energy? (Often the heart chakra is over-working.) If you feel exhausted, where is the energy there? (It feels as if there is none at any level!) If you are in a packed train or bus and feeling claustrophobic and panicky, what is happening to your energy? (You are struggling to assert your own space but it is colliding with everyone else's aura and literally suffocating your energies. At this stage, you will tend to start pushing your energies higher into your head to compensate and this can leave you feeling dizzy and off-balance.)

Connecting with grounding energy

Basically, any strong emotion will set off a chain reaction with your energies, starting them moving at an exceedingly swift rate around and through your chakras. Your physical body will certainly notice this energy change, your mental body will acknowledge something feels very wrong, and your spiritual energies will be completely thrown out of sync. One emotion triggers off all of you. To help redress the balance, you can use your breathing to settle the energies. The first step in this is grounding. Do you remember the grounding energy we talked about earlier? This is an exercise to help you connect with that energy, which helps smooth any sudden emotional reaction. It fundamentally 'brings you back to earth' and you can then assess more calmly how you really feel. Let's look at how you connect with the grounding energy. Try doing this exercise after an experience which has upset you.

Whether you are standing or sitting, put your feet flat on the ground. If possible, feel the soles of your feet connecting directly through to the ground. Have your weight evenly distributed between your feet.

Now stop and take a really deep breath. Most emotions make us revert to shallow breathing. (Remember all those tiny alveoli, the minuscule sacs in our lungs? In this state, you won't be inflating any of them!) Breathe deeply. If you can, put your fingers around your ribcage and check how your diaphragm is working. Try not to lift your shoulders. Feel the air being sucked down into your stomach.

Now focus on your feet. Look at them. Imagine that long, long roots are growing out of the soles of your feet and burrowing deep down into the ground. Your feet are like the base of a large tree, rooted firmly in the soil. (It's irrelevant if your feet are resting on fluffy carpet as you do this, or if you're on the 18th floor of an office block! Your thought process transcends physical reality. Remember you are working with your subtle energies now and they respond to whatever 'reality' your thought processes create.) If it is more powerful for you, close your eyes and imagine yourself as the strongest, tallest tree in a large forest. Think of the wonderfully deep and complex root system under your feet. As you concentrate on your feet, your energy will stop rushing around all the other areas of your body.

On every breath in, feel the grounding energy coming up through your feet and sweeping over and through all of you. This really means all of you. Feel the energy go through your ankles, legs, hips, up your spine and through all of your torso, down through your arms, hands and fingers. Feel it sweep up the back of your neck and up into your head, meeting the energy at the crown of your head. Every time you breathe out, feel the grounding energy settle comfortably within your body, nurturing the areas which need it most.

Now remember the significance of the grounding energy. Think of the beauties of nature, of all the knowledge and gifts of life hidden within the secrets of our Earth's core. Remember the molten lava which is just 22 miles beneath our feet. Realise that you are part of a far larger whole. Realise that your present emotion – while being valid and very real to you – is a small part of a much larger scheme of events.

Now feel your emotion slowly washing away through your body. Feel it drain away through the soles of your feet and down into the ground. On every breath out, feel more tension go from you, knowing that it will disperse and evaporate as it goes into the ground. Feel yourself becoming calmer but keep concentrating on how heavy your feet feel.

After a minute or two, open your eyes. How do you feel now? Continue to take a few deep breaths. Can you feel the air going down into your stomach? How do your energies feel now? Are they still rushing around your body or do you feel more balanced? You might even feel a little foolish, when you balance your emotion against the larger backdrop of life. Try not to look at it in this way. You have a right to your emotions. You'll be working with your emotions all the way through this book, so you have plenty of time to learn how to handle them slightly differently. Acknowledge you are learning all the time. Feel contented with what you've just learnt and know there's more to come.

When you feel ready, wriggle your toes. Then give your feet a gentle shake. Take three more deep, comfortable breaths and then continue your day, enjoying your new sense of balance.

Of course, it will not always be possible for you to practise this exercise immediately. If you are in the middle of a row with someone, it is not exactly easy or feasible to say 'Hold it, I just need to connect with the grounding energy!' However, you can do this after you walk away. Find a quiet moment and ground yourself. You might want to do this before you go to bed at night. You might wake up in the morning and want to focus your thoughts. At any time, when you feel you are not connecting properly with reality, when you need to reassess what you have and where you are in life, stop and feel the grounding energy. Again, the more you do this, the easier it becomes. If you practise enough, you will be able to have your energy drop to your feet within a few seconds of standing still. It is a great tool to have and is useful in so many areas of your life. If you are someone who regularly has to give lectures, for example, and always feel nervous, a few minutes connecting with the grounding energy will always help balance you and prepare you for your talk. Notice that you still access the grounding energy through your breathing. Everything in life is accessed through our breath.

Connecting with cosmic energy

Now let's look at how you can access the cosmic energy to help relax and revive you. Just as the grounding energy is very good for steeping you in reality and bringing you back to earth, so the cosmic energy is very good for creating a connection with higher, spiritual energies and for giving you a lift into higher realms. Using both will help create a healthy, balanced system.

You can access this through either sitting or standing, but sitting is a better method to use initially. Cosmic energy can feel quite heady, especially at first, so you are better balanced in a sitting position. Again, sit with your feet flat against the floor. Choose an upright chair and sit comfortably. Try not to slouch forward and have your head raised, looking straight ahead of you. Take a few comfortable, deep breaths. Close your eyes. Continue to breathe deeply. Enjoy your breathing and feel it being taken deep into your stomach.

When you're ready, concentrate on your crown chakra. Remember its location at the top of your head. Remember that this chakra is always open. Tune into it and feel its light, gentle vibrations.

Now you are going to imagine a beautiful, pure white light streaming down from above you. It's unbelievably bright and comforting. It's infinite in supply. It's there all the time, whether you tune in to it or not, but by tuning in to it, it becomes brighter, lighter and more intense in form. Spend a few minutes acknowledging this strong energy. (Again, whether you have a roof immediately above you or ten storeys is completely unimportant. Spiritual energies transcend all physical matter.) If it helps, imagine you are sitting in an open clearing in a beautiful location. See the clear blue sky above you, stretching into infinity, into the spiritual realms of higher consciousness. Acknowledge your own personal religious or spiritual deity, whoever they may be. If you haven't yet found a name which feels right for you, just silently acknowledge this unearthly and perfect spiritual strength from above.

When you have become fully aware of the cosmic energy, feel it pouring down all around and over you. Feel bathed in its unique beauty with every breath you take, feel it becoming stronger and even more nurturing.

Then feel it coming through your crown chakra. Feel it coming into the top of you and sweeping through all of you. This sensation can be very powerful when it first happens. It can feel so beautiful and so invigorating and yet deeply relaxing at the same time. A strong sense of contentment and 'coming home' can wash over you. Enjoy whatever sensation you have. Feel the cosmic energy relaxing all of you as it washes over and through every muscle, every bone, every single atom of your body. Again, go through the parts of your physical body: through your head and all over your face, down your neck and your spine, through all of your torso, down your arms and out through each finger, over your buttocks and hips, down each leg and out through the toes and soles of each foot. Feel warmed, relaxed and yet energised.

Sit there for a few minutes, enjoying the sensation. You may have a sudden insight or flash of unusual thought. You may suddenly feel less alone or more alive or incredibly relaxed. Notice which sensation you have and notice how it changes on different occasions with the cosmic energy.

After a few minutes, you can withdraw. Feel your crown chakra slowing down its vibrations. It is still open, remember, but moving at a slower frequency. If you feel light-headed after that, you can access the grounding energy through your feet to help you balance. You may have taken in too many 'gulps' of cosmic energy! This is easy to do initially. So concentrate on your feet, breathe in deeply and pull the grounding energy through your feet and up through your body. Feel it meeting the cosmic energy at the crown chakra and feel them fusing and balancing all of your body.

When you feel balanced, open your eyes and focus on an object. Do you still feel slightly light-headed? Close your eyes, remember to take several deep breaths, concentrate on your feet again for a few minutes and then open your eyes again. Remember which day of the week it is and what you have to do today. Take three more deep, comfortable breaths, wriggle your hands and feet and then get up. You may have a sensation of well-being that lasts with you right through the rest of the day.

Cosmic energy is very powerful. It can be used as a quick top up of energy at any time, if you feel you need a boost. It can help take you out of mundane, routine tasks and give you a sense of perspective about the whole of life, not just your life. It is enriching, uplifting energy that is particularly useful when you feel life crowding in on you, when you feel depressed over unfulfilled aspects of your life. Often through breathing in this cosmic energy, you can have insights about your own life or human existence in general. The less you try to have results and experience extraordinary sensations, the more will come your way! Spiritual work shows good results with a relaxed mind and body.

Sometimes, you simply need to cleanse yourself of thoughts, emotions and physical sensations. You know the grounding energy and cosmic energy are good for balancing your energies. They're also energising and uplifting. However, if you are still storing away negative feelings or images, you need to get rid of them before you can fully appreciate other energies. The same is true with Breathing into Stillness which is really your meditation for relaxation. The more you have let go of troubling aspects of your life, before you start these exercises, the more beneficial the exercises will be and the more you can enjoy them. So how can you cleanse some of the negative parts of you away? Earlier, it was mentioned about letting anxieties drain away in the ground and feeling them wash through you. Let's create a more powerful visualisation to assist you with this task.

Creating your cleansing sanctuary

This is basically a very private space that you are going to create for yourself. This will be personal to you; no two cleansing sanctuaries are the same. The more time you spend creating this space, the more powerful an energy it will create and the more effective your cleansing sanctuary will be. All you need is to relax and to let your thought processes create something beautiful that is absolutely right for you. Suggestions are contained within this exercise but you can basically create whatever is right for you, as long as it is cleansing, beautiful, private and utterly relaxing.

Start by closing your eyes and relaxing. If you want to lie down for this exercise, fine, as long as you don't fall asleep. If music soothes without distracting you, put on a favourite piece. Light some incense if smell is very important to you. Make sure your clothes are loose and comfortable. Come to the exercise with your physical body both alcohol- and drug-free. Concentrate on your breathing. Use the 'in' and 'out' thought processes if you have trouble stilling your mind. Feel your body becoming heavier and more relaxed with each breath out. Remain in this state for a few minutes before you move on.

Next you are going to create a space in your mind by allocating a certain personal area for your cleansing sanctuary. Remember how we use such a small proportion of our human brain? Imagine that this sanctuary is going to take up just a small area in your brain, one that you can access quickly and easily. The stronger your visual creation, the more powerful it will be for you.

What do the words cleansing and purity mean to you? You may already have an image that fits them. If you've had a wonderful spiritual experience (at Lourdes, for example, or another holy place), perhaps that symbolises perfect health and cleansing to you. It might be the image of your perfect bathroom. You might find the ocean your ultimate cleansing ground or a small, private pool of water. If you have a fear of water, you might find wonderful, bright sunshine is your cleansing space. You might see warm, soft spring rain as more inviting. Perhaps you like a powerful waterfall gushing down a bank. Maybe a marble jacuzzi appeals to you better. Spend a few minutes creating this space which represents complete cleanliness to you. The only rule is that you must have some drainage system for your water. This is vital. So, if you create your perfect bathroom, make sure you have a large plug hole or overflow. If it's a stream or river, see that it flows away into the distance or into the ground. If you choose the sunshine as your image, then see the rays being absorbed into the ground around you.

To make this space as vivid as possible, be specific with your choice. If you choose a bathroom, is it tiled or painted? What colour is it? Does it contain a bath or shower and what colour is that? Is there carpet or bare floorboards? Is there a soap dispenser? Are there bottles of incense in the space? What size is the room? Is there a window? Is it bright or dimly lit? Go through the whole space and make it come alive. Feel it actually vibrating and pulsing in front of you. If you choose a waterfall setting, how high is the waterfall? What is under your feet – moss or smooth stone? Is it a gentle trickle or a torrent of water? Where does it go? What is around the waterfall? Is it forest or open land? What colour is the scenery?

Keep questioning what you are creating and make sure it all symbolises purity and cleanliness to you. Anything that you decide you don't like, change. If you create a bar of soap and then prefer liquid hand wash, change it. You might find you prefer different objects around you at different visits. That's fine, as long as you are clear about what you see and it all makes you feel good.

You may have thought about colour and size, but what about smells? Is there air freshener in the bathroom? What are the smells of your ocean or lake or jacuzzi? Only create what makes you feel clean. Create a temperature setting, too. Some people like heat, others prefer a cooler environment. Turn the temperature up or down until it's right for you. Are there sounds which soothe you? Can you hear birds or dolphins or drums or your favourite piece of music? What means purity to you? What washes away your anxieties and tensions? Think about textures, too. Is your beach pebbled or sandy? Do you have soft, fluffy towels in your bathroom or big, rough towels? Absolutely everything matters and is relevant. Where possible, choose light, bright colours. This space is meant to uplift you as well as cleanse.

No one, absolutely no one, ever comes into your cleansing space. This is only for you and therefore it doesn't matter how strange or silly or inappropriate it might seem to anyone else. No one will ever know. Enjoy this unique freedom. If you love pink stuffed elephants, put one in your cleansing space. If you're passionate about roses, have them growing all around your lake or waterfall. Do whatever you want, as long as it's cleansing and purifying. When you're given so much choice, it can be hard to think clearly at first. Keep asking yourself what cleansing means to you and then add to your surroundings. If anything feels dirty or wrong, get rid of it straight away.

When you know you have gone over every inch of your space, when it feels, smells, sounds and looks just perfect, when it completely lives in your mind, then you can move yourself into the space. Go into this wonderful area and explore it. Touch different surfaces and substances. Smell everything. Is it all just as you want it? Move things around if you want to. You are the creator and you have the last choice in everything.

Now you are comfortable with your space, you are ready to really enjoy it. Run your bath, turn on your shower or jacuzzi, step under your waterfall or into your ocean, lake, river or stream, walk into the beautiful sunshine or gentle rain. You are completely safe in this space. You are alone and have complete freedom. Choose the temperature for your water or sunshine or rain. Add bath oils, soap or scents if you want, and then step into this cleansing space.

Now enjoy it. Really enjoy it. Feel the water or sunshine on your skin. Feel it penetrating deep into all your subtle bodies, into all your energies. Be aware of any place inside you that feels uncomfortable or unpleasant. If you are a visual person, you might see this as a dark patch or a grey mist. Feel your chosen method of cleansing wash away the unpleasantness or discomfort. If you want to put some soap in your hand and use that to help you, go ahead. If you are cleansing yourself of a specific emotion, or a mental obstacle or a physical pain, use some visual image to imagine the difficulty. It might be just a patch of colour, or it might be a monster with ugly teeth or a flame of anger or a roaring beast. You might hear your difficulty as an unpleasant, discordant sound. Perhaps you feel it as a dull ache within you. Whatever it manifests as, use your cleansing instrument to wash it away. This is where the drainage is important. See the monster disappearing down the plug hole, hear the uncomfortable sound gurgle away into nothing in the water, see the rain extinguish the flame or feel the revitalising sunshine burn the ache out of your body. Let the image be appropriate for whatever it is you want to cleanse. You might feel there are so many aggravations and anxieties plaguing you that you do not know where to start. Just imagine yourself filled with all sorts of images that are then washed away. Make the shower or rain or sunshine stronger if you need more help. Sometimes it helps to affiliate the action to your breathing. Breathe the purifying substance in and as you breathe out, feel all the unpleasant sensations going with it. Pick up a loofah or pumice stone or scrubbing brush if you need a more vigorous action. Keep repeating this process for as long as you can.

When you are ready, step out of your water or sunshine. Now take a moment to dry or cool off. Sit somewhere pleasant within your cleansing sanctuary. You might have to create a comfortable armchair or a bench or fallen log, or whatever you want. Use your chosen instrument to dry you: the sun or a towel or bathrobe. If you are cooling down after the sunshine, pick up a large palm leaf or a fan and let it bring you back to normal body temperature. Sit there for a few minutes and enjoy your sensation of cleanliness. Does your skin feel tingling and clean? Does your body feel like a freshly washed, empty vessel? Do you feel ready to face any challenges that lie ahead? When you feel ready, step out of your cleansing sanctuary, with the clear knowledge that it is always there for you at any time.

Move back to your present space now. Remember which room you are in, what time of day it is. Check that your feet feel nice and heavy. Take a few comfortable breaths and open your eyes. Are you grounded and centred? Wait until you feel ready before you get up and continue with your day.

You may find you need several visits to your cleansing sanctuary before you can see it clearly. You may choose one environment and then still not feel completely happy with it. Change it. When you do find what feels right, you will know it inside and you will want to keep it. The cleansing sanctuary is your sacred space for spiritual healing, particularly for your own health. Visit it regularly and it will suddenly seem to be a part of you that's very real and very near. You will want to slip into it for a quick 'wash' quite often. It becomes a comforting space which is constantly there for you.

After a while, you will not even need to close your eyes to experience it because everything about it is so real that you can sense it without closing your eyes. You will be able to step off a crowded bus or train and have a quick wash in your cleansing sanctuary as you walk away. A colleague will annoy you and you will have a little cleanse to get rid of it. Your neck and shoulders will feel stiff after a long day and you will nip into your cleansing sanctuary to soothe the ache away. It is a constant, infinite source of spiritual healing. It should become your holy place which you use as your own personal space to wash away unpleasant sensations and feelings. Remember never to bring anyone else into your cleansing sanctuary. That is extremely important. Anyone else's energies would change the space considerably, no matter how lovely they might be. Keep it all to yourself.

Releasing physical tension

By this stage you have learnt about using three different methods to help relax you: grounding energy, cosmic energy and your cleansing sanctuary. You might still believe that you are a naturally relaxed person and very good at unwinding and letting go. You might wonder how much you really need these relaxation techniques. So let's look at a simple exercise which checks just how physically tense you are.

Lie down on your back on a comfortable surface. Close your eyes and breathe deeply. Make sure your body is comfortably spread out. Keep your legs and arms straight but your legs slightly apart. Let your arms fall away from your sides. Tuck your chin slightly into your throat so you are not straining your neck. Feel your body sink into the surface on which you are lying. Feel it getting heavier and heavier and every time you breathe out, feel tension seeping into the ground.

Now bring your attention to your left foot. How do your left toes feel? Crunch them tightly and feel them tense. Now release them. Does that feel looser? Did you notice another part of your body relaxing at the same time? Tense your whole left foot, trying not to tense any other part of the body. Now release it. Does your left foot now feel differently from your right foot? Work up your leg, tensing the whole of the left leg, remembering all your muscles and the knee. Now release them all. Does your left leg feel heavier than your right? Now repeat with your right foot and right leg. Then work your way through different parts of your body: left buttock, right buttock, stomach, spine, chest, left shoulder, right shoulder, left arm, left hand and fingers, right arm, right hand and fingers, the back of the neck, throat, jaw, lips, eyes, forehead, whole face. Notice how much heavier your body feels. Can you still feel tension? Concentrate on the area, tense it, then release. Now tense your whole body. Release. Take several long, deep breaths. Then open your eyes. Wriggle your feet and hands, then draw your legs up to your chest and hug them with your hands and arms. Rock gently back and forth, side to side. Then roll onto your right side. Wait a minute. Take three deep breaths and then slowly revert to a sitting position. Take three more breaths before you get up.

Most people have no idea that we store so much tension in our bodies. The more you do this exercise, the more aware you will become of your own body and the easier it will be to recognise that physical tension is creeping up on you and take steps to let it go again.

Now that you are learning how to relax and why it is so important, let's look more specifically at those aspects of yourself which might benefit from spiritual healing.

It may sound a rather odd phrase: loving yourself. It may also not sound very spiritual to you. Surely, if you love yourself, you are being selfish and indulgent. Is spirituality not all about giving to others and not concentrating on yourself? In fact, spirituality is all about loving yourself. Many would say until you learn to love yourself, you cannot heal either yourself or others. Loving yourself is also a very emotional issue for a lot of people. It is up to you to be gentle with yourself during this chapter and work at the pace which feels right for you. If you become too emotional while doing some of the exercises, you can leave them until a later stage. On the other hand, you may find this area deeply rewarding and illuminating and it may help to clear blocks which you have created in your energies over the years. Clearing blockages does not have to be distressing or difficult. It can be uplifting and leave you feeling absolutely wonderful about yourself and others.

Have you ever thought about what 'love' really means? Most people only consider the word when it is in relation to someone or something else. They think about it in terms of their relationship with a family member, for example, such as a parent or sibling. They start to question the meaning of love when they embark on an adult, usually sexual, relationship. But how often have you asked yourself what it means to love *yourself*? Let's look at some of the dictionary definitions of love – 'a deep affection . . . for someone', 'good will towards others', 'devotion for someone or something'. These seem to add fuel to the idea of love as fundamentally something which relates to others, not to yourself! No wonder so many people grow up believing that to love oneself is somehow unhealthy and narcissistic.

So let's look at what loving yourself does not mean. It is not about only thinking of yourself all the time. It is not about ego and feeling you are the most important person alive. It is not about feeling superior or arrogant. It is not about spending endless hours in pursuit of what you enjoy without consideration to others. It is not about filling your life with material and financial riches. It is not about preening yourself in front of a mirror constantly. It is not about telling everyone you are a terrific person all the time, while a gnawing doubt eats away at you inside. It is not about pushing people away from you with the excuse that you need no one in your life because you are self-sufficient.

All the above have nothing to do with loving yourself. Truly loving yourself is a simple unselfish act that comes from deep within. It takes the form of a deep, unshakeable sense of knowing that you are perfect just as you are. This is not easy for everyone. It means accepting all those apparently unappealing qualities in yourself that everyone can find if they look hard enough. These can be mundane dislikes, such as being too thin/fat, tall/short, introvert/extrovert, old/young, lazy/over-ambitious, a doormat/too aggressive. The list is endless. Most of us have dissatisfactions about some part of ourselves. Can you honestly look at yourself and say that you accept absolutely everything about yourself, exactly as you are at this moment? Almost everyone finds that hard to do. Basically, loving yourself is about reaching the stage where you truly know that you are perfect as you are.

It's also more than that. Loving yourself is about knowing your place within the larger scheme of life. This means knowing that the family you were born into or brought up in is the right one for you to have in your life, no matter what your childhood experience may have been.

Loving yourself means knowing that you have a special, unique part to play in the evolution of life and that you are willing to take part in whatever unfolds for you. You even look forward to the experiences ahead of you, good and bad. In fact, there is no such thing as a 'bad' experience in life; that is only a label we attach to some event whose significance we do not understand; we will look at examples of this as we go along.

It is only once we love ourselves at these levels that we can truly love others as well. Loving others means also accepting in them qualities we may not like. How many of your friends and family can you say that you love exactly as they are? If you had the choice to change certain qualities in others, would you like to be able to do that? Very few of us can truly say we would not change a thing about another person. Loving yourself means knowing that everyone else is perfect at whatever stage they are at in their life.

So let's list some of the benefits of loving yourself which will help clarify the importance of this act. You need to understand that loving yourself is an essential part of holistic health.

These benefits are that:

- *You have great self-esteem, knowing you are worthy of every task you set out to accomplish.*
- *You find it easy to love others and to accept people as they are, because you have already accepted yourself completely as you are.*
- *You can accept setbacks in your own life and see them as part of a learning curve, rather than punishments for not being a good person.*
- *You do not rely on others for praise and encouragement because you have your own in-built sense of self-worth.*
- *You do not blame others for problems in life, because you take responsibility for everything that happens to you.*
- *You take joy in the accomplishments of others, without envy or resentment.*
- *You know that everything you do is worthwhile and has a purpose.*
- *You love all of life.*

All the above states are difficult to achieve if you do not love yourself. It is the single, most powerful starting point for all spiritual healing. Loving yourself will render all of the above conditions possible for you.

Is loving yourself beginning to sound rather daunting? In fact, this journey lasts right through our life. Loving yourself has endless possibilities, for how we view life and for what we put into and get out of it. Life can be as wonderful or as dreadful as you choose, and your attitude to it is relevant to your ability to love yourself.

Starting to love yourself

So how can we start this process? Some of you may already feel you are well on the path to accepting and loving yourself because all of this makes a great deal of sense. Others may be feeling very uncertain about the experience of self-love. Check what stage you are at by doing the simple exercise below.

Sit quietly by yourself in a comfortable chair where you will not be disturbed. Close your eyes and take a few deep, easy breaths. Now take a moment to relax in your cleansing sanctuary. Let your chosen method of cleansing go through all of you and leave you feeling refreshed. Take a few more comfortable breaths.

Now say silently to yourself, 'I love you'. Pause. Notice what sensations come up for you. If they are negative thoughts or emotions, use your water or sunshine or rain and let it wash the negative away. Take a few more deep breaths. Repeat, 'I love you'. Now what comes up for you? If it is anything unpleasant, wash it away. Keep repeating this process. It may take a while, especially the first time you try this exercise. That's fine. It's natural. We don't realise how many negative concepts we have about ourselves until we start to probe a little deeper. It's not the fact that we have these thoughts which is important but how we choose to let them go.

Many people feel tearful at this stage. This is fine. Tears release and wash away negative images. Some people simply feel very silly. They can't believe it's good to love themselves. Others feel cross. Some feel a surge of relief and pleasure. If you feel a pleasant sensation, acknowledge it. Whatever you don't like, wash away. The stronger your image of your cleansing sanctuary, the easier this will be for you. Wash away all the emotions, thoughts and images which you don't want. If they come back, simply wash them away again. Remember to see them disappear down the plug hole or melt into the ground or whatever method you have chosen.

Sometimes people see images of others who have ridiculed them or hurt them in some way. Wash those away as well. They have no place in your cleansing sanctuary. You have to accept that you have let them come in and that you also have the ability to send them away again. Don't let anyone or anything stay that distresses you. This is very important. Part of loving yourself is discovering your strength to control your life. You needn't have anyone influencing you in a negative fashion because you have the ability to wash them away, especially in your cleansing sanctuary. Wash them away now. You brought them in and now you can let them go. Take control of this action now. You don't have to let them go with anger or panic. Just breathe comfortably and deeply and wash them away. You are in control.

When you feel you have washed away the negative and feel cleansed and calm, try the statement once more to yourself silently. 'I love you'. What does it feel like now? Perhaps less negative emotions hit you. Perhaps you just feel a strange emptiness. That is wonderful. You are like an empty vessel, ready to receive positive influences into your life. Some of you may feel a wonderful sense of peace and calm. A warm glow may steal over you.

Now pull in the cosmic energy from above you and let it filter around you and in through your crown chakra, slowly filling all of you. Notice how warm and loving this energy is. Cosmic energy is unconditional love. Let that sense of peace and contentment calm and energise you. Know that you have taken the first step to loving yourself and feel contented with this new stage in your life. It doesn't matter how small a step you have taken, because that first step is always a giant one to take.

Sit quietly for a few minutes with your eyes closed. Take several more comfortable breaths and wait until you feel balanced and ready before you open your eyes. Then concentrate on an object in the room to refocus yourself. Wait another minute or two before you get up.

This first exercise can unnerve some people and bring out new, unsettling thoughts. Others find it interesting but not very effective. A few can find it liberating and uplifting. Whatever the nature of your own experience, try to repeat this exercise. It really does become easier and more enjoyable with familiarity. Constant practice means you can reach the level where your statement of 'I love you' feels natural and obvious.

It does not mean you suddenly have an inflated feeling of self-importance or pride; this sense of loving yourself is an internal peace that comes from a higher level of awareness. It is not connected with earthly pleasures and attachments. Once you start to feel this sense of belonging and complete calm, you will be experiencing the difference between earthly and spiritual love. This then becomes the foundation for your spiritual work. This process of loving yourself cannot and must not be under-estimated or passed over as unnecessary. Everyone must learn to love themselves in the truly spiritual sense to become effective healers. The more you practise the exercise above, the easier it becomes to connect with this source of loving. Come back to it again and again and continue to work at loving yourself.

Loving yourself via the heart chakra

Now we are going to use your heart chakra to try to delve more deeply into any blocks you may have with regard to loving yourself. If you found the preceding exercise emotional, leave the exercise below for the time being. There is no law that says you have to work swiftly through all the exercises. You should work at the pace which feels right for you and be gentle with yourself. The process of being gentle with yourself and knowing yourself is all part of your self-healing. You have to take responsibility for your own emotions. If you are concerned that you are trying to open up too many sensitive areas of yourself too quickly, leave the exercise until later. You can always come back to it in a few months' time. If you know you are ready to work at a deeper level, then continue. You might want to re-read the details about the heart chakra on page 47, to refresh your knowledge before you do the exercise.

Sit comfortably in your chair and close your eyes. Take a few breaths and wait until you feel settled and comfortable before proceeding. If you are feeling stressed for any reason, wash away any problems by using your cleansing sanctuary before you continue. Don't rush your relaxation process.

When you're ready, concentrate on your heart chakra. Remember its location and that it opens front and back. Remember it is associated with the colour of green: soft grass green. Gently focus your thoughts on this particular area of your body. You don't have to consciously open this or any other chakra as you do this exercise. It will gradually open of its own accord as you let your images and thoughts flow freely without force or distress.

Think now about your heart and its function. Think about where it is in your body. What does that part of you feel like right now? Does it feel light and warm? Does it feel heavy? Is there a fluttering or tingling around the heart area? Is the chakra moving – either clockwise or anti-clockwise? Can you feel it front and back? How would you describe the general feeling around this area of your body? Just concentrate your thoughts on this area and let your body tell you how it feels. Remember to keep breathing deeply and comfortably. Don't become actively involved in any sensation in your body, just observe it in a slightly detached way. Always remember to wash away any unpleasant emotion or feeling. Never let it linger.

Do you have images which come through as you concentrate on this area of your body? They may be wonderful, loving images. They may be sad. Wash away what you don't want but notice what they are.

Now think of the colour green. What does green mean to you? Do you like it as a colour? What is green naturally on our Earth? What is your relationship to these objects? How much time do you spend with them? How much green do you choose to have around you? Do you wear green clothes? Do you have green walls/rugs/curtains in your home? Do the paintings you like have green in them? What fruit and vegetables are green? Do you eat many of these items?

Now say the word 'love' silently to yourself. What sensations do you notice around your heart chakra? What images crop up for you? As you focus on your heart chakra, what does the word 'love' make you feel? Ask your heart to give you more information. Say you would like to learn more about the word. Ask the heart chakra to help you in this path. Notice what information you receive without becoming actively involved in it. Notice if certain images or thoughts keep recurring. Keep washing away what you don't want.

Now say 'I love you' silently to yourself. What is happening now to your heart chakra area? If it's a lovely sensation, experience the pleasure of its warmth and notice how it makes all of you feel. If you don't like what you experience, wash it away. Repeat the words silently, if you want to experience more.

Then remember to slowly withdraw. Consciously close your heart chakra down. (It will have opened whether you were aware of it or not.) Wash through with your cleansing sanctuary. Remember where you are sitting, what day it is, what the time is, and slowly open your eyes. Wait a minute before you get up.

Was that a more emotional experience for you? Did you find other concepts and beliefs about the word love cropped up this time?

By working with your heart chakra you were delving deeper into your spiritual understanding of loving yourself. Some of you may have found it uncomfortable, others liberating. What is very likely to have happened, however, is that you found certain old statements and thoughts cropping up again and again. This is a natural process. When you ask yourself to love yourself, you will find that any negative belief you hold about self-worth and self-love will assail you. It may not feel comfortable and it may feel irritating. How much do you want those old, negative thoughts?

You see, the process of loving yourself involves letting go of old repeated patterns of thoughts. Most of us do not realise just how many well-worn phrases we have going around our heads. We accept them as part of the 'truth' about ourselves because they have been with us so long that we cannot believe they are not true! That is why as you start to let go of negative thoughts, they just keep returning. How many thoughts returned to you during the above exercises? You may have thought you let them go but did some suddenly resurface to haunt you?

You can liken it to an old recording or CD playing around in your head. You have forgotten how to press the stop button, so the thought keeps playing. When you do find the stop button, it then starts up again of its own accord. This can be deeply frustrating. A good solution to this is to re-record the thought. Replace it with another thought process so that the initial one is erased.

Affirmations
The word for this technique is 'Affirmations', which can be a valuable tool to aid the process of loving yourself. Take a look at some of the statements below. Can you apply any of them to your life?

- *I was often told as a child that I was useless/bad/ stupid/a pain.*
- *I felt a sibling received more love than I did/I still feel this way.*
- *I was useless at school/university.*
- *Everyone else has more money/love/fun than me.*
- *Other people have all the luck/I have no luck.*

- *I cannot find a loving relationship.*
- *I dislike my job.*
- *I have no real talent.*
- *Life is a hard grind.*
- *No one really likes me/understands me/wants me.*
- *I am not pretty/handsome enough.*
- *I am not good enough.*

Expressions like these run through the heads of most people from time to time, often because of past experiences. Later on, we will look at how we may have developed these attitudes and how to forgive those who may have influenced us. For now, we are just going to look at how we can let some of the negative images go.

Affirmations are basically positive thoughts that you use to replace negative ones. It is a thought which you say out loud and repeat at regular intervals. It does not have to be said loudly or with vehemence. It does not even matter if, initially, you do not believe it. All you need is a commitment to repeating the phrase often enough so it becomes believable. The repetition is what makes it powerful.

There is one important rule with an affirmation. It must be phrased in the positive. That means you say 'I love myself' as opposed to 'I don't hate myself'. You say 'I'm happy' instead of 'I'm not sad' and 'I am well' instead of 'I'm not sick'. The reason for framing the affirmation in this way is that our brains are programmed to pick up on the main word. Consequentially, if you have 'I don't hate myself', your brain picks up on the word 'hate', ignoring the 'don't' in front of it! You then continue to work with the image of hate as opposed to love. This is a crucial area of affirmations, so think carefully before you create one for yourself. The wrong phrase continually circling in your head will create further negative images for you.

If you are worried about making up the right affirmation, you can start off with one listed below. After a while, you may spontaneously discover your own, more powerful affirmation. You will know when this feels right for you. Say the following out loud and see how they make you feel. Does one feel stronger and more right for you than another?

- *I love my life.*
- *I enjoy holistic health.*
- *I love myself unconditionally.*
- *I love everyone unconditionally.*
- *I embrace all experiences in life.*
- *I embrace my spirituality.*
- *Everything in my life is exactly as it should be.*

Many people struggle with the last affirmation! We can always find aspects of our life to criticise and rebel against. The last affirmation is a very powerful one, if you feel ready for the challenge. You will notice that these affirmations refer very much to what we have been discussing during this chapter. We will look at other affirmations for other areas of life later.

So how do you work with affirmations? They need to be repeated out loud. They need to be repeated regularly. You need to be committed to saying your affirmation, even when you do not feel like it! Constant repetition is the key. Here is a suggested starting point for your first affirmation.

You say your affirmation when you get up in the morning, either before you get out of bed or shortly thereafter. You choose a suitable time during the middle of the day to repeat it. You repeat it again before you go to bed. On each occasion, say your affirmation ten times. Yes, ten times! This means that 30 times a day you are making a new playlist. Now, to make it more effective, also say your affirmation every time you need a boost of confidence, as well. For instance, you might be going out on a date and feeling insecure and nervous. Repeat your affirmation as many times as you like as you get yourself ready. Say it before an important business meeting. Use it to give you extra courage if you have a difficult personal issue to face. In other words, use your affirmation constantly.

It sounds so simplistic, doesn't it? You just say something often enough, and things start to improve in your life. Perhaps you are feeling sceptical as you think about this. Do you believe that any change in life is always a big upheaval, always difficult, always uncomfortable? Some changes in life happen without enormous effort; they happen because we are ready to embrace change. By choosing an affirmation and repeating it, all you are doing is making the space for changes to occur.

Let us refer this concept back to what we understand about energies. Remember the discussion about our human auras and how they change constantly according to what is happening around us and how we are feeling? Do you remember reading that if we are feeling suffocated in a crowded train or bus, we close down our auras? If we feel frightened or nervous, our auras change. Likewise, every single thought we have also changes our aura. If we are thinking openly and embracing all the possibilities in life, our auras (and chakras) open and expand. If we believe, truly believe, that we deserve positive experiences and influences and that everything has a purpose, if we embrace everything around us, good and 'bad', then our auras change. In other words, thoughts (which are affirmations) change our human energy. As soon as our own energies change, we can start to release those blocked, closed areas and repair torn or ripped areas within our subtle body. It is the thought process which starts everything working. If you have been developing your relationship with grounding and cosmic energy (see pages 71 and 74) and have been practising with your cleansing sanctuary (see page 77), you will know that the more often you create the thought of these areas, the more powerful they become.

There is yet another way to make affirmations even more powerful. You may find this daunting at first but it is well worth trying to see if you can deal with this. You say your affirmations while looking at yourself in a mirror.

Looking at you

How often have you looked at your own eyes in a mirror? This is not an easy thing to do. You might glance at yourself as you shave or put on make-up or comb your hair. You might check your clothes or shape in a mirror. But have you spent time really staring into your own eyes and seeing what they tell you? Most people do not like the emotions that crop up as they do this. If you have found the exercises in this chapter challenging, then leave the next exercise for another time. Remember, be gentle on yourself! However, if you want to look deeper, then try this:

Sit comfortably in your chair, with a hand mirror ready in your lap. Close your eyes first and relax. Cleanse if you need to, and remember your new commitment to loving yourself unconditionally. Take some deep, comfortable breaths and when you feel ready, open your eyes and hold the mirror up to your face. Look at your eyes in the mirror.

You may initially experience confusion because it's hard to look at both eyes at once! Concentrate first on one eye and then another. Notice if there is any difference between the two. If one is more comfortable to gaze into than the other, choose the more comfortable eye. Notice how beautiful your eyes are! If you have ever studied anything to do with the eyes, you'll already appreciate how beautiful and complex they are: their different colours and shapes, the way they actually glow and sparkle in different lights, how the white compliments and enhances the other colours, how looking into them is like gazing into an endless pool. Try to look into your own eyes without any judgment and without straining too much. Just appreciate how beautiful they are.

The eyes are often described as the gateway to the soul. One could say they are a path to acknowledging your spiritual self. They store our feelings, emotions and experiences. The eyes don't lie. If you look at a photograph of someone and cover up everything except their eyes, you will discover how they were really feeling at the time. Their mouth might be smiling, but their eyes could be sad. Or they might be looking stern, but you can see a twinkle in their eyes. Our eyes say who we really are.

Look deeply into your own eyes and you can look past all the trivial, outer parts of you and see right into your own soul. You can find the pure, perfect person that you really are. This is a way to access your true spiritual self.

However, there are often blocks to reaching this state. If you have difficulty in loving yourself, looking into the mirror will show this to you. Try saying 'I love you' out loud to the mirror as you gaze into your eyes.

Are you having even stronger emotions now? (Some people find this moment too emotional initially. If it's too much for you, put the mirror down, close your eyes and cleanse through. Wash away all the residue emotion. Return to this exercise on another occasion.) If you want to continue, notice what thought or feeling is cropping up. Is it the same as you experienced during the previous two exercises, or is something new happening? Notice if it is an emotion related to a particular person or an experience. Don't delve into the situation, but remain detached and observe what is happening. Wash away what you do not want.

Continue gazing into your eyes. Remember to keep appreciating the beauty that you see. Take a moment to acknowledge how unique you are. No two eyes are identical, just as no two fingerprints are identical. You are unique. Your place within the universe is unique.

Now say out loud the affirmation you have chosen, as you gaze into your eyes. Notice what happens. Repeat the affirmation. Do this ten times. Notice how the feelings change. If you want to repeat the affirmation more than ten times, that is fine. You might find a wonderful sense of self-worth and self-purpose as you do this. You might have a sudden insight into an area of your life that has been troubling you. You might just feel a warm glow through all of you. You may feel an unaccountable sensation of peace and tranquillity. Enjoy any positive reaction.

When you feel ready, withdraw your gaze from the mirror.

Put the mirror down and close your eyes. Remember to cleanse away anything unpleasant that may have lingered. Take several more deep, comfortable breaths before you open your eyes and focus on an object to balance you again. Wait a minute before you get up.

Mirror work is another exercise that you can benefit from returning to often. Again, it becomes easier with time. As you work with reprogramming the negative thoughts, it becomes easier and easier to shed them and to replace them with positive concepts.

One of the unsettling aspects of working with affirmations is that we end up realising just how often we phrase things in a negative fashion! It is not until we concentrate on what we really think of our life, that we acknowledge how many negative patterns exist. If you believe that the thoughts we send out provide their own energy, then it becomes even more important to concentrate on embracing whatever will offer you a full, holistic life.

Loving yourself is the starting point. We have looked at why this is important and some tools you can use to start this process, especially affirmations. However, affirmations are just one method you can use to embrace everything around you. There are many other techniques we are going to explore. You also need to start looking deeper at different areas of your life and discover what you can personally do to improve the quality of your life – on all levels. You need now to start assessing all of your life.

Just a word of warning before we continue, however. The process of learning to love yourself will continue through all your work during spiritual healing, which is a subject which we will return to constantly, because it is the source from which all positive actions will flow. As you will see through further work, holistic healing all flows back to acceptance of yourself, your life and everything around you. That acceptance stems from unconditional love. You cannot escape the significance of this chapter and it will be referred to again and again. Please take time to re-read this section if you have skimmed through it. It is just not possible for you to achieve satisfying and prolonged positive results in spiritual healing without having absorbed and accepted the concept of utterly loving yourself.

What areas of your life would you like to heal? That question brings up a major issue in healing. Honesty. You have to learn to be honest with yourself if you are going to tackle different areas of your life that you want to heal. By connecting with spiritual energy, you are dealing with the very core of you. It will not respond to lies or hidden agendas. It can only respond to the truth.

For example, you might decide you want to look at your relationship with your partner and to improve areas of communication between you. You have to face this scenario in the same way as you would face any other. This means unconditional love. You cannot create a healing force by saying any of the following:

- *It would work if only they would talk more/listen more.*
- *It would all be all right if only they were more patient.*
- *All it needs is for them to change a little.*
- *I know I'm right about this and they need to listen to me.*
- *They have to agree with me or else they're bad/wrong.*

None of those statements will change the energies between you and lead to a healing environment. It takes a new degree of honesty and searching from within to handle spiritual healing. You have to stop blaming others and look within for solutions.

For example, embracing some of the following might help you:

- *We can accomplish anything together.*
- *I am committed to improving our relationship.*
- *I love my partner and accept them as they are.*
- *Our relationship is wonderful and we can make it even more wonderful together.*

- *I am learning all the time about myself and
  how to change.*
- *I want to share all my positive thoughts with my partner.*
- *I am committed to understanding my partner better.*
- *Our love is getting stronger and more wonderful
  every day.*

Some of those statements may be very difficult for you if you are
having problems and cannot see your way through, but to
change the energies between you it is necessary to reconsider
how you approach problems in life. Blaming anyone else will
not lead to any kind of solution. Always take responsibility
yourself and work from that point.

This does not mean that you should take on the concept that
everything is your fault. Blaming and finding fault with yourself,
and feeling guilty, have no place in spiritual healing; these are
very strong emotions which govern many of us and we have to
learn to let them go before we can heal. So being honest with
yourself has nothing to do with thinking it is all your fault. Being
honest is saying you want to face the problem and learn from the
process without attaching blame to anyone, including yourself.

There is a wonderful saying, 'There is no such thing as a
problem without a gift for you in its hands. You seek problems
because you need their gifts.' So here is a new way for you to
consider any area you want to heal in your life. Until you learn
what it is you need to know, you will probably continue to make
the same mistake again and again. Once you have learnt whatever
spiritual lesson is necessary, you will move on. That same problem
is unlikely to occur again. What areas in your life have perpetual,
recurring difficulties? What do you need to learn from that?

Take, for example, someone who has constant difficulties in adult
relationships. They cannot find a permanent partner. They keep
having the same problems: partners who treat them as doormats;
partners who leave them; partners who cheat on them; partners who
abuse them. Is there someone around you who is in a continuous
cycle of disastrous relationships? This happens because they are

refusing to learn a lesson in life. If they took the time to sit in stillness, to access their inner, spiritual core and find out what is really going on, the true reason for their situation could become clear. Perhaps they have never learnt how to love and respect themselves. They may have had an abusive childhood and are simply repeating a negative thought in their head which says that they do not deserve a loving relationship. They might think they thrive on emotional upset and drama because they confuse that with the concept of feeling truly alive. Maybe they are searching for a perfect love that they think will solve all their problems in life. Perhaps they are terrified of being alone because they think they cannot cope. There is a long list of possible answers, but all that matters is that they find the truth for themselves. While they are in the frantic process of rushing from one partner to another and dealing with all the emotional upset, they are stopping themselves from pausing and going within to deal with the root cause.

The truth is that most people are frightened of this process. Fear is the greatest blockage we have in our complex energy systems. It has to be released before we can fully work at healing. Where fear stems from and how we can release it is dealt with in the next chapter, but at this stage you just need to be honest enough to admit that you feel fear over various areas in your life. Then you can start to shave away the outer levels of protection and blocks of fear and insecurity and be willing to delve deeper into the core issue. Again, you must concentrate on yourself first, others later. Once you can release some of the fear, you then learn to own every problem, every difficulty you face and take responsibility for it, but not any blame. Then you can move forward.

All our healing starts with loving our self and then moving into higher realms of consciousness and appreciation of life on a larger scale. The most frustrating and powerless struggle we can find ourselves in is to believe we do not have the ability to change different aspects of our life. Believing we can alter our attitudes and circumstances creates the arena for change, and change then follows as a matter of course. So consider the following affirmation before you start assessing your own life:

I welcome and embrace all changes in my life.

Say it out loud. Say it again. And again. Does it feel comfortable? Do you have all sorts of fears that crop up when you say it? Do you think that change is not necessarily good? Do you think that everything in your life really is all right after all so you had better not rock the boat? Do you fear what might alter in your life if you change your attitude to things? Are you nervous of approaching people in your life with whom you would like to change things? Consider this statement also:

We cling to our pain through habit and fear of something worse.

To work with spiritual healing, you have to be willing to change. You have to acknowledge that we are more than just physical beings, having a physical, earthly experience. You have already spent some time tapping into another, deeper part of you through recent exercises. You are like a flower opening to the sunlight. Remember, you do not have to let go of all your earthly, physical thoughts. Embrace them, but continue to open your mind further. Spiritual healing is about accepting that nothing in our lives is constant. Our human auras change every second through each day. We decide how much we want to change and open by expanding our thoughts all the time.

Embracing life

Try to see problems in life as just another chance to learn more. Think of a time in your life which was sad or difficult. Can you see something wonderful that came about as a result? Every difficult experience in life is tinged with some positive, joyful outcome. If you have not found it yet, it is purely because you have not looked hard enough. Try the exercise below to prove this point:

Close your eyes and relax. Breathe deeply. Think back to an unpleasant experience. Be gentle with yourself. Don't choose an experience which was deeply traumatic. Think of an uncomfortable situation rather than a deeply upsetting one.

Remember the circumstances regarding the scenario. Remember how old you were, where you were, the people around you. Remember how you felt. Then let the emotion wash away using your cleansing sanctuary. Now think about the period following that experience. What did you learn? What was the 'gift' you received as a result of that experience? Really think about it.

If you can't think of a good outcome, it's only because you aren't concentrating enough. Try repeating your affirmation of 'I welcome and embrace all changes in my life' to help open you further. Keep concentrating. After a moment, you will find a positive influence. There is always a good outcome. Always. Now think even further. What else happened that was positive as a result of that experience? After a moment, you will think of something else. Now think even deeper. Isn't there something else as well? Keep working with all the good results. The more you think, the more they come rushing into your thoughts.

If you focus deeply enough, you will reach the stage where all you will see is the positive outcome of a supposedly 'bad' experience. You will let the negative influence wash away of its own accord. You are left seeing that any unpleasant experience is far outweighed by the uplifting positive effects. If you haven't found more than half a dozen good results, you haven't been concentrating enough. Keep repeating your affirmation if you are struggling. Refuse to give up. All that knowledge is inside you. You just have to dig beneath a few layers to find it. Keep your thoughts firmly focused on the effects of that incident and a wealth of positive repercussions can be found.

A change then occurs at this stage. You often have a sensation of being lifted up, of leaving earthly frustrations behind for a minute. You have a taste of knowing where you belong in the higher scheme of life. You gain the truly powerful insight that no situation or emotion is 'bad'. It's not what happens to you in life that is important, it's how you react to what happens. Every sad or distressing experience is far out-weighed by a much stronger, more illuminating response of having learnt from whatever happened.

When you feel ready, withdraw from the memories. Wash in your cleansing sanctuary. Take some grounding energy up through the soles of your feet if you are feeling a little light-headed. Wait until you feel well grounded and balanced again before you open your eyes. Take more deep breaths and sit still for a minute before you continue with your daily work.

You may find yourself feeling overwhelmed by the residue of emotion from this exercise. If you have not had a powerful response from your first try at this exercise, go back and do it again, remembering another experience. Keep going back to areas of your life where you wondered why something happened and learn from it. Keep listening to the information you are given and the insights that crop up for you. This is you learning to heal yourself through spiritual awareness.

It is important to acknowledge that no experience is purely 'bad'. You need this not only to heal yourself, but also when working with others. It is a philosophy which, if you can develop it fully, allows you to let go of fear and to embrace all possibilities. It is fear which stops us from moving forward in so many areas of our life. Fear is from the unknown, not trusting in what is about to happen. If you know that whatever happens there will be a good outcome, you can let go of fear.

Of course, it is more difficult to embrace deeply distressing incidents in your life. However, if you start off with the less difficult incidents and then gradually work your way into darker ones, you will be amazed at the ease with which you can tackle what you thought were very difficult, challenging issues. It is the practice which enables you to work at deeper levels.

So what are the areas in your life that you want to look at? You know you want to be honest with yourself, you know you want to look at your life without guilt and blame. You want to take responsibility for everything that happens to you. You want to embrace change. You know all outcomes have positive repercussions. So what do you *really* want to work at healing?

What are the areas of your life that you feel need improvement, a radical overhaul or even a complete change?

Childhood

We are going to start with your childhood. It is in those very early stages that so many of our thoughts were recorded in our head. It is our childhood thoughts which we take with us into adulthood and which we continue to re-play until we learn to change them. Of course, some childhood thoughts are wonderfully nurturing. We only want to change those which debilitate us in some way.

So what was your childhood like? Do you have a sensation of comfort and warmth? Do you feel insecure and unhappy? Is there anger? Or sadness? Start writing some thoughts down as an exercise.

Take a large sheet of blank paper and a pen or pencil. Write the words 'My Childhood' at the top. Now underneath it put everything you can remember about your childhood. Write down memories, objects, emotions, incidents, feelings. It doesn't matter how much you scribble or how messy it is. Let your thoughts flow. No one will read this, apart from you, so it can be as personal as you like. If you start to get upset, either cleanse through with your chosen technique, or stop the exercise. Again, you can return at a later stage. If you have strong feelings for family members or friends, write those down, too. Make sub-headings if you want. If you moved around as a child, record how you felt about different locations. Are there periods of your childhood where you can remember very little? Why?

Include your adolescence in your childhood page as well. How did you feel about yourself during this period? What were your relationships like with family members or guardians? Can you remember a point when you felt as though your childhood ended and your adulthood began? What happened during that period? Write for as long as you like.

When you've had enough, put down your pen, close your

*eyes, and cleanse any distressing emotions from your aura.
You may just feel warm and contented after this writing,
but if you don't, then wash away the residue. You don't
need any negativity. Remember that all belongs in your past.
Those experiences are gone. Now you can look forward to
discovering the positive benefits of your past. Ahead of you
lies discovery and freedom from old negative patterns. Take
a few moments to balance yourself. Wait until you feel
composed again before you open your eyes and look down
at your piece of paper.*

*What is the first thing your eye is drawn to? Which aspect
of your childhood leaps off the page? Don't worry if nothing
strikes you initially. Just keep browsing over the page. The
right word or phrase will make itself known. It doesn't matter
what it is or how insignificant it seems. It might be someone's
name or an emotion. It could be a place you visited as a
child. It might be the word you've written in large, bold
capitals, or it might be a light squiggle at the bottom of the
page. Trust your instinct and know that the right word or
phrase will make itself clear. When it does, remember it.
Circle it, or write it down separately. This is what you have
chosen to start your healing process.*

Adulthood

Now you need to take another sheet of blank paper. You can do this
on a separate day if you prefer. You work at your own pace, remember.
It does not matter how long you take to work through the exercises.

*Now write the words 'My Adulthood' at the top of the page.
Repeat the process of writing down everything you can think
of about your adult life. Remember when you felt it started
for you and how you felt about having to be an adult. Write
down your feelings about your adult relationships. Write
down your present relationship with people from your
childhood. Has it changed much? If you want to do sub-*

headings, that's fine. If you feel certain issues, such as marriage or children or career, need separate sheets of paper, go ahead. This is a time of freedom for you. Write as much as you like. Remember no one else will see these scribbles and you can be as honest as you like. Remember that you want to be honest, to facilitate the healing process. If you want to draw something that represents how you feel, that's fine. Anything that helps you express how you feel about adulthood is good. Write for as long as you like.

Then put your pen down. Close your eyes and take a few deep breaths. Are you feeling relieved or suddenly overwhelmed by adult responsibility? Let any unpleasant sensation go. Cleanse it away. Again remember that all you have to learn from these experiences are positive outcomes. You might not be able to see the good influences yet, but know that you will. Remember to keep breathing deeply. Wash unwanted thoughts away.

When you're ready, open your eyes and look at your piece of paper. What hits you? Did you find that this time the process was quick? You are learning to trust your instinct. The important adulthood influence will show itself. Circle it.

Good! You have started looking at certain areas of healing in your life. Now you have opened the floodgates by looking at your childhood and adulthood, are there other areas you want to look at?

Your physical self

Let's approach your life from a slightly different angle now. Let's look at its physical aspects, and at the emotional, mental and spiritual spheres. We are going to work slightly deeper, using communication with some of your chakras to access more information about how you really feel about yourself and aspects of your life. Make sure you have plenty of paper and a pen ready when you do these exercises, but do not hold them in your hands while you are working.

Close your eyes and concentrate on your breathing to relax. Cleanse if you need to do so. During this exercise, focus on your base chakra. It's just below the base of your spine and has just one opening, downwards to the ground. Remember that red is associated with this chakra. Don't consciously try to open it or expand the chakra in any way. It is not necessary. Just be aware of its location and notice any sensations in that area as you work through the exercise.

Now bring your awareness to your whole physical body. How does it feel as you sit in your chair? Do parts of it ache? If they do, why are they hurting? Is it tension or just a lack of exercise? Do you feel sluggish or full of energy? How much do you nurture and love your physical body? How good are you at keeping it clean and exercised? Do you pamper your body with oils and lotions but ignore what you eat? Or are you conscious of having a healthy diet but of not exercising regularly?

Now think about the parts of your physical body which you like. (Usually, all you can think of suddenly are the parts of you which you dislike! Wash that away and think positively.) Have you got nice eyes? Are your feet nicely shaped? Do people say you have good hair? Is your complexion blemish-free? Perhaps you have small, perfectly formed ears. Perhaps your hands are attractive. It doesn't matter what part it is – just acknowledge that you have some areas of your body which you like.

Now what don't you like about your body? (The floodgates usually open here!) Think about why you don't like a certain part. Is it because you have been criticised or teased? Is it because you look at magazines and think everyone else has a perfect shape but not you? Forget what other people dictate. What do you feel deep inside? Does the size of your nose/waist/ chest really matter? Who says there's only one 'right' way to be? If you understand that unconditional love is the only way to move forward with spiritual healing, then can you see an opportunity for loving your physical body exactly as it is? Can you believe that you are perfect just as you are?

Consider the myriad tasks your physical body performs every day without you thinking about it. How much do you really appreciate your body? How much do you abuse it? What would you really choose to do with your body if you had the time?

Think about what you would like to eat, think about how you would exercise, think about personal hygiene and pampering your body. Create a situation where you totally look after your physical body, where you appreciate it and nurture it. Think about loving your body unconditionally.

Now tune in to your base chakra. How does it feel now? Is there any difference? Does your base chakra have any information to give you about how you feel about your physical body? Spend a few moments sitting quietly and see if any other sensations or images come to you. When you feel ready, withdraw from your base chakra. You may find other chakras have been working during this time. Gently withdraw your awareness from them and go into your cleansing sanctuary. Wash away anything you don't want around you. Sit for a while before opening your eyes. Make sure you are grounded.

Now pick up your pen and paper and start making notes. Write down the predominant emotion or thought you are left with after this exercise. Just put down what you honestly discovered about your relationship with your physical self – it doesn't have to look good. If you are upset or uplifted, put that down. Try to remember the good sensations and the positive thoughts as well as the negative. Write down any insight or break through that occurred during this time, and make a note of how your base chakra felt. How does it feel now as you are writing?

When you've finished, have another cleanse and then ground and balance yourself before you get up again. Remember to

pull some of the cosmic energy down into your aura if you
want to refresh or energise yourself.

Your emotional self

Were you surprised by the depth of your thoughts during that exercise?
Once you start working with your chakras, you are allowing yourself
to work at deeper levels. If you felt very little, that is fine, too. You
can repeat all these exercises again at other times. You will have
different responses depending upon how you are feeling at the time.
When you are ready, work your way through the next exercise.

Close your eyes, sit comfortably and take a few deep breaths.
Cleanse if you need it. Now concentrate on your second chakra,
the navel chakra. Remember it is located just below your navel
and it opens front and back. It is associated with the colour
orange and although this chakra is connected to your sexuality
and sensuality, it's also about your emotions and how you handle
them in relation to yourself and others. Again, don't try to open
this chakra, just focus on the area in which it is housed. Notice
any sensations or emotions which flow from this area.

Now think about your emotional self. Would you describe
yourself as a naturally emotional person? Do you cry easily?
Do you enjoy laughing and sharing humorous incidents
with others? If you are angry, can you readily show it? Do
you often have arguments with people around you, or do
you spend a lot of time pacifying people, disliking emotional
outbursts of any kind?

Were you brought up to believe expressing yourself was an
important part of life, or were you told to keep yourself in
check and that brave children do not cry? Were you always
longing to share experiences as a child and yet constantly
told to be quiet? Did you ever have meals together as a family
and discuss your day and share what had happened? Or
were your meals rushed affairs or silent, brooding periods?

What happens now in your adult life?

*How do you react if you hear an unpleasant piece of news?
Do you try not to think about it? Do you immediately react
with tears or anger? When you have had a wonderful
experience, do you rush to share that moment with others
or do you have a need to keep it to yourself? Do you admire
emotion in others or does it unnerve you? If you watch people
arguing or being volatile in some way, do you feel apprehensive
or enlivened by that energy?*

*Notice how your stomach area reacts as you are consider
these questions and try to answer them honestly. Is there
more activity through the front or back of your chakra? If
you feel your stomach knotting up in any way or feeling
uncomfortable, pull your cleansing energy right through
your body and feel the tension being washed away. Remember
to keep doing this if necessary. If your stomach suddenly
starts to gurgle as you work through this exercise, that is also
very normal. It means you are processing information,
digesting it, as you work, and you are also letting your
stomach muscles relax.*

*What aspects of your emotional self do you like? Are you
good in a crisis if someone else is very upset? Are you level-
headed and practical? Is your volatile nature good for
drawing other people out of themselves? Acknowledge the
emotional parts of you that are an asset to your life.
Acknowledge how you may positively influence others with
your emotional strength.*

*Now look at areas you may not like so much. Where does your
emotion hold you back? When do you stop yourself from
expressing your emotions, and why? Have you got other people's
words running around the tape in your head, criticising you
for some emotional reaction? Do you dread someone behaving
in a certain way because you know it will prompt a particular*

reaction from you? Do you ever long to express yourself but feel you cannot? Is this a recurring problem?

Now think of a moment in your life when you felt truly happy and fulfilled, emotionally. It might be when you passed a difficult school exam, when you fell in love, when your child was born, or when you were given a job which you really wanted. Remember a moment when your emotions felt good. Relive that moment again. Remember the sensation through your body. Did your physical body feel uplifted as well? How did your stomach area feel? Do you feel sensations in the other chakras as well? Enjoy the sensation for a moment, and then slowly withdraw your attention from your chakras.

Keep your eyes closed and breathe deeply. Cleanse anything unpleasant from your aura and physical body. When you are ready, pick up your pen and paper and start writing.

Put down your strongest emotions first. Note how your stomach area felt throughout and how it feels now. Write down the areas you feel good about and the areas you would like to work with. If you still feel upset in any way, write it out. If a person or situation is constantly cropping up for you and you're not sure why, write it down and look at it in detail later. Put down anything which feels relevant to your emotions. Notice the areas where you want to change your emotional responses and know that you will look at them later. Let any residual emotion come out through your pen.

When you know you are finished, put your pen and paper down and cleanse again. Thoroughly. If you had unnerving emotions, wash them away. If sexual issues came up for you which you aren't ready to deal with (this chakra also relates to your sexuality, remember), wash those away, too. Remember that you can always choose to look at other areas later. It's not the fact that you're not dealing with them now that is important; what matters is that you are acknowledging them but choosing to look at them at a later date. You therefore take control. You are always in control during these exercises.

Sit for at least three minutes before you get up. Remember to keep your breathing even and comfortable. Open your eyes and focus on an object to reorientate yourself before you stand up.

You may find yourself feeling more emotional than usual after this exercise. It is a normal reaction to working more deeply with your emotional chakra. Without consciously trying to do so, you have been shifting the energies within this powerful centre by means of your thought processes alone. That is good, but it can be unsettling. Remember that any change can initially feel strange so do not worry if you feel a little off-balance for a while. Your energies will shift again and settle. If you continue to feel uncomfortable, find a moment to sit down again and go into your cleansing sanctuary. Remember that you take control of everything in your life. You choose to let go of anything that you do not need at present. Wait until you feel ready before moving on to the next section.

Your mental self

Sit quietly and compose yourself. Breathe comfortably and cleanse if necessary. Wait until you feel relaxed before proceeding. Now focus on your solar plexus chakra. This is in your spleen area, just below and to the left of your rib cage. The colour yellow is connected with this chakra and it also opens front and back. Be aware of this chakra during this exercise but don't try to open or manipulate it in any way. Just notice the sensations which emanate from this area.

Now think about your mental self. How would you describe your mental health? Are you rational in thought? Do you enjoy sitting and thinking about things without acting upon them? Do you like problem-solving? This can include mathematical equations, crossword puzzles, lateral thinking questions, murder/mystery stories, philosophising about the meaning of life, or just sorting out problems in your own life or someone else's.

How much of your day do you spend actually using your powers of logical reason? Is your work challenging and fulfilling? Are your adult relationships changing and evolving so that you contemplate their significance all the time? Or does your day consist of constant, routine tasks which don't challenge you or invigorate you in any way?

Do you often get headaches? Do some areas of your life feel like a constant headache? Are there people whose company you leave feeling that your head is about to explode? Notice if you're having emotional reactions to these thoughts and if your stomach area is affected. Perhaps your head is pulsing slightly. If you have any sensation you don't enjoy, wash it away.

What does mental health mean to you? Have you ever had someone call you mad or crazy? How has that affected you? Have there been occasions when you felt out of control mentally, when you questioned your own mental health? Or do you always feel tightly in control of your thoughts and emotions?

Are there people you admire for their mental abilities? Do you feel mental astuteness belongs to others but is not necessarily something you possess? Do you relate mental abilities to being knowledgeable in an academic sense? Did you go to university, and if so, what sort of student were you? If you didn't go to university, do you feel you suffered from lack of mental stimulus as a result? Do you often feel inferior in the company of others, convinced that they are mentally superior to you? What happens to your emotions when you have that experience? Have you had people in your past calling you stupid or thick?

Now, when have you been made to feel good about your own

mental powers of observation? When have you had someone praise you for work well done, or for sorting out a difficult issue? Have you finished a crossword puzzle on your own and felt a great sense of achievement? Have you correctly worked out the solution of a murder/mystery book before the end? Has your IQ been tested and been proved to be impressive? Did you get good results from school and university exams? Remember a moment when you felt that your mental abilities had been acknowledged, including by you.

What was the sensation which accompanied that? How did your solar plexus area feel? Was your stomach also affected? What was the feeling in your head and heart? How does feeling accomplished mentally make you react?

What would you like to do in your life to improve your mental self? What do you enjoy doing which is mentally challenging? What do you find stultifying which you want to change? How could you create mental enjoyment from routine, boring tasks?

When you feel you have asked enough questions and tried to find enough answers, slowly withdraw from your solar plexus area. Cleanse through, paying particular attention to your head and solar plexus areas. When you feel ready, pick up your pen and paper. Write down your predominant thoughts first. Did you make any decision about what else you want to do to increase your mental state? Did you notice that you had a past where you felt mentally inadequate in different areas? If you have emotions that are strongly associated with this exercise, please write them down. Notice if your head is still pulsing or your solar plexus area is still tingling. Do you have the sensation of using your mental gifts more through your spiritual healing work? Write down how you see perfect mental health.

Then put down your pen and paper. Close your eyes and

pull your cleansing energy through all of your aura and your physical body. Take a good few minutes to do this. Notice if your physical and emotional bodies are storing any residual effects of this exercise. Wash them away. Then open your eyes, focus on an object and wait a few minutes before you stand up.

After this exercise you may often have the sensation of your brain working overtime for a while. You may start questioning more aspects of life and where you fit into it as a whole. This is purely because you are receiving and releasing yet more energy from the solar plexus area. You are probably also working with other chakras without noticing it. Enjoy the extra surge of energy this exercise has given you and notice how you feel more connected to everything around you as a result. If you have been thinking too hard and feel a headache coming on, sit quietly in your cleansing sanctuary. It will soon dissipate.

Your spiritual self
When you feel ready, move on to the last exercise in this chapter. It is particularly important that you are not interrupted during this, so make sure you have some free time on your own before starting. It is helpful if you have a candle burning during this exercise. However, do please make sure it is in a safe location where it will not cause any damage.

This is usually the moment when you start to feel uncomfortable that you are entering a unknown realm which is going to be difficult. Relax. Sit comfortably in your chair, close your eyes and spend a few minutes concentrating on your breathing.

Now you're going to focus on all your chakras, one after the other. You might want to refresh your memory by rereading about the chakra locations. Start with the base chakra and remember its location at the base of your spine. Visualise the colour red. You might feel a tingly sensation or a slight tickle in that area. Then move to your navel chakra which opens both front and back. Concentrate on the colour orange. Remember to breathe deeply and comfortably. When you're ready, move up to the solar plexus which is just to the left of the other chakras. Visualise yellow. Remember this chakra opens both front and back. You might feel further sensations of movement in this area. Now concentrate on the heart area, think of the colour green and focus on both the front and back openings of this chakra. This is where the energies start to change and feel lighter and brighter. See if you feel any difference. Don't rush yourself. Move on to the throat area when you feel ready. Think of the colour blue now. Again this energy centre opens both front and back. Don't worry if you feel less in this area. Move up to the brow chakra, in the middle of your forehead. Enjoy the rich colour of purple. Feel both front and back centres moving. Again, don't worry if you feel very little. Lastly, feel the crown chakra at the very top of your head opening upwards to the sky. Concentrate on beautiful, pure white.

Now pull the cosmic energy down into your crown chakra. Feel it filling all of you. As you move down through each chakra, notice if they feel different from one another. Work through slowly: crown, brow, throat, heart, solar plexus, navel and base. This is a wonderful sensation if you experience it slowly and really let yourself melt into the energy. The cosmic energy will soothe you as it goes through your body, gently washing away any tension or aches. Don't rush this process. It's important for you to enjoy it thoroughly.

Now you're going to visualise a flame just in front of your body. If you find it easy to imagine things, keep your eyes closed and let the flame come into your thoughts. If you're not a naturally visual person, you might want to open your eyes and take a look at the candle in your room. Gaze at the warm glow of the flame for a minute before you close your eyes again. You should still be able to see it in front of your eyes.

Let the flame flicker gently in front of you for a while. Notice how soft and beautiful the glow is. Feel its delicate warmth and enjoy its comforting presence. Now you are going to invite the flame to come into your aura. Ask it to come closer to you. Watch it move into your own energy field. Now ask it to come right inside of you, entering through whichever chakra feels right for you. Normally this is through the heart or solar plexus area. If you're fully relaxed, the flame will simply enter the area which is best for you. Enjoy the sensation of peace and stillness which comes with the presence of the flame within your body. You might feel a warm glow as well.

Whichever point the flame has entered, let it rest in that spot for a while. Let any pleasant emotions and sensations sweep through you. Is your flame still flickering? It might be gentle, but there will probably still be some movement.

Now you want to still the flame. There are different ways to do this. You might imagine a breeze that goes into stillness. You might want to focus on the flame and stop its flickering with your thought process. You might simply ask the flame to be still and it may do it for you. Still the flame by using whatever means is right for you. It doesn't matter if it takes a few minutes. Concentrate on the flame, nothing else.

As the flame becomes still and calm, so a change will come over you. It's difficult to explain until you feel it for yourself. You fuse with the flame; it becomes you and you become the flame. Everything becomes still and peaceful. You become a single shining light of energy. You enter a space where words aren't necessary. It brings a contentment and sense of peace which isn't like any other physical sensation. Rest in this state for a while.

During this time, insights will come to you without you asking. You'll have a sudden flash of knowledge, because in this relaxed state you don't have to question or worry or strain for any information. You may find your thoughts drifting into different areas of life without pushing yourself in any way. What comes to you will be right and appropriate for you at this stage in your life. You might find yourself pondering a situation in which you have found yourself recently that has been puzzling you; an insight will come to you that helps explain the situation. You might find an image or person coming into your thoughts; you'll be shown something which helps to clarify what you have been worrying about.

This state may be very brief or it may appear to last for some time. You'll feel as though you have little control over it because you will suddenly find yourself outside this thought process again. You'll remember where you are again and when you concentrate on the flame, you'll find it is flickering again in its gentle fashion. You may discover it has changed location during your meditation.

Wherever the flame has ended up, it is now time to let it go. Let the flame slowly withdraw from your body, through whichever chakra feels right for you. Let it move right outside your aura. Now watch as it slowly recedes into the distance and disappears. You may find the light never quite goes. It may still be there, rather like a star twinkling in the sky above. Whether you still see it or not doesn't matter. It is there for you to call down at any time when you need it.

Cleanse as much as you feel is necessary. Sit quietly for a minute or two and then open your eyes. The first thing you'll probably see is your candle. Let it continue to flicker gently as you pick up your pen and paper. Write down what you can remember from your venture into your spiritual self. Was it difficult? Did it feel strange and uncomfortable, or did you have a sensation of coming home, of everything feeling right? Can you remember very little but are left with a feeling of contentment and warmth? Did you feel particular sensations in different chakras? Which chakra did the flame enter first, and which did it leave from? Can you remember any of your insights? What areas of your life were you drawn to looking at during this exercise? Make a note of everything you can remember. Be honest about what you felt. If you can't remember much at all, that is fine, too.

Now put down your pen and paper and gently blow out the candle flame. Close your eyes. Cleanse again. Give thanks for your first exploration of your spiritual self. Realise it is not difficult at all. It just takes practice, as with any new skill you learn. Resolve to practise again soon.

Now you want to make sure that your chakras feel closed and protected. Go through each chakra, starting from your base chakra and working upwards. Make sure it feels comfortable. If it feels too open, too vulnerable, imagine your centre closing down. Use whichever visualisation helps you. Picture a flower's petals closing or a spinning wheel becoming motionless. Take your time with each chakra and work slowly: base, navel, solar plexus, heart, throat, brow and crown. When you have finished, do you feel balanced and earthed again? Draw up some of the grounding energy, pull down some of the cosmic energy or simply sit there quietly, breathing comfortably and evenly.

Before you open your eyes, you are going to add a form of extra protection. You have opened all your chakras and this is a very vulnerable position to be in. You may not have closed down completely, even if you feel you have. So now you want to imagine a light, shimmering cloak of beautiful light coming down over your shoulders and covering all of you. You can even pull a little hood up over your head if you feel you need it. This is not a heavy cloak. It has no weight. It is iridescent. If you want a colour other than white try a pure gold or silver or possibly a soft pink shade. Avoid dark colours as they can be oppressive in this context. Let your soft cloak settle around you and protect you. Feel safe and secure.

Sit for a few more minutes and then open your eyes. Are you well grounded again or does reality still seem far away? If you need to, close your eyes again and balance yourself. Do not rush this process. If you get up too quickly, you will feel dizzy.

How was this exercise for you? It is a powerful one and you are working at quite a deep level. Some of you may have found it quite difficult; your flame may have kept flickering despite your attempts to still it. Just continue to work at your own pace and refuse to give up. Return to the flame on another occasion. Sometimes people have no recollection of what happened after their flame became motionless; they just know they went somewhere else. Some people keep falling asleep during this exercise! You just have to learn to discipline yourself. Healing work can be quite soporific. It can be so soothing and relaxing that you drift off without realising it; sometimes you may drift off because you do not want to consciously face a certain issue in your life. The more you practise, the more you can learn to stay awake and reap the full benefits of your work.

Don't worry if your pieces of paper from the exercises in this chapter look messy or indecipherable; they are simply for you to use as a starting point. During the next chapter, we are going to rewrite some of them and decide what you really want to work on. You may not want others to know what you have written, so make sure you keep them in a private place.

In fact, you have already started your healing process. Your spiritual healing began the moment you accepted the contents of this book and you were willing to look at the concept of healing outside of conventional, orthodox treatment. This is not to say orthodox medicine is wrong or bad. If you are taking conventional medicine as you are reading this book, continue with your regular treatment. Remember that all spiritual healing can work as a complement to other medicine. If, at some later stage, your conventional treatment becomes unnecessary that is another matter, but one that can only be decided between you and your doctor.

Another very important message for you is to realise that this process of beginning to heal has to be handled slowly and completely at your own pace. Every human being has a different aura. Our energies all require individual handling. Sometimes the process of spiritual healing is uplifting and invigorating; sometimes it is emotional and unsettling before you clear blockages or repair tears in your energy field. Only you know how you feel, no one else. You must listen to your own body. This means your physical, mental, emotional and spiritual spheres. Listen to all of you, and in the process you will learn to love all of you.

Because dealing with your own individual energy is such an intensely personal, intimate journey, give yourself some private, personal space. You cannot work through the exercises if you are continually interrupted by family, friends or work colleagues. You need to find some time just for you. If you are starting to think that is not possible, you are simply finding excuses to delay your healing process. The busiest person in the world can find time for solitude if they are committed to doing so. It does not have to be a large period of time: even ten minutes a day will benefit you.

After doing the exercises in the previous chapter, you now have a sheaf of at least six pieces of no doubt messy, scribbled writing that you somehow want to restructure into a process whereby you can begin healing work on yourself. Although it is difficult to simplify the complex levels of spiritual healing, we are going to start with a basic three-step programme. This is:

- Learning to love yourself.
- Letting go of fear.
- Forgiving others.

All these stages are inter-related and become influenced by each other, as you will subsequently discover. You have already started looking at why all healing starts with loving yourself and have begun your own very personal journey. During those exercises, you were gentle with yourself and gave yourself space and time to embrace changes in this part of your life. However, you probably also during this time encountered resistance at some level. The resistance to change is what we call fear.

We have to learn how to let go of the fear which stops us from moving forward. The key to doing this comes from understanding our past (which is why we started with your childhood in the first exercise). Most of us let our past dictate our present and shape our future. We are born a certain way and then learn to respond to fear and negativity so that we quickly forget our true roots. This happens to all of us. We learn fear from adults at a young age but we are not born with fear. It is important to understand this to embrace spiritual healing, as fear creates the energy blockages which stop us from enjoying perfect health. We have to let go of the fear to move forward.

So where does this fear stem from? We are not born with fear. How can we prove this? Consider a newborn baby, including you, although you probably have no memory of yourself at this stage. A baby radiates unconditional love, is bursting with curiosity and wants to explore everything with fascination and zeal. Remember, you were like this. You used to express yourself freely. You would openly ask for love. In fact, you demanded love! You knew it was your right and did not question whether you were worthy of it or not. If you were upset, you cried effortlessly, without embarrassment. Every emotion was easy for you: glee and satisfaction were natural expressions of your everyday experiences.

If you cannot believe you really were like this, spend a little time observing a young baby. Babies embrace everything, and you can see exactly how they feel at any given time; they express every emotion clearly and without shame. Notice how relaxed and loose their limbs are as well. Physically, this lack of fear gives them great suppleness and a true ease with their own body. It is wonderfully uplifting just to sit and observe a child's uninhibited energy. You were like that, and it is only as you got older and started learning from and imitating adults that you began to hold back and to experience fear and anxiety. You began to pick up all these negative emotions from the adults around you, just as they picked them up from adults around them. Of course, there are some areas of life about which we need to feel frightened. For instance, a child has to be taught not to go near fire. The difference is how you teach a child this. You can do it with fear and say 'Arghh, dangerous! Mustn't touch. It'll kill you!' whereupon the child will back away in fear. Their little heart will thump, their muscles will tighten through their body, they may experience a sudden knot of anxiety in their stomach. Their auras will suddenly contract and that fear will create a blockage in their delicate energy system.

There is another way to teach a child. You can teach them to respect everything around them. Through respect, they can learn how to handle potentially dangerous situations safely. You can say 'Fire is wonderful. We use it for heat and cooking. We need it in our life. But it will hurt you if you aren't careful. You cannot go near or it will burn you. Let's see how far back we have to sit to be safe, shall we? I'll protect you and make sure you do not get hurt. Let's enjoy the fire together in a safe way.' If you feed a child's imagination and teach them to respect, they will appreciate what is around them. It will also reinforce their own sense of loving, not just for themselves, but for everyone and everything around them. You can explore any potentially dangerous situation with a child by explaining the power and purpose of something. Let them learn to respect everything, not to fear. You were probably brought up with fear. Most children are.

This fear that we learn through our childhood then becomes the reality through which we live our life. Almost everything we do becomes governed by fear. Take a look at the piece of paper which contains your childhood thoughts and notice how many of your words and phrases come from a fear of something.

We also learn something else through our childhood. We very quickly start to feel that we are not good enough at whatever we do. There will always be some things at which we excel, but how often are those the areas of your childhood you remember? When you were writing about your childhood did you not mostly remember the negatives, the put-downs, the criticisms, the insults? Most people remember feeling unloved or unworthy, coupled with fear. Take a look again at your childhood scribbles and notice how often you refer to things where you did not feel good enough. You have taken this feeling with you into adulthood. This is where your difficulty with loving yourself unconditionally stems from.

Once we start delving into this uncomfortable world, we then encounter another difficult area. We see that our fear and inability to love ourselves seems to stem from other people's influences. We start the process of 'If only I did not have that mother/father/brother/sister/wife/husband/lover/cousin/friend/work colleague/boss then my life would have been all right'. Resentment starts to creep in and create further, even darker areas of imbalance within our own individual energies. That resentment and anger ends up making us unwell. So how can it be proved that this is what has happened to you? You have just read some powerful statements in this chapter. How are they making you feel? Sceptical, irritated or perhaps confused? Do you feel now that you have had enough of this philosophy because it is not true?

The stronger your reaction to what you have been reading, the more you are harbouring resentments in your life.The more you want to fight against what you have been absorbing, the more you know deep inside that it makes sense. In fact, the more negative your reaction to this, the more positive it is for you! Anger and resentment are very powerful emotions. They can be rechannelled into a wonderful, positive energy that can have far-reaching consequences. The more fiery you feel about these concepts, the more energy you have to work with. Passion can be a powerful healer, as long as it is tempered with understanding and love.

If you feel quite complacent as you are reading this, if you feel vaguely interested but think that you know most of it already, if you think you might consider it later but not now, if you know other people who could benefit from it but you are all right yourself, then you are not likely to move forward at a great rate. The more you think you know, the less you do!

It is also important to acknowledge that not everyone has had a dysfunctional childhood! Many of us were brought up by loving, aware parents who nurtured us and guided us wisely without criticism. Yet are there not areas in these people's lives that still aren't 'working' as they would like them to?

Discovering your thought patterns

So how can it be proved that this pattern from childhood carries forth into our adult life? How can it be shown that no matter who we are, what our childhood was like and how our adult life is shaping up, we all follow a common set of beliefs until we choose to alter them? When you have a spare 15 minutes, work through the exercise below.

Take yet another piece of blank paper. Write at the top 'My Perfect Life'. Now write down how your life would be if it were perfect. Where would you be living, and who would you be with? What sort of work would you be doing? How would you feel, how would you look, and how much money would you have? Put down everything that you would like. Create your fantasy world of perfection that is personal to you. Embellish it as much as you like.

There's only one rule. You must be honest. Do you really want to be a multi-millionaire? Or is what you think you ought to want because everyone else seems to crave money? Do you really want marriage and children or is it that you've been told that you do? Take as long as you like, and cross out some things if you go back and realise they aren't true.

Now write down 'My life isn't like this because . . .' and fill in the reasons. Some of your life may be just as you want it, but for every area that is not as you wish, decide why. Keep writing down every reason you can think of, even if it sounds trivial. Cross out if you like, but keep writing. This can be the longest section of the exercise. There are so many reasons when you start to think about it, aren't there? Make sure you exhaust every possible answer.

When you've finished, look back over your reasons. Now think very carefully about each statement. Who told you that? Who made you feel that way? Where in your past were you told something related to that reason? It might be that you haven't got the loving relationship you want because you aren't special or good-looking enough. Who told you that? You can't find the job you want because you aren't clever enough. Who made you feel that way? You don't have enough money because it's hard to earn a lot of money and money is the root of all evil. Who told you that? You don't have enough holidays and leisure time because everyone has to work harder nowadays. It's just the way life is. Who told you that? Your life isn't perfect because life is tough and always a struggle, everyone knows that fact. Who told you that? Who made you feel that way? Go through every reason and find out where it's come from.

As you do this, you may notice certain names and sources cropping up again and again. Try not to become emotionally involved at this stage. It's hard if you are harbouring deep-rooted resentment (which most of us do at some level), but try to wash it away for the purposes of this exercise. Know that you'll return to these people at another stage. For now, just observe where your beliefs come from.

When you've finished putting a source next to each reason, pause for a moment. Ask yourself how all these reasons have made you feel. By living your life through these belief systems, what effect has it had? Write down the emotions or feelings which are relevant. When you've written them all down, what's the over-riding sensation you are left with? Write it down in large letters. This is probably the feeling, the belief, the thought which you carry around with you all day, every day. How does this thought affect your energy system and therefore your whole life on a physical, mental, emotional and spiritual level? What can you see that you might accomplish from your Perfect Life scenario if you could only change your thinking? (The answer is everything, but you may not have quite got to that stage yet.)

Now look again at this last sensation you've written down. How can you transform this statement from its negative pattern into a new, positive affirmation? Do this for yourself. Remember to phrase the affirmation in the positive. Avoid using 'do not' or 'no' or 'not'. Also try to make it in the present, not a future statement. In other words, don't say 'I will become more positive', say 'I am more positive'. The present gives it much more power and energy. Placing it in the future gives you an excuse for not doing it now. Your brain will hear the future tense and refuse to apply it to the present.

Write down this affirmation in large, clear letters on a new, fresh page. Write it down ten times. Now say it out loud ten times.

Close your eyes and wash away any negative residue, particularly if you are unnerved by a sudden well of resentment against someone in particular. You don't need it. You will learn in future exercises how to release this resentment. Let it go for now. Then repeat the affirmation another ten times, out loud to yourself. Notice if your feelings are slowly changing. Commit to saying this affirmation to yourself constantly over the new few days and weeks.

Did you struggle with this exercise? Are you upset by the outcome or do you feel a sense of relief? Do you now see how your pattern of life at present is shaped by thoughts from your past?

Chances are your reasons for not having what you really want in life fall into a fairly predictable pattern of responses. Did your list contain some or all of the following?

- *I'm not clever/attractive/good enough.*
- *I'm not confident enough.*
- *I don't know how to do it.*
- *I'm afraid of failure.*
- *I just don't have the necessary skills.*
- *I'm too old/too young/too tall/too short/too thin/too fat.*
- *Other people don't understand me.*
- *It's so hard to do.*
- *It's too complicated.*
- *I'm too confused to make up my mind.*
- *Money is hard to get.*
- *Everything in life is so expensive.*
- *I can't do what I want because I have dependents.*
- *My family/friends are so demanding and put pressure on me.*
- *Good things don't happen to me in life/other people have all the luck.*
- *Changing your life is very difficult and painful.*
- *I'm afraid to change.*

You probably had a lot of others as well. What was your overriding sensation after determining where all your reasons came from and how they left you feeling? This will usually be one of the following of this much shorter list. You feel:

- *A failure*
- *Unloved*
- *Trapped*
- *Angry*
- *Tearful*
- *Resentful*

Sometimes it is a combination of the above. But the bottom line always, always comes back to an overwhelming sensation of not being able to love yourself and accept yourself as you are. Some suggested affirmations for this are:

- *I'm successful in everything I do.*
- *I'm loved by everyone.*
- *I'm free to do whatever I choose.*
- *I release all my anger and I'm calm.*
- *I'm happy.*
- *I love everyone.*

Make your affirmations as short and concise as you can. Your thoughts respond well to simple instructions. If you cloud the issue, the brain wastes valuable time trying to digest the information.

Now we have moved on to this stage of understanding, you may face a new problem of resentment which you now feel for someone else or possibly even more than one person. You may not have realised you felt this way before you did the exercise, which can bring out all sorts of unacknowledged feelings and suppressed resentments. You no doubt created some blockage of energy or hole in your aura and possibly even illness as a result.

Releasing resentment

Yes, physical illness can be purely a manifestation of a deep-rooted resentment or fear from our past. Every energy blockage or disruption is caused by our response to something. How that upset manifests itself in our body can vary. We will look at this in more detail later. For now, you need to stop that resentment festering. Release it. You don't want to create yet another problem by not dealing with this new emotion. So the next stage of your healing is to look at someone with whom you may be struggling. The recent exercises may have brought this person into your mind or it may be a resentment which you know you have had brewing away inside you for some time.

The first time you try this exercise, it would help to choose someone who does not immediately bring up deep distress for you. Again, remember spiritual healing is about being gentle with yourself, so start at a level with which you feel comfortable. You are to remain in control during this exercise as with every other. Don't choose someone with whom you have a long-term difficult relationship. Leave them until later when you are stronger and have progressed more. Speed has no significance or value in spiritual healing. You must not be disturbed during this exercise, so find some quiet time for yourself.

Sit in your comfortable chair and close your eyes. Breathe comfortably and deeply. Cleanse if you need to. Wait until you feel relaxed and focused before you move on.

Now visualise a beautiful park with a bench in the middle of it. This can be your personal choice as long as it makes you feel calm and comfortable. This is your park. There is no one in it but you, sitting alone on the park bench. What sort of bench is it? Wooden or metal? What is around this bench? What flowers, bushes and grasses? Is there a pond or lake nearby? What is the wider view when you look out? Create a pleasing environment in which you are sitting. Notice the smells of the flowers. Hear the sounds of birds or animals. Make sure the sun is shining and it is warm. Sit there for a few minutes in your private oasis. Enjoy its serenity and calming energy. Feel at one with what is around you.

Then notice there is someone in the distance approaching you. Realise it is your chosen person with whom you want to sort out some conflict. If your first reaction is displeasure, let that emotion wash away. You want to sort out this issue. They have come to help you.

As they approach, really see them for the first time. Look past their exterior and see them properly. Realise that they, like you, are simply frightened, unsure of themselves. They, too, have their path to work out in life, and they are doing their best. It may not fit in with what you think you want. Yet it is right for you. Remember that everything in life happens to us for a reason. They have come into your life with a gift for you. Whatever potentially uncomfortable situation existed up until now, you have the ability to change that energy. You have the opportunity now to learn and move forward, and to dissolve the conflict.

Watch as they come nearer and see that they are smiling, although they look slightly apprehensive. Notice how vulnerable they are. They are as insecure as you are. Smile and ask them to sit down next to you.

You may find it unnecessary to have a literal conversation. Sometimes, as they sit next to you, your energies blend and harmonise and you can understand what the conflict was about without discussing it. You feel that you have been touched on a deeper level which renders talking unnecessary. You see what was going on and realise what you needed to learn from the conflict. Your resentment slips away as you are both sitting there. It's a gentle, painless procedure which leaves you feeling lighter and brighter. You've unblocked some energy just by this simple act of being willing to learn something new. You're left with a feeling of acceptance and unconditional love for this other person. Very often it's as simple as that. You end up wanting to hug or kiss or hold their hand. Or you simply sit there together and enjoy the peaceful surroundings.

If your conflict and resentment goes deeper, then you may want to have a conversation. You might want to ask them why they are behaving in a certain way or why they did something to you in the past. They will always talk to you. If in your earthly relationship with them they are reticent and unapproachable, in this spiritual scenario the situation changes. It doesn't mean they become someone different, it just means that your gentle way of dealing with them enables them to be more open and to tell you honestly what is going on.

Usually they will tell you that their behaviour stemmed from what happened to them as a child. They will explain their upbringing and how their present thought processes work, based on their past. As they do this, your sense of awareness and acceptance grows. Your resentment and anger dissolves because you can see them as a human being, as someone who's struggling as much as you to learn and to grow in their own way. People don't usually handle other people badly because they enjoy it. It happens through their own ignorance and fear. Often they don't even realise the effect of what they are saying and doing. So many people who have hurt us in life are completely unaware that they have done so. They thought they were doing everything for our own good, just as their family may have treated them in a like manner.

As you sit and talk together, notice how they seem to change and soften in front of you. It is impossible to stay angry with someone when you see their vulnerability and innocence. Realise that now you are seeing them as they truly are. Before there were blocks and barriers. Now there are none. Enjoy that comfortable state between you. Sit together for a while, even after you have finished speaking. Hug or kiss or hold hands, if that feels appropriate.

When the time is right, they will tell you that they have to go. Let them slowly walk off into the distance and disappear. You have no need to feel sad as this happens, because they will return on any occasion when you need them. As they go, realise that you feel no resentment, no anger, no tears. You feel cleansed and renewed by your experience.

Now slowly withdraw from your park. Remember you are sitting on your comfortable chair. Do you still feel any unwelcome sensations? Cleanse them away. Focus on how heavy your weight feels in the chair. Do your feet feel firmly weighted on the ground? Imagine the roots of a tree beneath your feet. Use grounding energy if you need it. Open your eyes when you are ready. Wait a few minutes before you get up.

Has that helped your resentment? Do you now feel you need to go through this process with someone else? Did it make you realise how many people you resent in some way? Does it make you want to let go of other negative emotions as well, such as jealousy and envy and vindictiveness? You start to realise just how many negative thoughts and images we carry around with us all the time. You also start to realise that it is not as difficult to let some of them go as we had imagined.

Your healing chart

Let's now look at how you can restructure all your pieces of scribbled paper into some sort of healing chart. This will be very personal for you, as everyone has different issues to deal with at different times. Your healing chart this month will also be different from next month's. Never compare your healing chart with anyone else's as it may make you think you are doing something wrong, which is untrue. You are working on what is right for you.

Have a large, fresh sheet of paper beside you but start by looking back through the pieces of paper which you have scribbled upon. You should have at least seven sheets, if not more. You will have your strongest sensation marked out on both your Childhood and Adulthood sheets. Do those two comments seem more relevant than ever, or do they seem to be clouding another, more truthful issue? Look through your physical, emotional, mental and spiritual sheets. How different are they? Can you immediately pick out areas which you think are more contentious for you than others? Can you see repeated patterns within them all or does each seem to be unrelated? Lastly, look over your sheet on Thought Patterns. Have some of these comments been repeated in your previous sheets? Study everything for a little while longer. Now you have some choices to make. Don't worry if these choices seem difficult because whatever you choose will be right for you at this moment.

On your clean sheet of paper, draw a line halfway across the paper so it is divided into two. In the top half you are going to write up to seven statements or words.

Start with your childhood. Choose the one word, phrase, or statement that feels most powerful for you. It may have changed from when you initially did the exercise, but this does not matter. Write this on the top of your new sheet of paper in large, clear letters. It can be just one word. It might be someone's name, an emotion or a physical illness. If you suffered from asthma as a child, that may be your dominant memory of childhood. If you had a difficult time with your father, that may seem most important to you. If you were lonely or frightened or shouted at, you may just want to write words that reflect that. Anything is right, as long as it is truthful for your childhood experience. You might write 'asthma' or you might want to put 'suffocation'. You might write 'father' or you might write 'fear'. You could put 'I hurt' or 'tears'. Use anything that is expressive for you. (If during this process you are wondering whether there are people who can only remember wonderful, positive childhood influences and have no negative images, you can rest assured that everyone can remember awkward moments from childhood. You might feel their concerns seem minimal in comparison to your own, but it is all relative. Everyone has fears tucked away inside them which create energy imbalances.)

Now move on to your adulthood. This often seems more complicated because other issues such as career and relationships come into focus. If your main point from earlier still seems truthful to you, write that down under your Childhood statement on the new piece of paper. If you feel it's impossible to choose just one because there are so many, choose up to three to write down.

Now turn to your Thought Patterns page. Look at what you've written at the end about how you were left feeling. Write down the strongest emotion from that on the new paper. If you feel you need to write down more than one, choose up to three, but no more.

You now have up to seven statements or words on the first half of your paper. If you've only three, that is fine.

Now draw a large circle on the bottom half of your paper. Section the circle into four quarters or four equal 'pie' shapes. Mark each one separately: physical, emotional, mental and spiritual. Go back to your four pieces of paper which related to those parts of you and study each one thoroughly. Try to choose just one dominant comment from each area. Again, choose up to three for each if it is absolutely necessary, but try to be discriminatory. If you tune in to your writing, you should be able to work out which is the strongest sensation for you. Write these words down in the relevant quarter.

You can now destroy all the other pieces of paper, if you wish. If you want to keep them for further reference, remember to find somewhere private and secure for them. These contain some of your most personal thoughts and you don't have to share them with anyone unless you make the choice to do so.

Look at your new healing chart. This is what you will be working from during the next chapter. Does it contain phrases or words which you find challenging or unsettling? It's good if it does. All change is unnerving but it's the change which will allow the energy blocks to clear and the torn areas to repair themselves and thereby create a new, holistic health for you. If you find your new piece of paper messy and want to rewrite it that's fine. You will be referring back to this quite often, so it's better if you like your artwork. If in rewriting it some new challenge occurs to you regarding some aspect of your life, add it if you wish. Your healing chart can be fluid and changeable, mirroring your energy and new ability to embrace change. Feel free to decorate your new healing chart with colours and motifs, if you like.

You have been encouraged to look at some powerful concepts during this chapter. You may want to reread it or to repeat some of the exercises before you move on to the next section of the book, which looks at further healing techniques.

HEALING AT A DEEPER LEVEL

You now have your healing chart as your new guide to help you focus on areas you want to heal. As you continue to work further on yourself, this may change. You may discover new insights and new areas on which you want to work. It does not matter how you change as long as you stick to your principle of being honest with yourself. Remember, honesty will move forward the healing process. Are you changing some aspect of your healing chart because you are too scared to look at some area of your life, or is it because you know you need to look at another area first? Keep questioning your actions and keep being honest with yourself.

With the further healing techniques in this chapter we will be working at yet deeper levels again. Remember to continue working at your own pace. Skip exercises and return to them later if you know that is right for you. Reread other chapters if you need to refresh your memory regarding the chakras and the human aura. As always, through all exercises, and particularly the ones coming up now, remember how important your breathing is during spiritual healing. You must take time to calm yourself, relax and breathe deeply before every exercise. Rushing anything diminishes the outcome. The breath is the means through which we access all spiritual information and, therefore, healing. Continue to practise your breathing techniques, especially the Breathing Into Stillness on page 68. Use the grounding and cosmic energies constantly to help balance you. Continue to constantly improve your relationship with your cleansing sanctuary. Use it every day whenever you need to cleanse and refresh yourself. Remember to practise your affirmations daily and that means at least three times throughout every day. Everything you have learned so far remains a relevant and important grounding for everything which follows.

Your other hand

We are going to start by doing an exercise which has proved very powerful for a large number of people. It feels a little strange at first, but most people completely lose themselves in this experience once they get used to it. It is an extremely effective method for loosening blockages within your energies. It is especially useful for work with childhood upsets, but it is also relevant for any area of your life.

You are going to be working with writing again so take a sheet of blank paper and a pen. Make sure you are relaxed and comfortable. Now write down an area of your life you want to heal from your healing chart. It doesn't matter which one it is. You can eventually do this with all areas. However, phrase your healing desire in the form of a question. For instance, if you have a question mark about your mother from your childhood, write something like 'What do I need to learn from my relationship with my mother?' If you just have an emotion like 'fear' or 'I'm not good enough' then rephrase it into 'What am I frightened of?' or 'Why do I feel I'm not good enough?' If your healing comes in the form of a need such as 'I need love' then ask 'Why don't I feel loved?' or 'What does love mean to me?' Choose just one question at a time and write it down.

Now move your pen to your other hand and place it on the paper. Close your eyes. Wait a minute. You will feel very odd at first. You will think you're not capable of writing with your other hand and you certainly won't think you have anything interesting to say. Just keep your eyes closed. Concentrate on your breathing and try to forget about your hand.

At some point, your hand will start to write something. You can then open your eyes if you want, or continue with your eyes closed, if that feels safer. You can suddenly start to feel rather vulnerable at this stage. Keeping your eyes closed can feel better. Others may want to open their eyes to see what their hand is saying or to check they are writing on the paper and not the table or their clothing.

In the beginning, it might just be a scrawl which you can't understand. Give yourself a moment to adjust to this new form of writing. It really feels very peculiar on the first occasion, rather as though someone other than yourself is doing the writing.

After a few minutes, you begin to enjoy the experience and it doesn't feel so alien. The writing will start to become smoother, more legible. Just let yourself keep writing. Don't try to censor what is being put down and don't try to impose your own conscious will on the words. Let it flow. You may find yourself writing for a long period, or you may have only a few words come out the first time. Try not to put a time limit on this exercise.

When you think you've finished, put down the pen and look back over what you have written. After a few sessions, you'll probably be able to clearly decipher what you've written. Does it help explain the question? You may find the answer quite emotional or simply enlightening. It may also leave you wanting to understand more. Often one answer leads on to another question.

If that is the case, put your pen back in the hand you normally write with and phrase another question that is relevant for your healing process. Then switch hands to write again and notice what replies you are given. You can repeat this process for as long as you like.

Remember to cleanse thoroughly whenever you need to. Always, always remember to close down properly and ground yourself. If you're aware that a particular chakra has opened a great deal during this work, close it again. Balance your energies again. Always sit for a good few minutes before you open your eyes, focus on an object and remember what time it is and what else you have to do that day.

Whatever you accessed from this exercise, it will no doubt return back to a childhood experience or teaching. This is a means through which you get in contact with the unhealed part of you from your past. It is doubly powerful in that it often explains why you feel hurt or confused or angry over an area of your life. Look back over your healing chart every time you finish this exercise. What else is there on your chart which may have come about as a result of this childhood hurt? We are going to cross-reference this healing process a little later on, but start becoming aware now of how some of your supposedly separate areas are in fact interrelated. This becomes more and more noticeable as you continue working.

The results from this exercise can be quite astounding. They can offer deep insights into a troubled area of your life which you might have been struggling with for some time. The process through which this happens is not quite as esoteric as it may seem.

Did you know that the left-hand side of our brain controls the right side of our body? Conversely, the right-hand side of our brain controls the left side of our body. When we switch hands to write, many people would describe it as a means to access information within the other half of our brain. The two halves of the brain are known to control different psychological aspects. The left side of our brain controls the logical, analytical part of us. The right side deals with the intuitive and instinctive parts of our being. It is interesting to note that most people are right-handed. In other words, they may naturally find it easier to access their logical and analytical traits because they are working with the left part of the brain. They may not necessarily be using their intuitive and instinctive abilities. In spiritual healing we are trying to work more with our intuitive gifts, which could also translate as being in touch with our spiritual self. This does not mean to infer that if you are left-handed, you are more spiritually aware than a right-handed person! Remember all of us needs to be balanced for the energy to flow freely.

Working through anger
You may notice some recurring emotions as you work through these exercises. This is quite normal. We talked about coping with resentment towards others and you need to continue using

the Releasing Resentment exercise on page 130 to help you with this. If you do not work through these emotions, they will stay in your system, causing you further discomfort in some form.

You can also start to fall into the trap of being too hard on yourself. You may believe that you are not progressing quickly enough. Your frustration turns into anger and you forget to be gentle and nurture yourself. This is a natural process. It is also damaging. Take a moment to stop and consider the scenario below.

Imagine you have a young child. Place him in the centre of a circle with a combination of children, teenagers and adults surrounding him. Now imagine everyone around this child is criticising and shouting at him, telling him he is no good, he is stupid, he is lazy, he does not work hard enough, he is slow at learning, he is not attractive, that he is a pain to be with, that he is on his own and better learn for himself. Everything this child hears is a criticism and a put-down. How does he end up feeling?

Now take this identical child and place him in the circle again. Again surround him with the same group of people. Now imagine everyone around him is praising him, encouraging him, loving, cuddling him, holding his hand and stroking his head, supporting him through his learning process with enthusiasm, constantly telling him he can do whatever he wants to do, reassuring him that he is smart, bright, attractive, a joy to be with and a very special person who is utterly unique; that no matter what he does in life he will succeed. Now how does this child end up feeling?

Which way were you brought up? For most people, it is a combination of the two. We were all supported in some way. Even if you feel your immediate family 'let you down', can you not think of someone who was there for you? Perhaps it was a teacher who believed in you, or a cousin who listened to you, or a friend who shared your dreams and fears. It is just that we tend to forget the instances when we were supported and concentrate on the difficult areas.

Now consider this. Forget about other people, *how do you treat yourself?* How often do you nurture yourself with thoughts and words of praise, encouragement, love and support? How often do you stop and tell yourself that you are doing really well with some issue? Do you ever stop to properly acknowledge that you did a job well, or handled a person effectively, or made some positive change in your life? Do you often give yourself a little treat or a proverbial pat on the back and tell yourself that you are terrific, unique and a joy to be with? Does all that sound sensible and healthy, or are you struggling with self-praise still? Are you still telling yourself that you are stupid or boring or unattractive? What is happening with your self-love? How on earth can you possibly blossom and enjoy holistic health if you don't believe you are worthy of it? *Go back to your affirmations and continue working with them.*

Now ask yourself how often you feel angry with yourself. Be honest. Have you felt more angry than usual during some or all of the recent exercises? Have you also been noticing increased anger towards others during this healing process? This is very common. You do not have to worry or feel that there is something wrong with you if you have been having sudden, hot flashes of anger which unnerve you with their intensity. Let us now look at anger in more detail and at different ways of coping with it.

Although we try to forgive others and understand our own shortcomings, in the process of change we all have to deal with feeling angry. Many people have difficulty with this area. Sometimes it is because they were taught that anger is bad and unhealthy, so they learned to repress it and in the process created all sorts of uncomfortable blockages and imbalances. Others may have had episodes of violent anger in their past which lead them into believing that all anger is bad and needs to be suppressed.

In fact, anger can be a very healthy experience as it creates a great energy which, when rechannelled, can be used constructively to bring about change. The fact that we feel angry is not what is important; it is how we channel that anger that determines our learning process and, ultimately, our healing process.

So, what can we do with anger to turn it into something that is helpful? You may have encountered anger during the Releasing Resentment exercise and discovered that your anger evaporated through seeing your contentious person as someone very vulnerable and innocent. You therefore were able to dissolve anger through understanding. That is a wonderful way to work and very healing. It is an ideal to which we can all strive. However, human beings do not live in the ideal world all the time and sometimes it simply does not work that way, especially if you have a deep-rooted anger towards someone from your past. You might actively want to let go of your anger, but it might seem impossible to do so. Your brain or your heart may tell you to do something, but somehow you find yourself feeling or thinking in direct contrast to what you know would help you or someone else. You can also be convinced that you have managed to let go of your anger, only to have it suddenly resurface on another occasion when you least expect it. It can be frustrating and upsetting.

Anger is one of our greatest blocks that stops all sorts of change. You may now be gaining an understanding of why you have this anger, in other words where it stems from in your past. Yet knowing all about something does not always dissolve it. So we are going to look at a couple of methods which are practical and, if practised, powerful methods of releasing anger.

Physically releasing anger

You absolutely must be on your own for this process. It would be very damaging if someone were to interrupt you. Wait until you have that free time before you try it. The best location is to have a bed upon which you can work. If that's not possible, then place a large, thick duvet and/or blankets on the floor; the thicker the blankets or duvet the better. Now place a large, thick pillow on top in the middle of the pile. Make sure you have loose, unrestricted clothing on.

Now sit on the bed or floor-pile with the pillow in front of you. Close your eyes, breathe deeply and relax. Promise yourself that for the purposes of this exercise you will remain on the bed or floor. This is important. Discipline yourself to that rule. Agree you may do whatever you wish within that area but you will not move outside that safe space. When you have committed to that, you can start to access that well of anger inside you. If you know exactly where it stems from, remember the occasion or person involved. Let your anger build. Know that you're in a safe environment in which to express this emotion. Notice which chakra is being affected by this process; it may be more than one. Don't consciously work with it, just observe it.

Now feel your anger increase and swell. Know you are going to let it out physically. Look at the pillow in front of you. Punch it. Punch it again. Harder. If there's a person involved, you don't have to imagine the pillow as that person. It can be inhibiting to your release of anger as you can get caught up in the belief that you shouldn't be feeling that way. This is about releasing anger from deep within using physical actions. You don't have to analyse it. In fact, the less you analyse it, the more powerful it becomes.

Initially, you might find hitting the pillow uncomfortable. You might even feel silly. Just keep hitting. After a minute, it starts to feel more natural. Then it starts to feel quite good. Then you start to lose yourself in the process. You might be amazed at how much anger comes out of you. Hitting the pillow starts to feel powerful and invigorating.

You might want to express yourself vocally, too. If this isn't possible because of other people in close proximity, promise yourself you will release vocally at another time. For now, keep using your physical actions to release emotion. Increase your physical activity if that helps you.

When you feel ready, stop. Often you simply stop of your own accord, physically worn out from the experience. Sometimes, you feel the need to dissolve into tears. Tears are good. They are another form of releasing energy blockages. When you've finished, then lie down on the bed or floor-pile. Put the pillow comfortably under your head.

Now relax and close your eyes. How does your body feel now? How angry do you feel? Breathe deeply and evenly. How does the chakra or chakras you were aware of at the start of the exercise feel now? Are other areas affected now? Notice how much more relaxed your body feels. Do you feel calmer emotionally, and how do you feel about the person or incident now? Observe any insights you have relating to this area. Let yourself lie there for a few minutes. Notice that the pillow on which you were venting such anger is now a wonderfully soft, comforting item which supports and cradles your head. Can you see by releasing anger that you're now in a softer, more nurturing environment?

Now cleanse thoroughly. Pull down the cosmic energy to refresh you, too. You may need it to replenish you after such physical activity. Use the grounding energy to help balance you again. Close down your chakras if they feel too open. Wait a few minutes before you get up.

You may discover a new physical side of you through this exercise. If you found it difficult on the first occasion, go back at another time and see if it becomes easier. People who are naturally very active physically such as athletes or fitness trainers are often very much in touch with their physical side. Others can take a bit longer.

A word of warning now. If, during that exercise, you found yourself breaking your rule of remaining on the bed or floor-pile, if you found yourself going outside that boundary and doing more damage to your environment, you need to find a trained professional to help you release this anger in a safe environment. This is extremely important. If you accessed an uncontrolled anger inside you, it is not bad. It simply means you need some extra counselling and guidance to help you to release it. If this happened to you, please see your doctor, phone the Samaritans or a similar help-group or talk to a friend or family member for advice. Don't leave the situation to worsen.

Verbally releasing anger

If you found this exercise helpful and were able to stay within its boundaries but still want to release more, try the next exercise.

This again has to be conducted alone, but you need even more solitude for this experience. An excellent way of doing this exercise is to be alone in your car. Drive to a remote place, park the car and turn off the engine. Don't consciously think about someone or something which makes you angry as you do not want to be going within to work with your anger. This exercise works on a much lighter vibration, but it can still be very helpful. Just let out a really loud scream. How did that make you feel? Relax the muscles around your throat. Take a deep breath. Let out another scream. Make it as loud as you like. How did that feel? There is a wonderful freedom about screaming. Children do it all the time because they know it feels good. Adults shout at them and tell them to be quiet, or tell them they're naughty. The difficulty we have is finding time and space alone in which we have the freedom to scream, particularly if you live in a crowded city. If you have access to a soundproof room one day, let rip in there and see how it feels. We have actually forgotten how to scream. It can feel wonderfully freeing and uplifting and you do not have to concentrate on anger to do it.

Another method is to use singing. Why are there so many aspiring singers around? We are using our voices to release emotions verbally. Is there a song which always makes you feel fired up and angry? I Will Survive, I'm Still Here and I Am What I Am are all very powerful modern songs. You might find a rap song really affects you, or an Indian love song. Start noticing music and the effect it has on you. If a song really affects you, use it. Sing it out loud to yourself when you're alone. Use physical gestures as well to accentuate your feelings. If you're singing along to other music, you won't be as likely to unnerve people in close proximity to you. They needn't know the true purpose behind your singing.

There is also a third method which can help and can be practised more easily. Simply sit down in your comfortable chair, close your eyes, and spend a little while concentrating on your breathing. Then think of something which makes you feel angry. Let yourself feel that well of emotion. Then on your next out breath, sigh. Sigh deeply. You can vocalise it into a groan. It doesn't have to be a scream or a muffled yell of frustration. A moan or groan can work wonders, as long as it is heartfelt and honest. Now every time you breathe out, groan. Enjoy the sound. It may sound awful. It may sound animal-like. It doesn't matter. You'll probably notice the groans becoming longer and longer as you continue. That also indicates that your breathing is becoming deeper and more relaxed, too, which is excellent. Remember to keep your throat and jaw relaxed during this process. After you've let out one final, long, throaty groan, stop.

Go back to concentrating on your breathing without making any sound. Do you feel differently now? How does your body feel? Is your throat tingling? Always cleanse thoroughly and when you close down, pay particular attention to your throat chakra. Protect it. Give yourself a moment to reorientate yourself before you stand up.

There is an interesting side effect from this exercise. You may find that you suddenly want to verbalise or feel able to verbalise some aspect of your healing path. It may be that you simply understand something for the first time or that you want to verbalise it to someone, yourself or otherwise. You have activated your throat chakra during this exercise, even without trying to, and you are quite likely to gain some insight as a result. Do not be surprised if you end up feeling that you want to talk more after this experience. You will simply have released yet another blockage during your healing process.

Mentally releasing anger
Sometimes, verbally and physically releasing anger, although helpful, is not enough because we still have negative scenarios running around our head. It is rather as though the mental part of us is working separately and cannot quite let go of the anger. You may know logically that you want to but the brain keeps ticking over,

relentlessly feeling angry or bitter towards someone or something.
Below is a very effective, simple way of releasing mental anger.

*Sit down and take a pen and piece of paper. Now choose
someone with whom you still feel angry. You are going to
write to them. Again, there is a rule with this exercise. You
may never send this letter to the person concerned. Never. This
rule can never be broken. Agree to this rule before you start.*

*Then close your eyes and relax for a few minutes. Breathe
deeply. Settle comfortably into your chair. When you feel
ready, concentrate on your chosen person. Think about why
they make you so angry. What do you want to say to them
that you have never said before? What do you need to release?
What has been eating away at you in your relationship
with them that is making you harbour anger or resentment
or bitterness?*

*Now pick up your pen. You are going to tell them exactly
how you feel about them, what they have done to you and
how angry you feel. You are going to criticise them and call
them names and be as foul as you like during this process.
You are completely safe. No one will ever read it. You can
release all the darkest, most unpleasant emotions you have
and know that as you write they will help dissolve your inner
conflict. All you must do is be honest with yourself.*

*If during the writing you seem to veer off the track and start
talking about something else, that does not matter at all. Let
your thoughts move on to other areas. Let other anger come
out. If halfway through you want to start a letter to someone
else, do so. Often you discover the person with whom you
started is only a smoke screen for another, deeper issue. Let
it all out. Don't worry if it seems to show you in a less than
favourable light. You don't have to look good. If you feel full
of negative thoughts towards this person, write about it.
Be honest.*

When you've written all you can think of about this person and criticised them in every possible way you can think of, then finish with the question 'Why are you in my life?' Now move your pen to your other hand.

Let your other hand be this person. Trust. What comes out? The more relaxed you are, the more open you are to learning how to heal, the more information will come through to you. They may tell you what happened to them, they may simply relate what you need to learn from this process. You may write it and feel you knew that all along but somehow it was tucked away in your subconscious. You may be amazed by what comes out. Write for as long as your hand allows you to.

When you've finished, read it over thoroughly. What insights have you gained about this other person? Have you learnt something new about yourself, too? How angry do you feel now? Study it for as long as you like, and then tear up the paper. Tear it into tiny pieces so that it is not legible. Shred it if you have a shredder. Burn it if you have a safe means of doing so. As you destroy it, feel your anger ebbing away even further.

Then close your eyes and cleanse. You may find the process has released a lot of your pent-up emotions anyway, but regardless of how you think you feel, cleanse in your cleansing sanctuary. Then close down and protect yourself. Make sure you are balanced and grounded before you continue your day.

You may realise that there are other people with whom you want to repeat this exercise. You can come back to it on different occasions. Notice if you still harbour anger after this exercise has finished. Try using the physical and/or verbal exercises as a contrast. By comparing them all, you will start to learn which is most powerful for you.

Your progress

When you have worked through all these exercises, go back again to your healing chart and start making further comparisons. What connection can you make between your emotional and mental spheres and how does one affect the other? Have you discovered an inner calm which you did not know existed before? Maybe you have had some spiritual insights. What about physically; are there still physical conditions you want to release? Has some physical condition improved as a result of you working with a specific emotion? Let's assess your progress.

Take another piece of paper and on the top half of it draw a large circle, which you again cut into four quarters or 'pies'. Mark them physical, emotional, mental and spiritual. Put into each segment what you now feel you have learned about yourself. Therefore, instead of looking at areas you want to heal, and concentrating on what doesn't work in your life, you're now going to take a look at what you've learned so far and recognise all the improvements either in your well-being or in your concept of how spiritual healing works. What does the spiritual side of your life now mean to you? Is there a deeper understanding of certain issues in your life which you wanted to heal? Are you calmer, less irritated, less anxious? Maybe you've been feeling more alert mentally. As you start to fill in the blank spaces, you will realise you have learnt more than you first thought.

Now below your circle, on the bottom half of your page, make two headings: 'What Worked for Me' and 'What Didn't Work for Me'. Fill in both sections, noting which exercises were more powerful for you; the areas where your energies seemed to stick and where breakthroughs happened quite painlessly. Again, be honest. Even if you found something uncomfortable, but it still achieved a result, put it down. You'll probably find you are quicker to note the areas which didn't work as opposed to the areas which did! Write down which affirmations worked for you and which didn't.

When you've finished, look back at your progress and really study it. Where you still feel stuck on something, is it related to some other area of your life? When you had a breakthrough, did something else shift in another area of your life? Lastly, acknowledge what you have accomplished and how far you have already journeyed in your healing process. Acknowledge yourself. Don't finish this exercise until you've given yourself a gentle pat on the back.

The one sphere that often ends up being quite empty at the end of this exercise is the physical part of you. This is because you have spent a great deal of time working fundamentally with your emotions and accessing your mental, emotional and spiritual realms. However, physical illnesses are all part of energy imbalances. The next chapter concentrates on physical illnesses, what they really mean and how to heal physical conditions through gentle spiritual teaching.

SPIRITUAL HEALING FOR
PHYSICAL CONDITIONS

You will notice that up until now, not a great deal of emphasis has been placed purely on physical illnesses and disease. You may have done some work on a childhood physical illness and gained some insights, or noticed that when you feel down emotionally, mentally or spiritually a physical illness creeps in during that time as well. We are going to look now at what physical illness means.

Again, you are warned that whatever information or healing techniques you find beneficial, particularly during this chapter, these are not in any way meant to replace any conventional, orthodox medication which you may be taking at present. If you discover some healing has taken place which seems to render your prescribed medication unnecessary, *you must visit your doctor to verify your healed state. Do not discontinue medication without prior consultation with your doctor.*

During this chapter, you will need to concentrate on a specific physical condition which you would like to learn more about. This can range from anything as slight as developing a cold, through to having a potentially life-threatening condition such as cancer. Whatever your personal position is at present, you can work at your own pace. Some of what you read may make sense and seem obvious to you; some statements you may find challenging and uncomfortable. If you feel angry or irritated as you read on, remember they can be useful emotions. Some of the concepts you may choose never to embrace. All that really matters is that you are willing to consider the possibility of thinking a different way about your physical illnesses and to see the possibility of healing yourself by opening your thoughts to larger, more universal truths.

Tuning in to disease

Another word for illness is disease. In fact, the word 'disease' is very illuminating. If you break it down into 'dis-ease' it means a state of not being at ease. That is all physical disease is: a condition where you are not comfortable. It does not have to be bad or distressing or very frightening. It simply means you are not in a state of ease. It means that, as well as your physical energies being depleted, your energies from your subtle body are also out of alignment and need to be gently manipulated back into a holistic state of health.

Why do we become physically ill? The orthodox approach is not to question why but simply to treat the condition. Yet if we take complete responsibility for our own life and believe that everything happens to us for a reason and because we need to learn something, why do we fall ill? We do so for a variety of reasons, but the bottom line is always because we need to learn something. So what can we learn by falling ill? Does it feel odd to approach illness as a positive learning curve rather than something bad or undesirable? Let us look at what we can gain from physical illnesses:

- *Growth of spiritual awareness.*
- *Greater compassion for yourself and others.*
- *Losing the fear of dying.*
- *Appreciation of your body and how not to abuse it.*
- *As a lesson for others.*
- *Understanding personal responsibility and how to apply it.*
- *Ridding your body of toxins and blockages.*
- *Increased attention from others.*

Can you see there can be enormous benefits from illness? Can you see the possibility that we might actually choose to make ourselves ill? Consider the last point about gaining attention from others.

Can you think of a time in your life when you were feeling either ignored or rather sorry for yourself? Can you remember that feeling of 'I'll show you and then you'll be sorry' which we have all fallen victim to from time to time? Can you remember thinking that someone has been taking you for granted recently and that you are fed up with it? Or maybe you have had a phase of working too hard and feeling it is deeply unfair. Think back to any occasions like those above. Can you remember any illness that came about at that same time? Perhaps it was even an accident of some sort which left you incapacitated for a while and more dependent upon others.

Now think back to times in your life when you were ill or had physical problems of some sort. What was going on in your life at that time? In fact, can you think of situations which relate to those mentioned above?

Or perhaps you were on another spiritual path. Were you abusing your body and not nurturing it enough so that it had a mini revolt and refused to work properly for you? Did you then learn to offer your body better nourishment and exercise and to handle it with more respect? Did that lesson last or did you then slip back into old habits and not look after yourself properly? Have you been ill again since, and how are you treating your body now?

Or were you working in a particularly polluted environment for a period of time and did that disagree with your personal health? Were you working on a crowded, polluted city street, or in a double-glazed, air-conditioned office with no access to fresh air?

Would you say that other people around you have learned something from your condition when you were ill? In other words, did you offer someone else the opportunity to learn some lesson by observing your illness? How often have you walked down the street and seen someone with a particular physical disability and felt an overwhelming sense of gratitude for your own health? The only sad point with this is that so often we immediately forget that moment and continue with our present life full of destructive energies. If only we could learn to maintain that sense of awe about our own state of health and nurture it even more.

You can also learn a great deal from someone you are very close to being ill. How many people have experienced taking someone for granted until a potentially dangerous illness strikes and then they are suddenly forced to really address what they are feeling for someone else? It can also work in reverse, with someone believing they had a close relationship with someone and then learning through the energies which develop during an illness that someone has not been honest in expressing their emotions. It is said you can find out who your true friends are when you are going through a difficult period in your life. Illness often qualifies as a difficult period.

The process of being ill also offers many people the chance to really stop and think about their own individual purpose within the larger scheme of the universe and its laws and truths. It is true that being physically incapacitated for a while offers you an unique opportunity to increase your awareness and appreciation of life. Whether your illness is a temporary, slight affair or a more major imbalance, physical disease ensures that you have to reduce your workload for a period of time. That enforced rest gives you the chance to reflect about your life and make fresh decisions about future paths you might want to take.

Have you ever been privileged enough to be in the company of someone who is terminally ill and not afraid of their impending death? There is so much ignorance and fear surrounding death, and being with someone who is calmly facing the end of their life can be a truly humbling and enriching experience.

The most common reaction when facing an illness, whether minor or major, is to say 'Why me?' Many people are taught to change that to 'Why not me?' as a means of acceptance. In fact, 'Why me?' is an extremely positive question which can lead to myriad helpful answers. The difference only lies in your motive for asking the question.

If you ask it feeling full of bitterness and anger, convinced that the world is out to get you and that you are a victim of bad luck, you are unlikely to find inspired answers. Remember, what you give out as thought processes will be what you receive back. You are therefore only likely to find constructive answers in changing your attitude. You have already been working on this during your Embracing Life exercise and you may already have applied this to some physical illness. However, physical illness is usually (many healers believe always) an indication of some other issue which needs addressing in your life.

We are now going to look at the stage at which a physical illness comes into our life. There is a commonly held belief in spiritual healing that the physical illness is actually the last manifestation of an energy imbalance. This is a powerful concept to embrace as we can then see that physical illness has come about as an energy imbalance which we have been holding for some time and it will actually have tried to manifest itself in another form prior to the physical condition occurring. This implies that we are given warning signals en route to any illness; the reason we may not heed them is purely because we have not yet learned how to successfully tune in to all of our energies and discover where we are out of balance. If this is true and we can treat energy imbalances before a physical illness occurs, what need is there for us ever to be ill physically? If physical illness is the last expression of energy imbalance, can we not learn to heed the warnings *before* we become ill? Yes, we can. Holistic health is learning to look at and treat all of you in a loving and completely nurturing manner. Holistic health can therefore also be preventative. All we need to do is learn to listen in the right way.

Reading the signs

So what can physical illnesses possibly tell us about ourselves on another level? Look at some of the statements below and see whether you relate to any of them or whether they seem connected to one another. Before you read them, you must understand that these are only examples and not always to be taken literally. We create illnesses for many reasons and none of the statements below should be taken as the absolute truth. Illness works on many levels and below are very basic simplifications of complex issues. They are only concepts to be considered and digested. Keep an open mind as you read them.

- *You feel smothered and suffocated by overprotective and possessive people around you. You develop asthma.*
- *You are feeling overworked, put upon and very unsupported in your life. You develop back problems.*
- *You are harbouring a deep sense of unrequited or spurned love which you have never been able to release. You develop heart trouble.*
- *You are surrounded by people who continually shout at each other and criticise you. You develop ear infections.*

- *You are feeling very vulnerable and frightened and eat more in an attempt to form extra protection around you. You develop a weight problem.*

- *You see the outside world as negative, sad and depressing. You develop poor sight and need glasses.*

- *You are continually overwhelmed with the sensation that you are not good enough. You develop ulcers.*

- *You want very much to express how you feel about someone or something but you cannot. You develop a sore throat.*

- *You are afraid of moving forward in your life, making changes and exploring new territory. You develop leg problems.*

- *You are deeply critical both of yourself and others, and are constantly striving for perfection. You develop arthritis.*

- *You are rigid in your belief that there is only one 'right' way to do anything in life and refuse to change. You develop stiffness in your joints.*

- *You feel guilty over someone or something and believe you deserve to be punished. You develop physical pain somewhere in your body.*

- *You are desperately clinging onto someone or something, afraid to let go. You develop aches in your hands.*

- *You are frightened of sex and have been taught that it is dirty and unpleasant. You develop sexual infections.*

- *You are deeply resentful and overwhelmingly angry towards someone in your life. You develop cancer.*

Some of these statements are extremely powerful and bring up strong reactions. Again, it is extremely important that you remember these statements are *not* meant to be used as personal diagnostic tools. They are simply intended to be thought-provoking and to let you see the *possibility* for creating illness. They are not irrefutable outcomes of a given situation. They are not predicting your future. In fact, they are *not* necessarily personal to and relevant for you. Let us be very clear about this to avoid dangerous repercussions.

If you are feeling deeply resentful towards someone, it does *not* mean you will develop cancer. If you are scared of sex, it does *not* mean you will end up with some sexual illness. It is very dangerous to read statements such as those above and then let your imagination run wild. We can all think of areas of our own life which need healing. Feeling anger, fear, resentment, insecurity, and self-hate do *not* instantly guarantee physical illness. It may, however, show a *tendency* towards some imbalance which *may* result in a physical disease *if it is left to fester long enough*. It is crucial you make this distinction. Now. You know how strong your thought processes are and if you have read the statements above and can see there is some truth in them, it is utterly counterproductive for you to then see a process whereby you will develop a physical illness. It is vital that you see the distinction between the potential for an illness to develop and the certainty that one will occur. This last sentence is extremely important and deserves emphasising. *It is vital that you see the distinction between the potential for an illness to develop and the certainty that one will occur.*

There is no certainty about any illness occurring in our body. We know that energy imbalances are created by our reaction to experiences that we have. We can choose to change our reactions at any given time, and therefore change our energies and release blockages and repair holes in our aura. That is why you need to keep working on your affirmations and other energy-releasing exercises. It is to take control of your own health and to learn how to create a holistic, loving environment in which you can live every aspect of life to the full.

So have you decided which physical condition of yours to look at? You may be enjoying good physical health as you read this and not be able to think of a particular area you want to concentrate upon. If this is the case, then you can choose a period of your life when you did have an illness and look at what lessons you learnt from that. You might find you still have something to learn.

You may also know that you have a particular physical area which often seems to be a weakness for you. It is interesting to note that our birth signs (which are of course astrologically linked and therefore connected to our universal laws of health) are often linked to individual areas where we may have a tendency towards imbalances. Are any of the following accurate for you? If you know your rising sign, you can also check that for further information about your own personal tendencies to physical weaknesses.

Astrological signs and the parts of the body to which they correspond

ARIES:	Head/Face
TAURUS:	Neck/Throat
GEMINI:	Hands/Lungs
CANCER:	Breasts/Chest/Stomach
LEO:	Heart
VIRGO:	Intestines
LIBRA:	Kidneys/Ovaries
SCORPIO:	Sex organs
SAGITTARIUS:	Hips/Thighs
CAPRICORN:	Knees
AQUARIUS:	Ankles/Calves
PISCES:	Feet

To make this even more comprehensive, there are also physical associations with the different planets which rule each sign. Here are the planetary associations.

Planetary associations with parts of the body

SUN: (Leo)	Heart/Back
MOON (Cancer):	Stomach/Breasts/Chest/Digestion
MERCURY (Virgo & Gemini):	Hands/Arms/Nervous system/Solar plexus
VENUS (Taurus & Libra):	Throat/Voice/Loins/Veins/Kidneys
MARS (Aries):	Head/Sex organs/Muscular system
JUPITER (Sagittarius):	Hips/Thighs/Liver
SATURN (Capricorn):	Skeletal system/Knees/Teeth
URANUS (Aquarius):	Ankles/Shins/Cerebrospinal system
NEPTUNE (Pisces):	Feet
PLUTO (Scorpio):	Generative organs

Has this helped you to decide which area you want to focus

upon? You might realise after some thought that you have always had a weakness in one particular area of your body. Are you prone to sore throats or chesty coughs? Have you often had headaches? Do you frequently suffer from indigestion? Perhaps you are prone to leg cramps. Once you have acknowledged and chosen your physical area, you are ready to work.

You are going to be going within, past your physical body, to understand the true root cause of your physical condition. It takes some time, patience and plenty of unconditional love to work at this level. If you find it difficult to begin with, that is only natural. The key to moving forward into this deeper area of spiritual understanding is simply to be gentle and to let yourself work at your own personal pace. All the information you need to help you with this spiritual healing process is already contained within you. The trick is to learn how to access it.

You can liken it to sitting down in front of a computer for the first time. You know it is capable of doing a large number of tasks, but you have no idea how to access all that information. Your spiritual healing process is like learning to use your own personal computer. As with all learning processes, you need to have breaks from time to time. Do not worry if you need to have a break from some of the deeper exercises after a few sessions. Just listen to yourself and know when you have reached your limit and remember to be gentle on yourself.

One of the great joys and benefits of spiritual healing is that it is effective long after we have finished a particular exercise or thought process. Spiritual healing is a continuous process. While we sleep, we are healing. While we are doing our daily tasks, not particularly focusing on healing ourselves, we can continue to heal spiritually. Once you have opened your thoughts and heart to healing and to loving yourself unconditionally, the positive repercussions never cease. Therefore, when you think you are taking a break from your spiritual path because you have had enough for a while, it still continues in its own gentle, unassuming way.

Understanding your physical illness

You need to create your own space for the next exercise. You do not want to be interrupted. Ideally, you want at least half an hour to explore your chosen physical area. As you are now working at a deeper level, you might want to add some extra dimension to your quiet time. You might want to add some soothing music, a little incense, a candle, some flowers or a soft fabric around you. You need to nurture yourself. Make sure you are wearing loose, comfortable clothing. Be alcohol- and drug-free, as with all the exercises.

Now sit in your comfortable chair and close your eyes. Focus on your breathing. Use your Breathing into Stillness exercise and feel yourself moving into an altered state of consciousness. You become aware only of your own breath, moving gently in and out. Don't rush this process. All healing is in the breath. All knowledge is in the breath. Everything is possible through the breath. When you feel completely relaxed and your body feels heavy and centred, then say silently to yourself, 'I embrace all spiritual knowledge'. Repeat this slowly, ten times.

Now go through your chakras, starting from the base and working through your navel, solar plexus, heart, throat, brow and crown and consciously open them up. If you experience any unpleasant sensation as you do so, wash it away in your cleansing sanctuary. Don't let anything uncomfortable remain. Remember that you are in control at all times. Do you feel properly open and balanced? If you need to, go back and repeat the opening process with your chakras. Don't rush this process and remember to continue your deep, comfortable breathing.

Now pull down the cosmic energy from above. Concentrate on it and feel its power, beauty and purity. Let every part of you be bathed and energised by it. Pull it down through all of you. Fill every cell of your being. Let it surround your whole aura with protective love and light. Again, don't rush this process. Let yourself luxuriate in its unique joy.

Repeat your affirmation again, ten times: Believe it. Know you deserve all the love, help and guidance that is possible for you to help heal yourself. Know you deserve it all. Every bit of it.

When you feel properly opened, cleansed, relaxed and ready to move forward, then you want to bring all your attention to the physical area you are concerned about. If it's easily accessible, gently place your hand or hands upon the area. If that's not possible, just draw all your thoughts and attention to this area.

How does it feel now? Is it pulsing, is it still and quiet, or does it feel ominously dark and brooding? Is there a particular colour attached to it? Maybe it is trying to tell you something. Sit quietly and focus completely on that area of your body. Don't strain during this process. The more relaxed you are and the less you actually try, the more you will learn. Strain creates further energy imbalances. Can you actually sense a blockage in your energy as you sit there? Is it like a dark mass or a short circuit of electricity? Perhaps it feels as though some separate energy is within you, causing the imbalance. Have you taken something extra on board that you don't need that is affecting you?

What do you know about this area of your body? What physical function does it perform? It doesn't matter if you don't know the finer details, just try to work on the basics. Then ask yourself how this physical function could relate to other areas of your life. For instance, if it's your stomach, is there some aspect of your life you're having trouble stomaching or digesting at the moment? If you are working on your throat area, what do you need to say or express which would release that blockage? (The throat area also assimilates changes in life. Are you undergoing a major life change at present?) If you have arthritis in your hands and are concentrating on this area, what are you reaching out for that seems beyond your grasp? Or perhaps your hands are tightly clenched, refusing to receive what someone wants to offer you. If your lungs feel congested, who or what is not giving you room to breathe properly?

Take every physical condition and relate to it more deeply. This is an intensely personal experience and no two will be alike. You cannot generalise and say one physical condition always relates to just one root cause. It is different for different people's energies. You have to do your own personal work before you will know what is true for you. Remember to commit to honesty during this time. Listen to what your heart and soul is telling you, not what you want to hear because it makes life easier.

Which chakra is nearest this physical area? What do you know about that chakra already? What more do you need to learn? As you focus on your area, can you feel other movements in different chakras? Follow the movement,

if you can. A physical condition in one area can often be linked to another, just as every part of our body is linked to something else. Let your focus be shifted, if you know it is right, and go through the questioning process again. Keep relating the physical condition to other areas of your life.

Whatever insights you may glean from this process, hold onto them. Give thanks for their presence. Then you want to wash away any uncomfortable sensations which were created during your question time. Physically cleanse through all your body. Stop focusing on the physical area concerned and go back to concentrating on your breathing. Take your time to refocus again on your breath.

Now breathe even more deeply. Imagine every breath in is being sucked straight down to your navel area. Every breath out comes up through your body and out through your nose. Repeat this thought process of breathing down into your navel area. If you concentrate long enough, you will find yourself entering an even deeper, quieter state. Rest in this space for a while. Keep breathing deeply. Repeat your affirmation ten times: 'I embrace all spiritual knowledge.' Feel safe and secure in this gentle world of stillness.

Now ask yourself what you have to learn from this physical condition. You may have to wait a minute or two for the response or you may be told right away. You may be told that you have learned what you need to know already from your exercise or you may be given further insights. You may be given a deeper, more spiritual understanding of what is happening. You may simply be shown a flashback of an incident in your past which you did not realise was connected to your condition. Give yourself the time to explore what you are being told. You may only have an increased feeling of love and support without any words to accompany it.

Now ask what you can do to help re-balance your energy system. Ask how you can best heal yourself. This is often the moment which becomes very emotional. It does not mean that it is distressing. It may simply be a feeling of release, either through tears or a deep sigh. You might have a sensation of a great weight being lifted from your shoulders or from your heart area. You might suddenly feel lighter and brighter. You might feel a grey blanket lift from your head. Again, this is always a very personal experience and you cannot generalise the reaction you will have. Always, the answer to healing yourself is couched in very simple, gentle terms. Often you are given just one or two words. It can be 'forgive', 'love yourself' or 'let go'. They sound simple taken on their own, but during a healing meditation they have a far deeper meaning because you see them in their true, spiritual context. Ask for a new affirmation. You will be given what is appropriate for you.

You will know when it is time to withdraw from your healing centre because you will either be told or you will know it instinctively. Go back to your breathing and start focusing on each breath in and each breath out. As you concentrate on your breath, bring your awareness back to your physical body. Notice how heavy and relaxed it feels in the chair. Focus on your feet and notice how heavy they feel on the floor. Now cleanse again. Thoroughly.

Then close your chakras, one by one, starting with the base chakra. Work slowly and concentrate. Your chakras will have opened a great deal during this work and you need to make sure they are properly closed and protected. If you complete the process and still don't feel balanced, go back and close them down all over again. Pay particular attention to your heart and crown chakras.

Then cleanse again. Wash through every part of you. Enjoy the refreshing sensation. You also want to add some extra protection. Use your long cloak of spiritual light and wrap it securely around you. Pull a hood up over you as well, if your head and neck feel too vulnerable.

Check you are grounded again. Imagine long roots from the soles of your feet anchoring you deep into the earth. When you feel ready, open your eyes. Are you balanced? Focus on an object. Think clearly about where you are, what day it is, what time of day it is. What else do you have to do today? Wait another two or three minutes before you get up.

You may want to make a note of what you learned from that exercise. You may find you forget and slip back into old ways without a constant, written reminder of your experience! Although it may be the most powerful experience you have had so far, unfortunately we are programmed to let positive influences slip from us, unless we have constant reinforcement. Have a commitment to your new affirmation and repeat it regularly throughout each day. Note what improvement occurs with your physical condition as a result.

Sometimes physical conditions are slow to clear. You have learnt that forgiving, releasing and loving yourself are all part of the process and it is true that they alone are often enough to release the physical pain. However, there are occasions when you may need extra help. This is where visualisation techniques can work wonders.

Releasing blocks through visualisation

Visualisation is another form of training your mind to create positive energies and eradicate unwanted forces. It is a very powerful force which can shift all sorts of energy imbalances; it is often used with people who have cancer. It is fundamentally the way through which people can take responsibility for and 'own' their own conditions. This enables them to take control and work constructively with their physical disease. So often when we first learn we have something wrong with our bodies we panic and start to feel as though we are the victim of some evil force. That only disempowers us further. We also often feel as though we want to run away because we have a desperate hope that if we ignore it, it will disappear of its own accord. A healing process takes place once there is recognition, acceptance and the desire to move forward. Visualisation techniques are helpful because they encourage you to fully accept your condition and take control of the situation. Feeling powerful again releases a lot of energy blocks. Work through the following exercise in your own time.

Relax in your comfortable chair and close your eyes. Concentrate on your breathing and wait until your body feels nicely heavy and relaxed before you continue. Have a cleanse if you need to refresh yourself.

Now concentrate on your physical condition. How does it

actually feel to you? How do you 'see' this state of being unwell? What does it look like to you? This is different for everyone so you need to create your own image. Does it seem to be one dark, indefinable mass, or is it pulsing or moving? Maybe it seems to have a life of its own. Or perhaps you see it literally as some kind of monster with an evil face and grotesque body. Does it show itself as shards of bright light all clashing against each other, creating short circuits and electrical storms, or is it simply a dark well of nothingness?

Whatever you see, face it. Don't back off. Really look at your 'monster'. It can't hurt you. You see, you have created this image and you therefore have power over it. It's not some outside force that has entered your body. You have it there to help teach you something. Choose to learn. Choose to change its shape into something which pleases you, or choose to let it disintegrate into nothingness.

If you have a monster, what does it look like? Has it got enormous teeth which are biting you? Turn your monster into a toothless creation. Is it leering madly at you? Change it into a warm smile. Is it full of warts, wrinkled skin and hairy moles? Create a smooth complexion. Change your monster into a gentle, helpless creature who has no power to hurt you. Change it into a warm, positive force which is working with you instead of against you. This may not happen immediately. You have to put some work in. You have to constantly keep altering the tape in your head. You are in control of your monster and you can change it. You just have to prove this to yourself by doing it. Refuse to let some negative energy have more power in your thoughts.

Are you finding it difficult to even define your illness? Is it a well of nothingness? Go into the well. You have nothing to fear. You have created it only because you have something to learn which will nurture you. Go into the darkness and see what you find. You will create whatever you need. Remember you have control over everything. Nothing can hurt you. See what you find in the darkness and then work with it.

If your physical condition is a mass of clashing lights, then slowly untangle the lights. See them separating and standing on their own. See them as beautiful and helpful in their own way. It's just like you are untangling some of your energy lines and restoring them to full power again. Notice the sensation of calm which descends as you do this.

Is your disease a dark, pulsing mass that has no distinguishing features? Then imagine your dark mass changing colour. What is your favourite colour? (Choose a light shade, not a dark one.) See this unfriendly, ominous mass turn into something beautiful. Change its shape. Make it into a star and see it twinkle with a beautiful, clear light. Change it to the sun or moon or whatever you find a pleasing shape. See it becoming your friend and a positive symbol of hope and peace. See it as nurturing. You are learning about the gift each illness brings with it. You may have a flash of insight as to the purpose behind your disease at this stage. Give thanks for your new knowledge.

Now, whatever your shape has become it is time to let it go. *You do not need it any more and to hold onto it will only stop you from moving forward on your own spiritual path. Now you have to say goodbye. If it has become a friend to you, it will seem quite difficult. Whatever your relationship is now, you are going to let it go.*

You can imagine this in different ways. You can see your shape now slowly disintegrating, becoming smaller and lighter and more transparent until it finally melts into nothingness. You might imagine your shape getting into a hot air balloon and going off into the universe, and watching it become a tiny dot which eventually disappears. You might see the shape being soaked by rain and disappearing into the ground. You might choose to let the sun's rays melt it into a puddle which then disappears into the ground. If you've been working with shards of light, let the ones which you don't need shoot off into the universe or watch them slowly disintegrate into nothing. Use whatever technique works best for you. Create one of your own which is powerful for you. Work with your image until it is nothing. Give thanks for the lessons you have learnt from your illness as you work through this process.

Now cleanse thoroughly. Notice if there are any areas which are aching or pulsing uncomfortably. Wash away what you don't want. Take your time. Have a longer relax than usual in your cleansing sanctuary. You deserve it. Feel all your muscles relaxing. Feel every cell in your body being cleansed and rejuvenated.

Then call upon the beautiful cosmic energy and bring it down into you. Let it wash through every part of you. Know how much you deserve this blessing and its gifts. Give thanks for everything you have in your life and all the lessons you are learning and the improvements you are making to all of you: physically, emotionally, mentally and spiritually. Feel truly blessed and enriched by everything around you.

Now withdraw, remembering where you are and what you've been doing. Concentrate on your physical body. Does it feel different now? Do you feel differently about your illness? Open your eyes when you feel ready. Sit quietly for a few minutes before you get up.

Was it easy for you to visualise your disease? Perhaps you might struggle on the first occasion. Go back and try again another day. Notice how much fear crops up initially and how you can gradually let it go.

You will notice there is nothing aggressive in this visualisation exercise. It is not about blasting unhealthy cells with a machine gun or smashing a tumour into tiny pieces with a sledgehammer. Some people use aggression and anger to treat illness, even in visualisation. However, this can lead to other negative images cropping up. If you find yourself still feeling angry as you work with this exercise, then you need to deal with your own anger first and rechannel it. Go back to the exercises for releasing anger on page 140 onwards and use one of those techniques, particularly Physically Releasing Anger, to process your emotions. Once you have found a mechanism for letting go of anger, then the visualisation work will be most effective.

Did you find that you learned more about your physical condition by your ability to truly face up to your state and not be afraid to learn from it? Now go back to your healing chart and study it.

What else in your healing chart actually relates to your physical condition? Can you see that one of the phrases on the top of your chart actually relates to what you learned from your physical condition? Is there something in your mental or emotional sections which is relevant to what you have recently learned? Perhaps you can see where your physical condition has purely stemmed from an emotional or mental pattern which you have been carrying for some time. Can you see where you have repeated patterns from childhood in adulthood?

Now look at your progress chart. What is left under 'What Didn't Work For Me'? Does something in that section relate to what you have been working on in this chapter? Are you now starting to understand how all the seemingly different spheres of your life are all interconnected and interrelated? Really study your healing chart and your progress chart and see where your links are. Also notice where you have shifted and made energy changes which have brought about positive results. Always stop to acknowledge your progress. When you really study your chart can you not actually connect almost everything to something else? Sometimes, it is suddenly so glaringly obvious that you wonder why you have not noticed it before.

Healing the whole

In case you are still struggling with all the connections on your healing chart and progress chart, let's summarise how the different aspects of human energy are linked. This following paragraph sums up how we make ourselves ill and how we can redress the balance again. It is important you study it as a concept and work repeatedly with it.

We have an emotional response to a situation as a child. If it is repeated or especially if it was unpleasant, we create a mental thought process to accompany it. The combination of the emotional and mental processes creates negative thoughts patterns all around us, infiltrating our complex energy system and imbalancing it. If we do not clear it, finally we create a physical disorder to force us to look at the issue properly. We then access our spiritual being to help us recognise this and use our spiritual knowledge to help us clear the energy blocks and restore ourselves to holistic health.

Now read the previous paragraph again. Is a thought forming from this concept? Can you see an obvious solution to this cycle? *If we had only accessed our spiritual being from the very beginning, we would not have gone through such an arduous process of emotional, mental and physical stress.* This does not mean to imply that spiritual awareness then bypasses all emotional, mental and physical spheres. It simply means that it will allow us to approach all experiences in our life from a different angle. Instead of seeing life as fraught with problems and as a frequently unpleasant process which we have to endure, we can embrace all our experiences and learn from them on a physical, mental and emotional level using our spiritual teaching as a firm foundation. Remember, holistic health means letting all of you operate fully, not just your spiritual body.

There is one last point to make before we leave physical illness. There have been several references to the fact that we need to pay attention to all spheres of our life in order to attain perfect health. Many people, once they start on a spiritual path, can temporarily let go of their physical awareness. Whether you are healing yourself or others, always pay attention to your own physical condition. Don't neglect personal hygiene and physical exercise. They are just as important as spiritual awareness. How you look after yourself physically is just as important as how much time you spend in quiet reflection. A lack of cleanliness and no physical exercise also leads to energy imbalances.

How much time do you spend on your hygiene? Do you clean

and floss your teeth regularly, do you keep your nails trimmed and clean, is your hair and body washed regularly? Unwashed conditions often lead to a lack of self-esteem and often demonstrate a huge lack of self-love. Do you exercise frequently? It can be any form of exercise which agrees with you, whether it is sport, the gym, an exercise class or running up numerous stairs on a daily basis. Do you eat sensibly and regularly, is the food you consume compatible with your physical needs and spiritual beliefs? Continue to address and constantly reassess your own physical needs, no matter how deeply you delve into your spiritual world. Keep trying to balance your spiritual self harmoniously with the other physical, mental and emotional spheres. They are all important. Why else would we be here on Earth?

That question brings up another contentious area which has been debated by humans for centuries. Let us go further into this in our next chapter and explore what our individual purpose for being here on Earth might be and what we each have to learn in the process. Or, to phrase it more comprehensively, what is this source from which spiritual healing stems and why is it so powerful, so all-knowing?

OUR INDIVIDUAL SPIRITUAL PATH

We are now going to look further at what we have to learn from the process of life. You have been delving deeper and deeper into your spiritual self, but where is all this leading to? It seems an appropriate time to formulate further ideas. It does not mean that you have to embrace them all, but considering some of these concepts may help you to broaden your thought processes and lead you into a yet deeper understanding of what you can accomplish during your time on Earth.

What are your thoughts about why we are born and then die? Have you ever thought about it before? Are you thinking about it more through your work with spiritual healing? Do you spend much time thinking about the position of the Earth in relation to the entire, infinite universe? Does it make you wonder if other intelligent life forces exist on other plants or in other galaxies? Do you believe we are the only human life in the entire universe? Why? What other energies and powers exist which we might call upon?

You have spent considerable time now getting in touch with other energies.You have been tuning into and working with grounding energy and cosmic energy. You have also been working with your spiritual energies, which are much lighter and finer in vibration than your physical energies. Where do all these forces come from and why are they there? What else is there for us to call upon, energy-wise, which we have not yet explored?

From your spiritual healing work so far, you will now be able to recognise that you appear to have this well of complete information from within you that you have not accessed before. Many of you will feel it has a separate energy and vitality and yet it also seems to be part of you. You will be discovering that it has an enormous power and a great sense of peace and calm associated with it. It is loving and nurturing in a way that does not seem earthly. Material things cease to have such significance in this realm. Physical worlds seem to be put into perspective when you are here. It does not mean that they are unimportant or trivial, but Earth is seen in a much larger context and is considered just part of a whole.

Part of a whole. Perhaps that is why we are all spending a little time on Earth. It is because Earth is just part of a much larger whole. It does not mean it is not important. It simply means it is only a percentage of our whole learning process.

There is a lovely saying which sums up this concept:

We're not physical beings having a spiritual experience.
We're spiritual beings having an earthly experience.

What are the possibilities if we consider this statement further? If we are fundamentally spiritual, then why are we here? Let us recap what we know about illness and spiritual healing.

Living to learn

We know every form of imbalance occurs because we have something to learn. We accept we are all part of a learning process. So if every imbalance or state of being unwell is purely so we can learn, can you extend that thought process to see all of life as a learning process? In other words, from the moment we are born (some believe it is from the moment of conception) we are here for a purpose or purposes. We spend our lives learning what we need to know and then when the time is right, we depart again from the Earth, taking our spiritual body with us to continue its learning curve.

Have you ever had the learning experience of being with someone as they die? In fact, it is not a 'death' because the spirit cannot die. As their life force ceases, as they take their last breath, there is a very tangible feeling of their spiritual core actually leaving the physical body behind. Their lifeless body is simply that, a body. It is not the essence of what that person truly is. That spiritual essence lives on in another form as a lighter, higher vibration. People have often reported being able to see a light or mist actually leave someone's body and disappear upwards as they die. It is not just trained psychics who see this phenomenon.

Does that not explain why spiritual experiences seem to be part of us and yet separate? They are connected to our physical being for the time that we are here on Earth. However, our spiritual core never dies. It simply changes energy constantly as we evolve and learn. When we die, that spirit continues its path in another realm of consciousness.

There are many levels of intelligence out there. There are many energies working in different areas of the universe and we are guided to the sphere which is right for us. We are all on our own individual path. This does not mean that one person is better, wiser or smarter than another. We all have to go through all phases of learning to progress. This process of learning and evolving takes a long period of time. We have to come back to Earth many times to learn different lessons. Every time we bring our spirit back into another human body we are getting ready for another set of learning experiences. Sometimes we do not always learn what we need to in one life. We have to come back and try again.

Our spirit also chooses what is right and appropriate for us each time we come back to Earth, or each time we 'reincarnate', as it is commonly known. That is why every experience we have is important and valid. It has been predetermined for our own spiritual path. That is also why what happens is not really important, it is how we react to what happens to us which determines our learning curve.

Of course some spirits are more evolved than others. Some spirits have reincarnated a larger number of times. Do you know the expression 'What a wise old soul?' People who say this are unconsciously tapping into higher awareness. Have you looked into a newborn baby's eyes and been amazed by the wisdom you see inside? Many young children have that odd characteristic of seeming to be wiser than their years dictate. It is not really odd at all. It is simply that they have spent time on Earth before and are now approaching another new lesson or series of lessons to learn.

Are you struggling with this as a concept? Do you feel better going back into the realm of 'We are born, we live for a bit and then we die and that is it'? Did you also struggle with the concept of energies and thoughts affecting our energies? You may have made the jump forward from being sceptical about energies to accepting them as commonplace by simply working with them and becoming familiar with them. Reincarnation works along the same vein. You need to develop some sort of relationship with this concept before you can feel comfortable with it.

Reincarnation is also difficult for a lot of people in that they have no concrete proof. Without that physical proof, humans loathe to take it on board as a truth. The American philosopher and psychologist William James puts it beautifully when he says:

> *'A new idea is first condemned as ridiculous and then dismissed as trivial until, finally, it becomes what everyone knows.'*

Yet reincarnation is definitely not a new concept. Did you know the following people all believed in reincarnation: Plato, Pythagoras, Jung, Nietzsche, Goethe, Blake, Napoleon, Schiller, Dante, Kant, Franklin, Emerson, Thoreau, Whitman and Wordsworth. This is just a handful. The more you study people from all different walks of life, the more you realise that reincarnation is a commonly held belief. A wealth of religions all follow reincarnation as part of their belief system. To name but a few: Shamanism, Buddhism, Hinduism, Taoism, Native American and Theosophy.

Understanding reincarnation is not about looking at a new concept, it is all about rediscovering an ancient universal truth that has been buried away in many of us and has not resurfaced until recently. Your spiritual self knows all about it. If you have an inquiring mind and want to try to understand reincarnation more fully, or if you know that you need more proof before you can accept it as a belief, there are many documented cases of people who have experienced past-life recall. In other words, they remember being here on Earth in a past time and living a past life. Some of the cases have been difficult to prove as genuine; others are simply staggering in their attention to detail of past eras that could not possibly have been known to the person in question. If you want to read more, ask your bookshop or library for more information on reincarnation.

People often ask why we cannot all remember past lives, if it is true that we have all lived before. Why should the vast majority of people have no recollection at all? If you read autobiographies of the people who have been plagued with memories of past lives, you will understand why we are not able to remember. Can you visualise the stress caused by living in one time and yet having constant memories of a past life? This means all the attendant emotions, mental thoughts, physical symptoms and geographical imprints of an area, all battling for place within one brain that is already full of another present life. You can liken the experience to one body trying to live two separate lives simultaneously. It will cause deep distress and trauma.

Many cases of reincarnation have only been successfully discovered under hypnosis where the conditions for past life recall are created under strict control and without distress to the person involved. If you are interested in exploring this area for yourself, make sure you find a reputable hypnotist for such work. Personal recommendation is always safest.

What you give is what you get

The concept of reincarnation also ties up with our earlier discussions about thought processes and how they work, sending out energies which we then attract back to us in like form. In fact, it is not just thought processes which carry their own energy. Every action we take, every decision we make in relationship not just to ourselves but to others, also creates a different energy. The fluctuating energies all affect our spiritual progress and determine how we evolve. This cause and effect of energy exchanges is known as 'karma'.

Karma sounds complicated but the basics of it are not. Whatever you give out in life, you will receive back. If you are kind and loving, you will attract kindness and love back to you. If you are helpful to others, others will be helpful to you. Conversely, if you are dishonest and lawless, you will only attract people who will treat you dishonestly and lawlessly. If you have negative, resentful thoughts towards people, you will only attract people who are negative and resentful towards you. You can also put it this way: if you love yourself, others will also love you.

So when people say 'it's karma' about a situation, all they mean is that the appropriate reaction is occurring, based on something the person has done before. Can you think of times in your own life when karma seemed to be taking effect? Have you behaved thoughtfully towards someone and then had some act of kindness given back to you? Have you felt spiteful towards a person and then noticed someone else be spiteful to you? Or maybe you have ended a relationship badly and then had someone else finish with you in a like manner. If you think hard enough, you can usually balance each situation with an appropriate reaction.

Then we come to a difficult area. There are also people with whom karma does not seem to be quite right. They may be very pleasant, helpful people who do not in any way seem to be causing harm to others, and yet their own path in life is very difficult indeed. Can you think of someone you know who always seems to have a tough time, without ever apparently doing anything to justify it? You might think it applies to you. Now often this may occur simply because there are blockages in their own energy system and they may not be aware of them. There may be a number of major issues going all the way back to early childhood which they have chosen to blank from their conscious memory and which are affecting their adult lives. Is this applicable to you?

Then there are other reasons. Karma is not restricted to each individual reincarnation. It is continuous and it is the spiritual soul itself which is following a karmic path. Something occurring in this life may be a repercussion from a past life about which you have no conscious memory. You may have done some wonderfully selfless and nurturing act in your previous life and you reap extra benefits, if you like, during this lifetime. Conversely, if you committed certain atrocities in your previous life, you may have a somewhat 'heavy' karma to work with during your present reincarnation.

There are also occasions when you need to have some earthly experience because it will help you to progress spiritually. It does not mean that you are having a 'bad' experience because you are a 'bad' person. Karma is not about good and bad. It is about cause and effect and learning how to progress spiritually through those means. There is no 'good' karma and 'bad' karma. There are simply the basic, irrefutable laws of karma. What you give out, you will get back. Once you really accept that principle, there is nothing to battle or fight against. You simply get on and make do with your own karma.

Now there is a danger during the early stages of understanding karma that you might erroneously reach a level where you think nothing really matters because your path in life has been preordained and therefore you need make no personal effort to effect changes in your life. You can also try to make excuses for present situations by using 'Well, I wasn't a terribly nice person in my last life, therefore I can't help it now'. Basically, you can use karma as an excuse for just about anything, if you want to do so.

The laws and powers which govern karma are constant and unchanging. That means every action always has a reaction and those reactions are always relative to the initial action. You always carry your present karmic state with you and you cannot escape it by suddenly deciding you have had enough or that you will abandon your karma. However, you as an individual spirit can alter your karma constantly by every thought, intention and action you make. How you react to everything that happens to you is extremely important. You have your own free will and your own power to change your karma through positive action. It is not ever ordained that you will react a certain way to the tasks or lessons which are set before you. You and your spiritual self make the decisions as to which paths you will tread. You can change paths at any time by acquiring the will to change and the ability to transfer that will into constructive action. You are not a small pawn in a chessboard game of life; you are the player who decides which move to make.

So what is your own karma? Again, every individual is unique. We are all here for different reasons, even those tiny babies who live such a short while before passing over again. Every person on this planet is here in the evolution of their own karmic path. You do not need to spend time trying to work out other people's purposes and aims. It is quite enough to concentrate on your own.

It is not necessary for you to understand your entire karmic pattern and where you are at present within that pattern in order to be a fully functioning, healthy human being. True appreciation and full cognition of karma and your own karmic path comes from a higher level of consciousness which most of us have not yet grasped. So if we were suddenly given all the information, it is pretty likely we would not understand most of it anyway. However, what can be helpful and nurturing for you during this lifetime is to gain an understanding of who you are in the larger scheme of the universe and its laws. This process can also help clear other imbalances along the way.

Universal consciousness

We are all part of the whole universal consciousness. Each one of us is part of the whole and each one of us contains everything we need to know. We just have not learned to access it yet.

That paragraph may seem nonsensical at first. Words such as universal consciousness have a dangerous ring to them, don't they? Change the words into 'worldly awareness', if you feel more comfortable. The words are not important, it is how you grasp the possibility of wider concepts which matter.

To access these deeper thought processes, we are going to use the image of a hologram. The physical workings of a hologram can be used to help you make the jump from thinking in a rigid, linear fashion to thinking holistically.

You may already know what a hologram is as you may have seen one before. It is an image on a single piece of paper or card which appears to have a full 3D, realistic image. Now there is an interesting truth that applies to every hologram. If you take a hologram image and cut it in two pieces, both images still appear in full on each piece of card. They are not quite as crystal clear, but they are still there. Cut it into four and now there are four individual complete images. They are more blurred again, but they are still there. Cut the card into 16, 32 pieces and it makes no difference. No matter how small the piece of card becomes, each individual piece still retains the whole image. It becomes more and more blurred, but nevertheless it is still there in indistinct form.

Now think of human beings as holograms. When we are fully put together, we are beautiful, crystal-clear images of perfect health. All of us is working together. When we start to take bits of ourselves apart, however, such as when we shut down a part of us because it hurts or we do not want to know, then, although we are still operating, we are becoming more indistinct, less vibrant, with every part of us which we chop off. We can still survive, even if we are only using a tiny percentage of our true holistic self, but we are not living life to the full. Now how much of your life represents the full hologram? Are you a complete hologram? Or are you a half or even a quarter of one?

Now consider this. To enjoy communication with all of you and to exist as a complete, undivided hologram, you need to be in contact with universal consciousness. Universal consciousness is the highest form of pure thought. It is also contained inside of you. It is contained inside every single life force in the universe. You contain all of universal knowledge within your grasp, if only you learn how to access higher truths. This means suspending your complete involvement in earthly matters for a short period of time. When you have that time, try the exercise below.

I am a hologram

Sit in your chair and close your eyes. Concentrate on your breathing. Feel your body becoming nice and heavy in the chair. When you feel comfortably relaxed, then open your chakras. Go slowly through each one: base, navel, solar plexus, heart, throat, brow and crown. Then pull down the cosmic energy and feel it entering into all of you. Take your time during this process. If it takes five or ten minutes that is fine. Keep concentrating on the cosmic energy. When you are open, relaxed and balanced, you can continue.

Now you are going to gradually let your thought processes follow the cosmic energy upwards through to its source. Follow the path of light upwards. As you travel, notice what is happening. Look down on the area in which you were sitting. Watch it slowly recede. You can see the whole of the building you were in, as from a bird's-eye view. Now you can see the area surrounding it. Move higher still and notice how small it is becoming and how insignificant it seems in relation to all the other buildings and landmasses around it. See your part of the country and then see your country as a whole. What else is going on in the rest of your country that you know about? What do you think is happening that you may not know about? How many other people are living their lives, wondering about the meaning of life and where they fit into it? Watch as you fly higher. You can see other countries surrounding your country now. What do you know about these countries and how people are living their lives? Move higher and you will see yet more countries and bodies of water. What do you know about all these people and what they want in life? What do you know about how they live and their belief systems? Realise how rich and diverse your whole planet Earth is and how little you have really appreciated it and studied it. Notice how small and sheltered an existence you have led within your tiny section of a whole. You shouldn't ridicule yourself for this. Just appreciate the difference now you have something to compare it to.

Now you soar higher and planet Earth is receding. The landmasses and bodies of water are becoming vague squiggles on the surface of a round ball. How trivial do your thought processes and material concerns seem now, as you soar ever higher? You are passing stars now, flying higher and higher, passing planets and galaxies you didn't even know existed. You are enjoying your flight into new territory. You would like to return and explore some of these other planets one day.

Now you see a vast, bright golden glow above you. It is enormous, shimmering with a beautiful light that pulses and radiates with an unearthly, iridescent beauty. Move upwards and fly into the centre of the warm golden glow.

You realise you are in the centre of your own golden hologram. You are suspended in an iridescent bubble of knowledge and beauty. All of you is contained within this sphere and you have access to all spiritual and universal knowledge and truths. This is because this golden well of knowledge contains the energy of every thought, every action, every experience within the universe. Not only is all of you within this golden sphere but everyone and everything is here in energy form – every human being, every animal, plant and life force within our entire universe. You now understand that when you connect fully with your spiritual self, you are tapping into universal knowledge. With this universal knowledge, you are living your human life as a true hologram. Every part of you is vibrating on a pure energy level which resonates in harmony with all energy forces.

Enjoy your time within this golden bubble. Remember to keep breathing deeply and to feel heavy and relaxed in your chair. You may have further insights and flashes of understanding over areas in your own life. Ask for more information about your own karmic path. See what you are given. You may suddenly understand why you chose the parents or guardians in your life and what they are teaching you. You may realise you knew certain people before in other lifetimes and that you have met them again now to work through further cycles of karma. Soak in the knowledge you are being offered and give thanks for its presence.

You will know when the time is right to leave. You'll be told or you'll want to go of your own accord. Now see yourself slowly leaving the golden ball of universal knowledge behind. Start your descent back to Earth. You are flying past all the outer galaxies and planets. Now you see your planet Earth approaching in the distance. You fly closer and closer and can now see different landmasses and bodies of water. You are effortlessly taken back to your own country and then back to your own building in which you are now sitting.

Remember where you are sitting, which chair and in which room. Think what day of the week it is and what you have been doing. What time of day is it?

Keep your eyes closed as you cleanse thoroughly. Then go through your chakras and gently close them down, one by one: base, navel, solar plexus, heart, throat, brow and crown. Take

your time. Then protect yourself thoroughly with your cloak of
beautiful light. Have you chosen a different colour for your
cloak this time? Then open your eyes. Focus on an object. Make
sure you are balanced and grounded before you get up.

You may want to make some notes about this experience. Write
down any strong sensations or insights which came about as a
result of visualising yourself as a hologram. What were the
difficult areas for you? Did you find it easy to float upwards but
hard to see the golden sphere of pulsating light? Was it hard to
move upwards at all? Or maybe your golden bubble was very
beautiful but you felt little difference when you moved inside it.
Or perhaps you had a strong emotion of changed energies when
you became a hologram. What were your insights? Were you
given any information about your karmic path?

Don't feel you failed if you received little information. We are
told about our karmic route when the time is right for us to
know. Sometimes it is unhelpful for us to know too much too
soon. You also have to learn trust and patience when dealing
with your intended future. Are you someone who needs to
develop more trust in your spiritual self? How patient are you
when dealing with and learning about new issues?

Of course, you can return to this exercise on other occasions. It is
again important that you aren't interrupted during this time and that
you really make sure you are properly grounded before you finish.
This is a particularly 'heady' exercise because you are letting your mind
energies soar higher than they have probably gone before. Pulling them
back down again can take a little while. People often feel they would
prefer to remain with 'their head in the clouds' rather than return to
Earth with its attendant responsibilities and pressures. Continue to
practise discipline and pull your thoughts back down gently but firmly.
Always take a minute or two before you get up again.

We are now going to take a look at increasing your relationship
with your seven chakras. This is in preparation for considering
how you may be able to help others with spiritual healing. As you
will always work with these chakras when you heal others, you
need to begin by reinforcing your relationship with your own.

DELVING DEEPER INTO CHAKRAS

You have, of course, been working with your own chakras for some time during all these exercises and you will hopefully now be developing a much closer relationship with them. However, there is further work you can do to increase your understanding of these energy centres which will facilitate you when you feel ready to help others. Naturally, the process of learning more about the chakras will help your own healing process, irrespective of whether you feel drawn to healing other people. You can never know enough about the chakras. Their wealth of meaning and power is so intense and so complex that you could spend a lifetime studying just one energy centre and still feel you had more to learn.

The depth to which you delve into each chakra is up to you but the greater your commitment to learning more, the more effective you will become in healing, both for yourself and others. It is also very important that you develop a greater sensitivity towards each chakra as it is through these energy centres that you will be tuning into and helping others. You need to experience for yourself just how vulnerable these areas are in you, so you can handle others with the necessary awareness.

You can read books about the chakras, you can study pictures of what they are said to look like and try to learn about them in a practical manner. The difficulty with the chakras is that they are not easily discussed and understood using everyday language. As they are vibrational energy centres and deal with the energies which most of us cannot physically see, we have to use other means to study them. As we are dealing with a very sensitive, personal form of energy, it is also fair to say that two people will see the same chakra very differently. Exploring the chakras is like taking a long journey into higher consciousness.

This is a personal journey and different for every person. No one is right or wrong in this process. For instance, the fact that you might visualise the base chakra as a red ball of twirling energy and someone else might see it as a multicoloured wheel or a pulsating terracotta cone does not matter. Everyone's perception of the reality of chakras is different and this does not diminish the strength of your knowledge of the chakras in any way. All that matters is that what you see, sense and create feels absolutely right for you and helps you in your journey into understanding higher consciousness.

Again, honesty is of the utmost importance. If you are given information or some vision, do not re-create it just because you want to make it look nicer or more pleasing. Work with what you are given honestly and do not embellish through imagination. Awareness is not imagination. You should know the difference by now. You should now know yourself well enough to realise when you are being honest and when you are trying to deceive yourself. Usually, deceiving yourself comes about because you are trying to avoid looking at a particular area of your life which you find uncomfortable or emotional. Always keep checking that you are being honest with yourself.

Finding meaning in the chakras

So now is the time for you to do some more work. Rather than reading more about what they mean, you are going to use a couple of methods of going within to discover more about the chakras. You are going to start by drawing or writing about what each chakra means for you.

Have seven pieces of large, blank paper and coloured pens or pencils next to you. Before you start each drawing, you should prepare yourself in the usual way. You should sit comfortably in your chair, close your eyes and concentrate on your breathing until you are relaxed and ready to work. (If you want to do the physical exercise associated with opening each chakra before you start, then refer back to the physical exercises to open chakras illustrations shown between pages 52 and 60). Then open and concentrate only on the applicable chakra. It is better and more balancing for you if you have the time to work through all seven at one sitting. It can feel unnerving to spend time focusing on just one chakra and ignoring the others. You can end up feeling off-balance for the rest of the day.

Drawing the base chakra

Open your base chakra. Focus just on that part of your body at the base of your spine. Now try not to concentrate specifically on what you feel in this area but more on what that area of your body tells you about the base chakra. What functions occur in this area? What does the spine mean to you? What emotions comes readily to you? What images? Red is the associated colour but does it feel accurate for you? Is it more than one colour? You already know the base chakra is connected to physical vitality and a love of earthly matters. What does this indicate in a universal sense, as opposed to you personally? What images seem synonymous with earthly matters? Is there a colour which seems powerful in this context? What about an animal or plant or object which relates to the base chakra? The words connected with this chakra are 'I am'. How would you finish this sentence to relate the base chakra to spiritual awareness and knowledge?

Now open your eyes and draw or write what the base chakra represents according to your understanding of its energies. If you want to enclose everything in a shape because it feels right, such as a circle or cone-like shape, then do so. Use the relevant colour pens. If you think you cannot draw, write the names of animals or plants which you see. Write down any words which seem to sum up this chakra. If you believe a particular emotion is important here or even an affirmation, write it down. Notice how your own base chakra feels as you write. If you are relaxed and tuned in properly, your base chakra will let you know if anything you write is not honest or relevant.

When you have finished, study what you have put down. Does it really represent how you see the base chakra at this time in your life? Have you missed out something? Write 'Base Chakra' across the top of the page.

Now cleanse thoroughly, particularly through the base chakra, and close the chakra properly. When you're ready move on to the navel chakra.

Drawing the navel chakra

Now you want to open your navel chakra, which is just below your navel. Make sure you open both front and back centres. Now concentrate on this area. What is contained within this part of your body? How do those functions relate to this chakra? You know this chakra is about emotions. Where do you see the effect of emotions within the universe as a whole? What does 'I feel emotionally' really mean? What symbols or images make this chakra come alive? You also know that it is considered the sexual centre. Disregard your own personal views of sex and see its purpose within the universe as a whole. Is orange an appropriate colour for your present understanding of the navel chakra? If not, what colour is true for you? Is its shape different from the base chakra? Does it move differently? Is there an image or emotion which sums up this area for you? Are there different functions for the front opening from the back? What might those differences be for you and how would you relate that to everyone?

Open your eyes and write what feels appropriate. Again, try to keep your own personal views out of the picture. This is your opportunity to think in a broader, more universal context. Choose your colours carefully. If you want to split the picture into two for the two openings, do so.

When you have finished, check that the drawing accurately represents your perception. Make sure you write 'Navel Chakra' at the top. Then cleanse and gently close your navel chakra, front and back. Move on to the solar plexus when you are ready.

Drawing the solar plexus chakra

Open your solar plexus chakra, front and back. What do you know about this area of the body? What does the spleen mean to you? What activities go on in this area of the body? How do they relate to the solar plexus chakra? You know this chakra represents your mental sphere. What power do thoughts have *within the universe? What sort of image comes with this concept? Complete the phrase 'I think' in keeping with universal truths. Self-esteem is also important here. Where does self-esteem come from and how might it be expressed within this chakra? This area also deals with how people see themselves in the larger context of life and its purpose. What does this chakra tell you about one's sense of purpose and destiny? Is yellow appropriate or are there more colours? Is there a flower or animal which seems relevant to this chakra? Anger is often stored within this chakra. What does anger represent to you? How does it affect energies? What controls and releases anger? Can that be found within this chakra?*

Create a shape and then write within that, using colours which sum up how you see the solar plexus chakra. Put down everything which feels right and check whether your own solar plexus area agrees with what you're doing. Remember not to become involved with your own solar plexus chakra. You are trying to relate to the chakra in a more universal context.

Check through the drawing when you have finished. Add more if you wish or cross out what isn't right and mark it 'Solar Plexus'. Then cleanse. Take a minute to wash away any accumulation of thoughts which might be building up. Gently close your solar plexus, front and back. Concentrate on your breathing for a minute before you move on to the heart chakra.

Drawing the heart chakra

Open your heart chakra, front and back. This is considered the hinge between the physical and spiritual world. What image comes to mind when considering the heart chakra in this light? Think of the heart and its function. What parts of the body does it connect with? What does the word 'love' mean in the larger context of universal, spiritual love? How does the heart chakra help you to access this higher emotion? Is there a particularly powerful image that encompasses love? What about an animal or another life force? How does earthly love differ from unconditional love and when can the two be brought together? What can love accomplish as far as energy changes are concerned and how does the heart chakra assist this task? Does green resonate powerfully for you in representing this chakra, or perhaps other colours seem right? Consider the phrase 'I love humanly' in the context of spiritual enlightenment and see where it belongs.

Now draw your shape and start filling it in. Tune in to see what colours are right. How different is the function for the front opening from the back opening? Split your shape into two if you want to. Put down any overriding emotion or sensation which seems to sum up this chakra. Remember to keep being truthful. The vibrational energies become lighter and finer at the heart. Is this reflected in your drawing? How is it different from your previous chakra drawings? Name it as your 'Heart Chakra'.

When it feels right to withdraw from your heart chakra, do so. Cleanse any residue emotion away. Close your heart centre gently, concentrating on both the back and front. Move on to your throat centre when you're ready.

Drawing the throat chakra

Now open your throat centre, both front and back. The vibrations are higher again. You have to increase your concentration to focus purely on this area. What functions are performed by the throat? How can this be applied to acknowledging a higher truth and living by it? Fulfilment in your profession is also found in this chakra. How does that relate to the throat area? Creativity is another important aspect of the throat chakra. What does creativity mean in a larger, universal context? What do truth and integrity really mean? What image or symbol is compatible with these thoughts? Blame is often stored in this chakra. How do we alleviate blame and how can the throat chakra help us in this act? Can you relate any animal or life force to this chakra? How

*do the words 'I will' follow the path of higher spiritual truth?
Is sky blue the right colour for the throat chakra? Notice if
anything else is right for your interpretation.*

*Draw when you feel ready, remembering there are two
openings to the throat centre. Have you been discovering an
affirmation for each chakra? What is suitable for the throat
area? Use the colours you are drawn towards. Notice if you
want to change the shape here. Be aware of ever changing
vibrations in your work. Does this drawing feel different
again from your heart chakra? Remember to mark your
drawing 'Throat Chakra'.*

*Now cleanse fully and wash away any sensations from your
throat area. Close your throat carefully. Take a moment to
pull some Cosmic Energy down into your system to refresh
you. You may be feeling a little tired now. When you're
ready, move on to your brow chakra.*

Drawing the brow chakra
*Open the brow chakra in the middle of your forehead. Open
both front and back centres. Focus on the area in between the
two openings. What functions does your brain perform that
you already know about? What else might the brain be capable
of? What power may this give to the brow chakra? The brow
relates to our spiritual awareness and also our ability to move
forward with that knowledge and work on our place within
the universal realm. What images and colours become powerful
in this context? Can you find an earthly symbol for a spiritual
experience? Is there an emotion or expression which is adequate?
What does 'I love universally' really mean? Is purple the right
colour for you? You might want to change the shade slightly
or add more colours. You may change it completely.*

*Write when you're ready. This is much harder, as you climb
into higher consciousness. Colour pens and paper don't seem
to offer enough substance. Sometimes it feels as though the*

brow chakra itself is not clear, so how can your drawing do it justice? It's more elusive, more intangible in thought. Do not worry if you feel you are now struggling. Simply write what you know is honest for the way you view the brow chakra at present. If it's relatively empty or sparse in content, it doesn't matter. Just be honest.

When you've finished, don't criticise what you've written. Close your eyes and let the thoughts wash away. Cleanse through all of you. Gently close the brow chakra. If you have a slight headachey feeling through concentration, wash it away. Pull down some more cosmic energy and then continue with the last chakra, the crown.

Drawing the crown chakra

Focus now on the top of your head and feel your crown chakra opening a little further. Notice how light and fine the vibrations are now. What is contained at the top of your head? Again, what is happening in this part of your brain about which we know very little? What does the word 'bliss' mean to you in relation to universal knowledge? This is the highest vibrational frequency we can reach and it relates to the fusion between earthly and divine knowledge. Is there an emotion which sums up this experience? Is there an earthly word which properly explains this concept? If that isn't possible, can you think of an image which seems spiritually appropriate? What do the words 'I know' mean in the realm of universal consciousness? White is the associated colour. How is this pertinent to the crown chakra? Would any other colour be more suitable to you?

Now draw and write what you feel is right. You may have even less to put this time. It isn't important. If you end up with a completely blank page, that's fine. All that matters is that you are honest and put down what you see at present as being accurate for the crown chakra. If you only write one word, choose the right colour to accompany it. Take your time. Mark it as 'Crown Chakra'.

Again, don't criticise your work. Put it down and close your eyes. Relax now. Really relax. Cleanse through all of you. Spend more time than usual in your cleansing sanctuary and feel your aches and pains wash away. Don't forget to cleanse your fingers, hands, wrists, arms and shoulders, as they may be aching slightly from all your drawing. Then close down all your chakras again, one by one: base, navel, solar plexus, heart, throat, brow and crown.

When you feel ready, open your eyes and make sure you are fully grounded and balanced before you get up.

You may find you want to leave comparisons until another occasion. It can be demanding work to focus on one chakra after the other like that. Did you find some personal breakthrough occurred as a result of the exercise? You may notice a difference even a day or two later when you have a sudden flash of understanding. You will have facilitated changes in your energy system, even though you were not consciously concentrating on yourself.

When you feel ready, go back and look through your seven drawings. Lay them out, one after the other, and study them in turn. Were some easier than others to draw? You may have found some of the questions within each exercise difficult to answer. It does not matter whether you found what you thought was the right answer or not. The questions are simply meant to expand your thought processes and allow you to think in an ever wider circle. If you were to compare what you have drawn with someone else's, they would almost certainly be completely different.

You now have your own personal blueprint of the seven chakras which you can work with in the future. Keep them near you. Put them up on your walls or on a large cork board if you can. You are also encouraged to go back through the whole process in a month or so's time and completely redraw the seven centres. Notice then how they have changed as your perception has grown and widened to encompass even more concepts.

When you decide you want to heal another issue in your life, firstly go and look at those seven drawings. Is one more powerful than another for you? Is one making you feel uncomfortable as you look at it? Is that the chakra you need to focus upon?

This chakra work is also your foundation for the process of how you might be able to help others in their own individual healing. You are now about to enter the second part of this book, which deals with how to heal others. However, your own healing process will continue throughout. You have not finished with yourself, simply because you are moving on. Self-healing is a lifelong commitment which, as you can now begin to see, actually continues past what is called 'death'. It also continues and often accelerates as we work for and with others. It is said we only draw people towards us for healing when we also have something to learn from them. Through working with others, you clear your own blocks, sometimes without even knowing it. It's a two-way process.

Before you move on, stop to acknowledge how much you have learned and moved forward. Think back to all the concepts you have grasped and worked with during this time. Look back over your progress and be quick to notice where you have made positive changes in your life. Make a note of the exercises and meditations which you found particularly helpful for you. You may want to share them with others at a later stage. Really stop and take time to acknowledge yourself for what you have accomplished and what you know you will accomplish in the future. Commit to loving yourself unconditionally through your life.

Here is an affirmation with which to leave this part of the book:

I am perfect, whole and completely healthy.
I love myself and every part of my life unconditionally.
I love everyone and everything in the universe
unconditionally.
I embrace all changes as they, too, are perfect.
Everything is perfect.

PART TWO:

HEALING OTHERS

You have spent a considerable amount of time concentrating on yourself and looking honestly at ways to access your own spiritual power. Some of it may have been uplifting and encouraging. Some of it you may have found challenging. Some of it you may have wanted to run away from. The more emotions you experienced, the more you went through a roller-coaster of ups and downs, the better equipped you are now to help others. Whatever you have experienced for yourself will give you compassion and empathy for others. The more sensitive you are to others, the more you will be able to tune in and help them.

Some of you may feel you are not ready for the experience of healing others; you may feel that you have so much work to do on yourself first, that you cannot yet be of assistance to anyone else. Of course it is important that you work on your own healing process, but the truth is that healing yourself is a lifelong path which you can walk down forever. There will not be a time when you feel you know everything about healing and when you feel you are a perfectly healed person. All that happens is that you constantly discover more and more areas of your life which can benefit from healing. You go deeper and deeper into your own spirituality and uncover more and more aspects of a holistically healthy life and where you fit into the universal pattern. If you are expecting to reach a stage where you do not have to work on yourself any more and when you feel 'perfect', you are going to be disappointed. The joy of life lies in the process of discovery. Would it not be very boring and unfulfilling if there were nothing left to explore?

So if you are working on the premise that all healers are perfectly attuned and balanced individuals, you would be mistaken. They are learning how to follow their intended path in life just as you are. The only difference lies in their desire to help others on their way.

This does not diminish the fact that there is a certain stage you need to reach before you can consider healing others. If you are a particularly sensitive and vulnerable person, if you have a lot of unresolved issues and anger still within you, if you feel nervous about interrelating with others and lacking in confidence, then you need to work more with your inner self before going outward and touching others. You should have learned enough about your own personal energy system to know whether you are ready to handle other people's problems. It is only you who can make this judgment. It is a personal decision.

You also need to consider a further matter. This process of

helping to heal others does require certain extra abilities on the part of the healer. You have to develop some additional skills before you can benefit others. These can be broken down as follows:

- *Increasing sensitivity to others.*
- *Unconditional love for others.*
- *Letting go of your own ego.*
- *Wanting to help others.*
- *Knowing your limitations and responsibilities.*

You have been working on your sensitivity to others during your own healing process, particularly with exercises such as Releasing Resentment. There will no doubt have been many other occasions when different people cropped up during your healing exercises and you realised that you had conflicts which needed to be sorted out. The process of sorting them out involves your deeper understanding of them as individuals. This helps you in being able to tune in to others when healing.

You can liken it to having to break down some energy barriers before you can get through to the real core of the person underneath. You need to learn the tools with which you can gently work through to the real person, not the outer shell some people use as a defence mechanism. Part of your responsibility as a healer is to make someone feel utterly safe and secure in your presence so that they feel able to relax and let down some of those barriers which will enable you to help them more effectively.

Of course, that process involves them becoming much more vulnerable and open to your influence. Your job then becomes doubly important and also full of additional responsibilities. What you say and do then has more impact on their aura. You have to be extremely careful that what you offer as healing is truly beneficial and in harmony with their own energy. Just because you might want to do the best you can for someone, it does not necessarily follow that you will, unless you have been taught the necessary skills. Ignorance in spiritual healing can cause damage to others.

Increasing sensitivity to others
So the first aspect you need to embrace before you start healing others

is to learn how to increase your sensitivity to people around you. You can do this in lots of small ways just through your everyday contact with people. It is particularly useful when someone may have irritated you or when you are tempted to react angrily to a scenario.

Take, for example, an everyday situation such as someone taking the last seat on a train or bus, just as you were about to sit down. Most of us have that very human reaction of being cross. Instead, take a moment to let the irritation pass by taking several deep breaths. Wash away the emotion. Then have a quick 'tune in' to that person. Did they take the seat because they were feeling unwell? Were they lost in thought and did not notice that you were about to sit there? Or are you still sure that they did it because they are selfish and did not care what you wanted? Sometimes, you still end up choosing the last option. Then tune in further. What is their life like such that they behave that way? Can you see reasons why they may be selfish and that it is through fear or ignorance or insecurity or lack of self-worth? It is a very constructive way to pass a journey and you may discover by the end of the process that you end up feeling quite warm towards this unknown stranger who initially irritated you. There is one very important factor here. You must always remember to cleanse thoroughly when you finish your exercise. Otherwise, you may carry some of their emotion around with you for the rest of the day. With the additional sensitivity you develop towards others comes the added need for extra protection and cleansing. The next chapter covers that in detail.

By increasing your awareness of other people and developing a deeper understanding of them, you come to the second point quite naturally, of loving others unconditionally. It becomes so much easier to love others that way when we begin to see them as truly spiritual beings who are fallible and insecure and full of fears, just as we are. This leads to a nonjudgmental attitude.

Unconditional love for others

You cannot heal others if you are constantly judging them or criticising them in some way. Unconditional love is about complete acceptance of somebody just as they are. Now this can be difficult. You may not necessarily be immediately drawn to someone who wants healing from you. How do you feel, for instance, about healing someone who may have a strong, unwashed body odour? What about someone who is badly scarred from burns or suffering from a skin condition of weeping sores? If someone insists on talking negatively throughout a healing session and will not listen to a word you say, how would you end up feeling towards them?

This is not to put you off the healing of others because most people who come to you probably will not fall into any of those categories, particularly during your initial stages of healing. This is merely to demonstrate that loving others unconditionally is not as easy as you may first think. We all have areas in our life when we stop loving others unconditionally because it is so hard to lose our judgmental qualities.

A key to helping you become less judgmental is to go back to your understanding of reincarnation and karma. If you believe that we are each of us working along our own intended path in the larger concept of universal truth and awareness, then there is always a reason, a purpose, behind every individual soul's behaviour. You have to go back again to the belief that it is not what happens around us which is important, it is our reaction to that event which matters. You need to be able to pass on that concept to someone else without judgment on your part. So your role as a healer is not to decide why they are behaving a certain way; all that matters is that you are able to give them the tools to look at it truthfully for themselves and to allow them to come to some sort of conclusion or breakthrough for themselves. Whether you are party to understanding what they are going through, or what they have found to be true for themselves, is not important. You do not need to personally understand what breakthrough they have had. All that is necessary is for you to help facilitate that healing process.

Letting go of your own ego

The next important step is to let go of your own ego. This is another challenge all good healers face and it is a most difficult one. Whilst you have heard so much about how essential it is to love yourself and that, without self-worth and self-esteem, you cannot heal yourself, the subject of your own ego falls into a different category completely.

The ego in terms of spiritual healing is not about self-love or unconditional love or believing in yourself. The ego is about needing to look good and wanting to impress. The ego is about needing everyone to tell you that you are a wonderful person or a fantastic healer. It is about wanting to be proven right all the time and to have everyone bend to your will and to tell you that you are clever and know everything. This ego is a self-destructive force that craves power and needs to dominate to feel fulfilled. This ego is exactly what you do not want when working with spiritual healing.

It is quite difficult to know sometimes when this ego is actually working through you and when you have managed to let it go. As humans, we are all programmed to need this ego to some degree. We want to have people praise us and tell us we are worthy individuals, particularly if we had very little of that in our childhood. We all experience a certain glow when we are praised and told that we did well. The difference lies in knowing that you do something only because you are expecting and needing the praise. If that is your aim behind spiritual healing, then you are going to find certain areas a struggle. How do you know when you are acting purely with the best intentions for the person you are healing and when you are letting your own ego interfere? Consider the following scenario and be truthful about how you would react.

You have had a healing session with an individual whom you do not know very well but you find them negative and sceptical in their outlook. You have healed according to your best ability. At the end, when you ask them how they feel, they tell you that absolutely nothing happened and they feel as though they have wasted the last half hour. They ask you if you really know what you are doing. How would you respond? Would you:

- *Feel irritated as you explain that healing only works if they also want to help themselves and perhaps they are not ready to be healed yet?*
- *Appreciate their honesty, explain you are still learning yourself and that often healing can take place after a session has finished?*

- *Feel devastated, apologise and decide that you must have done something wrong?*

If your response would be the third choice, then you have some more work to do on loving yourself and increasing your own sense of self-esteem and self-worth. You are not working with an inflated sense of ego but nor are you acknowledging yourself and your unique place within the universe. You need to work through the Starting to Love Yourself, Loving Yourself via the Heart Chakra and I am a Hologram exercises in Part One. You are refusing to acknowledge your true potential and are stopping your own energy from flowing freely.

If your response was the first choice, then you are still not letting go of your ego. You have the need to put the onus back on them and make them feel as though they are doing something wrong and that it is their problem nothing has happened. This is not to say that you are not right by your comment that they have to help themselves and that they may not be ready for healing yet. However, any comment along those lines will always sound derogatory and leave someone feeling inadequate or ignorant. You only say discouraging things like that if your own ego feels bruised. Statements like that do not come from unconditional love; they come from wanting to prove someone else is wrong. If you would honestly react that way, then you need to do some more work on appreciating and understanding people as they are. You probably have areas in your own life where you still feel resentful and insecure. Who else would you like to prove wrong? Go back to the Releasing Resentment exercise (see page 130) and work through your feelings. You might also find working with Your Other Hand exercise (see page 138) might bring up some further issues for you.

If you truthfully would react as per the second choice, then you really are reaching a stage where you know that your own ego is not necessary for you to feel powerful. You are really embracing that every situation is just a learning process, which is positive. You are also able to be honest about your own stage in spiritual healing and have no need to try to cover up your novice status. You also want to nurture and encourage others by letting them know that healing is ongoing and not necessarily confined to the healing session itself. You have no need to criticise others to make yourself look better or more important.

Now the truth is that many people would initially feel irritated or inadequate by someone saying that they thought they were useless. That is just the human response which we are well-programmed to have. However, you can then learn to move past your ego very quickly by taking a deep breath, acknowledging your ever-constant learning process and seeing that any supposed criticism is merely the opportunity to learn something more.

You can take this scenario one step further by appreciating their honesty so much that you then ask them even more questions. Then you can really start to delve deeper. You may find that they did in fact have some sort of response to your healing, it is just that they are not tuned in enough to their own bodies to immediately be able to identify what was going on. You may also get feedback from them, such as 'You were standing too close to me', 'I didn't like the incense', 'The room was too hot/cold', or some other statement from which you can learn. Any criticism is only the chance for you to discover more. If they had said nothing but left, feeling disappointed but not expressing it, what would you have learnt from that scenario? Thank someone for being critical. They are helping you.

Letting go of your ego will be an ongoing process for you and it will get easier with time. It is wonderful to reach the stage where you actually welcome criticism from someone because you know you can then move forward. Can you imagine a situation where you actually feel disappointed because no one was able to offer any criticism? What a lovely position to be in!

Wanting to help others

The next point we come on to is simply wanting to help others. It is such a basic statement, isn't it? Yet it encompasses further the element of not needing your ego in spiritual work. If you want to heal others but do not need to do so in order to make yourself feel good/ powerful/ clever or to be acknowledged and praised all the time, why would you want to heal others? You have to want to do it for the simple act of helping others. There is nothing left if the ego is not acting in the equation at all.

If you do not want to help others, you will not find yourself effective in your spiritual healing. The intention to help creates a further energy of its own. The desire to do something positive for someone else acts as a sort of surge of energy, if you like, which makes your healing powerful. You could compare it to needing to turn the power on to make an appliance work. The power behind spiritual healing comes initially from your desire to want to help someone. The stronger your capacity for unconditional love of others and your desire to want to help, the more effective you can learn to become. If you are apathetic in your healing, if you take it for granted and do not want to continually work at it to become as effective as possible, that lack of commitment will be reflected in your results.

The other aspect to consider in this is why you might not want to help others. How much do you interrelate with other people? How much of your time is spent in communicating with others at more than a superficial level? Or is your work or home life geared to communication of practical, material matters which are unconnected to deeper communication? If you find close association or intimacy of any sort to be difficult, then you might benefit from looking at your own personal energies as far as communicating with others is concerned. Do you fear intimacy, sexual or otherwise? Do you hate feeling vulnerable or open to others? If so, how can you reasonably expect others to be open to your healing if you, likewise, cannot open yourself up? Where does this fear stem from? You need to look at your own issues more deeply before you consider healing others. Do you lack trust in other people? Who has let you down in the past? Do some exercises with Your Other Hand (see page 138) and look at where the fear has stemmed from.

Helping others with unconditional love and spiritual healing is a natural, loving, giving act which has many positive repercussions. If you balk at helping others, when you know inside that you can, look at the energy blocks which are stopping you from moving forward.

Knowing your limitations and responsibilities

The last area to look at before we move on towards healing others is to learn our limitations and responsibilities in spiritually healing other people. Particularly during your early stages, you cannot expect to work miracles with others. The most important aspect of this is that you must not mislead people at any stage during spiritual healing. No matter how powerful you believe spiritual healing is, no matter how much it has helped you personally, no matter how much you want to pass on its benefits, you are not qualified to decide what degree of power you actually possess.

This means you must always, at the outset, advise people that if they are on orthodox medication of any sort, they must continue to take the treatment. You must explain your healing is in addition to and as a complement to any conventional healing treatment. Even if you yourself personally believe that alternative medicine is much more effective and that orthodox treatment only leads to further problems, it is not your place to offer these personal opinions. You must remain neutral and give the person you are healing a chance to form their own thoughts and to make their own decisions, based on how they personally choose to view health. Always advise them that they must consult their own doctor before making any change in their medication.

If you have held a healing session and someone declares that they feel so much better that they are sure they are 'cured', insist that they consult their own medical doctor to confirm their belief. Never let anyone walk out of your healing session convinced they know best. Spiritual healing can have wonderful, short-term effects and can sometimes simply make someone feel relaxed and refreshed. It does not necessarily mean that their deep-rooted condition or belief system has been altered irrevocably. If they really are 'cured' of some condition through you helping them to re-balance some of their energies, let them have physical proof of that state by having an orthodox medical doctor endorse this for them.

Can you see yet again how important it is for you to let your ego go during healing work? It is so tempting when someone is complimenting your work and telling you that you have cured them, to be swept along by the euphoric flow of praise. It is wonderful to see someone who was in pain or distress be free of that condition when you have finished. But you are not medically qualified to say what has happened to their physical body, no matter how they may feel at that stage. Always, always demand that they speak to their doctor to establish the physical truth of what has happened. There are no exceptions to this rule, especially during your early stages of working with others. Discipline yourself to this routine. It is suggested that you have a small card on which you have written the following:

This healing session is not meant to replace any orthodox, medical treatment you may currently be undergoing. Under no circumstances should you stop taking prescribed medication without first consulting your doctor.

Rewrite it if you find a better way of expressing what you mean. It does not matter if you ask them to read it, or you read it to them, but you must never forget the process.

Also be honest in every way. Tell them that you are new to spiritual healing. Explain that you have a lot to learn still and that you appreciate them acting as your guinea pig. Never charge for your healing sessions until you are a fully trained and qualified spiritual healer. This does not mean that you should apologise for yourself and indicate that little will probably happen because you are not good enough! Make sure you do not end up sounding as though you have no abilities whatsoever. If you have the tendency to do this with the people you heal, make sure you have some quiet time on your own to work further on strengthening your self-belief. You see, your spiritual work continues on yourself throughout your process of helping others to heal! Always try to pay attention to how you sound as you work with others. It will tell you a great deal about yourself and quickly pinpoint any areas on yourself that you could benefit from looking at.

Part of your responsibility in healing others is to acknowledge that you are always in control. Through working on yourself, you will appreciate the advantages of learning discipline and accepting that you are always in control during your exercises.

You will have learnt that no one else dictates how you work and how you behave. You are responsible for yourself.

When you are healing others, you have to assume control. This does not mean to dominate or to impose your own will. The control we are talking about here is where you know you can deal with whatever arises. If someone is tearful, you know you can offer tissues and words of comfort. If someone is angry, you know you can help them to calm down. If someone develops physical pain, you know you can assist them in washing it away. If someone is being too demanding and draining your own energy, you know how to cleanse and refresh yourself and how to refuse to let them sap any more of your energy. Whatever happens within your healing session, you are responsible for everything and you must deal with it quickly and efficiently. Of course, you will shortly be learning different techniques for handling people to help you with this process. You are not expected to know it all now but you need to realise that you will always have to accept responsibility for that person while they are with you in a healing environment which you have created.

Lastly, there is your responsibility to yourself. You should never attempt to heal others if you are tired or unwell. That is very important and deserves repeating. *Never attempt to heal others if you are tired or unwell.* This is nothing to do with you being selfish or self-obsessed. You need to be in good health yourself before you are in a safe position to help others. Only heal when you know you are in healthy condition to do so. Also, healing others leaves you very open and vulnerable to everyone else's state of disease, whatever it may be. Whether their energy imbalances relate to physical, emotional, mental or spiritual disturbances, they are placing their aura within your own aura. You are therefore mingling energies. Unless you learn how to properly defend and protect yourself, you could end up taking on some symptoms of the people you are healing. As this is such an important issue, the next chapter will deal with it in detail and show you various methods you can use to increase your self-protection.

You already have several techniques which you know how to use to defend yourself against any unwanted bombardment of your energies. The areas you should be very familiar with are:

- *Your cleansing sanctuary*
- *Cosmic energy*
- *Grounding energy*
- *Closing your chakras*
- *Your cloak of protection*

By now, you should be so familiar with your cleansing sanctuary that you know every square inch of it by heart. It should make you feel relaxed and content just to be in it. You should also be able to transport yourself into the space within a split second of thinking about it. Whatever method you use to cleanse, whether it be water, sunshine or air, you should be able to call upon it instantly. It should be endless in supply. You should always be alone in your cleansing space and it should resonate with everything that you love. It is quite acceptable that this space may change from time to time according to your personal needs, but it should never be an effort to access the space in your memory. If you know you have not spent enough time getting to know your cleansing sanctuary, then set aside a little time each day to strengthen your bond with this very important space.

If you know that what you created initially is simply not right for you any more, do not be hesitant about changing your sanctuary completely. Did you have a marble bathroom but you now want seas pounding on a shore? Did you choose a waterfall but you now long for a private park where you can have the sun warm and cleanse you? Did you opt for sunshine on a deserted beach but you now realise you need soft, gentle rain? Change everything if you need to. Then make sure you spend some extra time in this new cleansing sanctuary and that you know it all intimately.

Your relationship with cosmic energy should be such that you can feel it immediately above you whenever you call upon it. You may not yet be clear about its source but you need to believe absolutely in its strength and unique power. You need to be able to call upon it wherever you are, whatever the circumstances. If you feel it is not strong enough initially, you must know how to strengthen its presence. You must have it come down easily to cascade around all of you. It must be easy to feel it penetrate your aura and then your entire physical body. If you are still struggling with the presence of cosmic energy and feeling its divine beauty and strength, then spend more time working with it. For example, every time you do a little meditation, concentrate on it. Always ask your spiritual self to guide you towards its divine source. Practise the I Am A Hologram exercise on page 181 and generally work with the cosmic energy until you feel happy and confident with its presence.

The same applies to grounding energy. Most people find this easier to access as we feel more comfortable generally with earthly concepts than spiritual ones. But make sure that you really are tapping into the grounding energy. Practice feeling the roots of a tree growing from the soles of your feet. The pull towards the ground is very strong once you have connected properly and it should feel a powerful sensation of being centred and feeling secure. If you suddenly feel sucked into the ground as though you are being swallowed up, you are not experiencing the power of grounding energy. You are using your imagination to create another scenario. Check that you are working properly with the grounding energy. Know its comforting source of practical, earthly vibrations will leave you confident and focused on everyday matters.

You will also have been closing your chakras on a regular basis during your exercises. You might become careless during this process. It is so easy to think that you have probably closed them all down when in fact you have rushed the practice and left yourself half-open and slightly imbalanced. If you wander around, particularly in crowded, city environments, with your chakras open and unprotected, you will be absorbing all sorts of different energies and they will affect you. You can close down all the time, constantly. You can be standing on a crowded bus or train and silently close your seven chakras. You might be in conversation with an angry work colleague who is bombarding your aura with their problems. You can swiftly close your chakra centres, one by one. No one ever has to know what you are doing but you can instantly help protect yourself. Get into the habit of doing this all the time so it becomes commonplace and familiar.

Your cloak of protection

You may not be so well-acquainted with your cloak of protection. It has been mentioned in a few exercises to help protect you when you feel particularly vulnerable and open, but you need to strengthen its presence more for your work in healing others. Work through the exercise below when you have the time.

Sit in your comfortable chair and close your eyes. Breathe comfortably. Feel your body and mind relax. Now imagine that you are sitting in the middle of a clearing in a beautiful forest. You are sitting alone in warm sunshine. You can hear distant birds singing or bees humming. You can hear the light wind in the trees. Without consciously trying to create it, feel the cosmic energy pouring down from above and filling the space around you with beautiful, pure energy. Feel it coming through your crown chakra and gently filtering through all of your body. Spend several minutes luxuriating in its comforting presence.

Now ask that you be shown the cloak of protection which is appropriate for you. Ask that it be brought gently around your shoulders. Sit there for a few minutes. Don't worry if nothing happens initially. Know that it will be given to you when you are ready.

After a few minutes, notice that something is happening. You may see your cloak as a mist which forms around your body and materialises into a recognisable fabric. You may suddenly realise your cloak is already around you. You may even be given the cloak by an angel or guardian who appears and then dissolves into nothingness again. You may suddenly feel a warm shaft of light above as the cloak slips down and encompasses you. It will be a personal experience suitable for you.

Now examine your cloak of protection. It will always be light in weight. It often feels without substance. Sometimes it does not seem as though it is a fabric at all. It can appear as shimmering, incandescent light which pulses around you. It doesn't matter if you can't describe it using normal words. All that matters is that you feel completely protected and safe within it. What colour is it? Gold and silver are frequent experiences but yours may be different. If it's a dark colour, ask whether that is really appropriate for you (dark colours can drain energy sometimes). You will be told if it is suitable; if it's not, you can change the colour with your thought process. Does it have a hood on it? Pull it up over your head. How does that feel? Does it have buttons or hooks or a zipper or a belt? Get to know your cloak and welcome its comforting presence.

You might want to get up and walk around your clearing in the forest. Notice how long the cloak is and how it protects all of you. Enjoy moving in it and realise that you can call upon your cloak of protection any time you wish. If you feel vulnerable on any occasion, it will be there for you to step into.

When you're ready, sit down again in your clearing and feel the spiritual folds of fabric settle around you. Give thanks for its presence. Ask that it remain near you at all times, to be called upon whenever you need it.

Now slowly withdraw from your clearing in the forest. Remember that you are sitting in your chair and what time

of the day it is, what day of the week. Cleanse and ground
yourself. Open your eyes when you feel ready and focus on
an object before you get up.

Could you still feel the cloak around you when you finished the
exercise? It should always feel warm and comforting and never
restricting. If it does not feel absolutely right for you, go back
on another occasion and re-create it so that it does feel right.
This cloak is a form of self-protection that you may need
frequently during healing sessions. Get to know it well.

Apart from these five forms of self-protection which you
need to work with continually to improve your relationship
with them and to subsequently strengthen their power, there
are many other techniques which we will look at.

If you are healing someone who is unconsciously draining
you of your energy, then you will learn to close your chakras,
balance yourself and give yourself some extra protection with
your cloak. However, there may be occasions when you feel
you want something more.

Crystal protection

You can imagine yourself within a large crystal. Crystals have amazing
properties which can protect, absorb, repel and cleanse energies.
(They are discussed in more detail in Part Three; see page 305.)
Imagine that you are totally encased in a beautiful, pure crystal which
you can see through and which allows you to send out your healing
vibrations, but prevents harmful energies from accosting your aura.

You can stand or sit for this exercise. If you stand, keep your
eyes open. Relax yourself by focusing on your breath and
feeling it deepen and become slower.

Now visualise this large, clear crystal around you, encasing
all of you. It is solid and feels immensely powerful. You are
completely protected and nurtured in its energy. It is
warming and comforting but you also know that no one
can touch you as you stand or sit within this space. You

can look out and your energies can penetrate the edges of the crystal and move out to others, but the crystal protects you from receiving any unwanted influences.

You feel secure and completely loved in this space. Spend some time getting comfortable with your crystal protection. Its energies are so beautiful that it can feel like another cleansing sanctuary when you are in here. Crystal protection can convert negative energy into a positive force. It is a very rejuvenating experience. Your crystal will resonate with your own energies and amplify your positive state. Feel free to step into your crystal whenever you need it. Always remember that you can give out lovingly to others in this space but others cannot invade you with negative forces.

When you have explored your crystal, bring your attention back to your breath. Remember where you are sitting and return to being balanced in your earthly world. Take a few minutes to ground yourself before you finish.

You can use your crystal when healing others if you feel that what the other person is giving off is having an adverse effect on your own energies. You can continue your healing whilst inside your crystal. It will not affect your own power to heal. It is a form of protection and does not mean that you are in any way shutting off from someone else.

If you are dealing with someone who is angry, there is a very quick and effective technique you can use. Imagine you are holding up a mirror for them to look at themselves. Just use your mind to create this thought. This allows the stream of powerful, angry energy to be redirected back at themselves. It deflects the energy from attacking you. They will not know what is happening, but once you have practised this a few times, you will soon spot a common response from an angry person. They seem to run out of steam quite quickly. It is hard to believe just how powerful a tool this can be until you try it for yourself and witness the result firsthand.

It is then helpful and nourishing if you can send a stream of unconditional love to them. Anger creates all sorts of rips and holes and blocks in our energy system and they could benefit from a dose of loving from someone to help them heal again. You can imagine a stream of green light coming from your heart or solar plexus chakra to their aura. You might prefer to imagine multicoloured streamers or simply a wave of energy enveloping their angry physical body. You will discover what feels right for you. It can work wonders to help soothe and balance their ruffled energies. If you get caught up in their angry diatribe, it will only imbalance your own energy field. Let go of your response to be irritated or feel threatened by them by offering that unconditional love. The act of your giving to them also helps to sort out your own energies.

Protective symbols

Do you find certain images also give you a sense of protection and calm? Symbols can be very powerful. Perhaps you have one already on a charm bracelet or a neck chain. There are many symbols known through the centuries as capable of warding off evil spirits. Our Western society is most familiar with the cross, but there are a large number of others. Look at the symbols opposite and see whether any of them seem protective and comforting to you. You can then draw or colour a shape on a piece of card and keep it with you. Prop it up on your desk, pin it to your wall, keep it in your wallet, do whatever makes you feel good. You can buy small amulets in many of the shapes if you want something to wear around your neck.

Finding your protective animal

Many people use animals as protective guardians. Animals, with their instinctive unconditional love, have very special energies and are imbued with protective qualities. Are you drawn to a powerful animal such as a lion, tiger, elephant or crocodile? Do you have a picture of one that you might want to have around you? You can take this protection further by using a visualisation to call upon your protective animal when you need it. We all have guardian energies or spirits which surround us and protect us, whether we are aware of them or not. Try this exercise below to help you connect with your own personal protective animal.

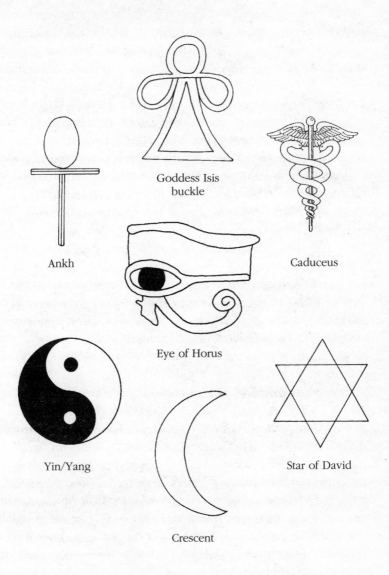

A selection of protective symbols.

Follow the usual procedure of sitting comfortably in your chair, closing your eyes and concentrating on your breathing. Wait until you are relaxed before you continue.

Then call upon the cosmic energy. Feel it pouring down in abundance from above. Let it surround you, penetrate your aura and then your whole physical being. Soak in its healing, protective rays for a while. Then remember its source from high above in the universe. If you have a name for the source: God, Buddha, Allah, Great Spirit and so on, then call upon them and ask that you be shown your protective animal.

Sit quietly and continue to breathe deeply. Don't push for anything to happen. If you are naturally a visual person, you might want to concentrate on your brow chakra for a few minutes. Imagine your eyes are actually positioned at the brow chakra itself. If you are more of a sensory person, imagine your aura reaching out to embrace whatever feeling or sensation is there for you.

After a little while, you will be shown your protective animal. You may be surprised at what is given to you. You might feel drawn to lions and yet suddenly have an elephant appear before you. You might find eagles a wonderful image and yet be given a crocodile or tiger. The animal your imagination creates is not necessarily the animal which is your true guardian spirit. If you aren't visual by nature, you won't perhaps see anything. You may just sense the animal's presence or smell its fur or hear the noise it makes. It doesn't matter how the animal makes its presence felt as long as you can recognise it.

If it's an animal that you don't have an immediate affinity with or which you find unnerving, work with the sensation. Realise that this is for your protection. This animal will love you unconditionally and protect you always. If, for instance, it's a lion and it's shown to you roaring and pawing at the ground, this is because this creature is proudly showing you how protective and strong it is. Your protective animal will never hurt you. It will only ever love and protect you. Spend some time with your animal. It may talk to you and tell you its name. You may communicate and decide how you will call upon your protective animal when you need it. You may only need to think about it and it will be there for you. Whatever form of communication you create, it will be instant and completely reliable.

When you're ready, your protective animal will say goodbye, but it will always be nearby. It will always be watching over and protecting you, whether you realise it or not. You can call upon it whenever you feel in need of extra protection and security.

Now withdraw from your meditation. Remember where you are sitting and focus back on earthly reality again. Cleanse and balance yourself. Wait until you feel ready, before you get up.

You may have the unnerving sense that your animal is still with you when you continue your day. This is because they are around your aura at all times. You have not actually created them by thinking about them; they were always there in the first place. The only difference is that you are now aware that they exist in energy form and this makes them seem more real to you. Does it make you wonder what other energies are all around you, protecting and nurturing and guiding you along every step of the way? We each have a great number of protective guides around us. It is not necessary to know who they all are, although a later chapter will discuss this in more detail. At this stage, it is enough to know that you have constant support and protection around you in energy form.

Auric protection
Awareness of your own aura will also allow you to protect yourself better on an everyday basis, whether you are healing others or not.

Have you been spending more time concentrating on your aura or has that been left in the background while you concentrate on your chakras and your inner healing? Our aura is the energy which extends from our physical body and which is constantly bumping into other people's auras. We are exchanging different energies all the time. Sometimes, it would help us to shut down more and close our auras more tightly around us. This is useful especially if we are with someone who is draining our energy. In case you have been neglecting your auric awareness, try this exercise to increase your powers of self-protection. If you feel you cannot sufficiently remember the aura and its functions, you might want to reread the section on the human aura starting on page 26.

You can sit or stand for this exercise. You might find that standing is more effective for your awareness. If you stand, make sure you keep your eyes open throughout; you may feel dizzy and sway otherwise. You can close your eyes if you're sitting. Start by taking nice, deep breaths. Feel the air being sucked all the way down to your navel on the in breath and then feel it being expelled up through your nose on the out breath.

After a few minutes, notice what is happening to your aura. Remember there are at least seven layers to your aura, stretching out from your physical body, each layer becoming lighter and finer in vibration as it moves outward. Can you feel your aura expanding and contracting on each breath? Start to focus on the energy field around your body. How wide does it seem to you? Is it stretching to the corners of the room you are in, or is it reaching up to the ceiling? Does it feel comfortable? Keep breathing deeply in and out and notice what is happening to your aura. Are you beginning to feel more relaxed and open? Is your aura widening and expanding in every direction? When do you feel too open? Perhaps you can think of instances in your life when you felt you were too open, too vulnerable to someone else.

Now practise withdrawing your aura so that it contracts closer to your physical body. On each in breath, feel your aura coming closer towards you. This should be a pleasant, comfortable feeling. There should be no effort involved. It shouldn't feel restricting or uncomfortable. Your aura is as flexible and pliable as a balloon that inflates and deflates. It's your own breath which controls your aura. You are now choosing to bring your aura closer to your own physical body. Keep working with your breath, until it feels quite securely wrapped around you. How do you feel now? Do you feel better protected? Does this feel a safer way to step on to a crowded train or bus? Are you naturally able to do this contracting of your aura or do you believe that you spend a lot of your day walking around with a very expanded, open aura?

Now bring your concentration back to your breath. Cleanse and close down. Make sure you are balanced again. Wait a few minutes before you continue with what you were doing.

Especially as you work healing others, you need to be aware of your aura and how open it feels. It will naturally expand as you heal. It will not necessarily contract when you finish the healing session. You may have to consciously bring your aura closer to you. It is also extremely important that you cleanse thoroughly after a healing session. You can see why.

Your aura expands as you heal, mingling with the aura of the person you are healing. Your aura can easily absorb some of the person's problems and anxieties. This will not harm you as long as you recognise your own responsibility for always cleansing yourself properly afterwards. Make sure you close down tightly and protect yourself with whatever means you find most effective.

Your protective shield
You may find during a healing session that you want to close yourself off for a moment because the person's energies are attacking you too strongly and you are aware you are too open. Simply take a step or two away from them, and move out of their aura. Cleanse yourself

in your cleansing sanctuary. Use your breath to retract your aura a little more. Ask for protection from your animal and other guides before you move forward again and continue healing. Remember to send some unconditional love to the person you are healing as you move back into their aura. If you are feeling anger from them, use your mirror to deflect the anger back at them. You may not always want to deflect the anger back, you may simply want to protect yourself a little more. You can then create your own protective shield.

Again sit comfortably, close your eyes and focus on your breathing. Feel the cosmic energy pouring down from above and let it cascade over, around and through all of you. Wait until you are really relaxed before you continue.

Now ask the source of this cosmic energy to help you. (If words such as God, Allah and Buddha still feel false to you, use simple words such as 'Divine Source' or 'Great One'.) Explain that you would like to be shown your protective shield so that you may call upon it when you need it.

Then wait and breathe deeply. Keep your eyes closed. Concentrate on your brow chakra if you want to see your shield. Expand your aura if you think you will sense or feel it only.

You will shortly be shown your own special shield. This will be personal to you. It may be large and heavy, made of brass or steel or iron. It may be light and transparent, seemingly made of energy in the form of light. It will be a shape that you choose: oval, square, oblong, rectangular or whatever. Is it enormous, does it cover all of you, or is it small? Look thoroughly at your shield, or let your other senses explore it. What colour is it? Is there a pattern upon it? Is it a protective symbol you had not thought about before? What sort of handle does it have on it? Maybe it has a scent. Is it soft or warm or cold to the touch? Get to know this shield. Hold it in your hand. Which hand feels right for it, or does it simply hang suspended in front of you without your holding it?

Examine what you are being shown so well that you know it intimately. This is your protective shield and you can call upon it at any time. Realise what you need to do to bring it close to you. It may have a name. Ask it. It may just require the thought to bring it into your aura.

When you are ready, withdraw from your shield. Cleanse and close yourself down. Remember to retract your aura if you have expanded it. Remember which room you are sitting in. Open your eyes and focus on an object before you get up again.

You may find your shield staying within your aura for a while after you have finished. Again, this shield has always been available to you before. You just did not realise until you asked it to make itself known to you. This will remain with you, within your reach, whenever you need extra protection. You do not have to physically imagine the shield in your hand when you feel vulnerable and want some additional security. Your visualising the shield will bring it in front of the part of you that needs protection. It may be one particular chakra which is too open or it may be the whole of your body which needs shielding. The more you develop your sensitivity to your aura and chakras, the more efficiently you will be able to use your protective shield.

There are a number of protective methods you have learnt about in quick succession. You have increased your relationship with your protective cloak. You have also heard about:

- *Using a large crystal in which to encase yourself.*
- *Visualising a mirror in front of someone's face to deflect negative emotions.*
- *Sending a stream of unconditional love to someone.*
- *Protecting with a symbol.*
- *Finding your protective animal.*
- *Increasing your own auric protection by withdrawing your aura.*
- *Discovering your protective shield.*

There are many more techniques for self-protection and some will be discussed in other chapters as they become relevant. For now, it is enough that you practise these different methods and find which ones work best for you.

It is important that you acknowledge all of these tools as a support and complement to your healing work. Protecting yourself does not mean shutting yourself off and slipping into your own private world to retreat; it means remaining in contact with others but knowing when you need to add some extra protection around yourself to prevent imbalancing your own energies. Self-preservation is essential, not a selfish act. You will not be an effective healer unless you protect your own energies first. If you let your own energies constantly go out of alignment through being affected by other people, then you will find yourself becoming less and less successful in your healing work. Never confuse self-protection with being selfish. It is a selfless act which enables you to be more effective in everything you do.

Now you are going to consider something further to help your healing work. This applies both for your own healing and healing others. You are going to think about creating a space, however small, which is used solely for quiet, healing practices. The next chapter explores this in more detail.

CREATING A HEALING SANCTUARY

It is not essential that you carry out the suggestions in this chapter. You can heal others without creating a special, holy place in which you work; you can heal anywhere if you are relaxed, committed and experienced enough. However, there is a lot to be said for being gentle with yourself and encouraging your early stages of healing work. Whilst you can accomplish anything, anywhere if your healing energies are powerful and focused enough, you need as much help as you can get during your initial steps. You know healing is all about energy and creating the space in which people feel safe to shift their own energy patterns and make changes. The more safe, the more inviting, the more helpful an environment you can create, the more you assist their healing process.

It is also worth mentioning at this point that your whole home can benefit from the following exercises, irrespective of whether you want to heal yourself or others! Creating a healing sanctuary is just another way of showing you how you can make your own living space more harmonious, comfortable and suitable for you. So let us take a look at what you can create with the minimum of fuss and expense.

Most people are not fortunate enough to have a spare room in their home which is available to decorate as they wish. That is the ideal. If money and space and time were no object, anyone could create an ideal healing environment. However, we will work on the basis that most people can find a small space, perhaps in their lounge or dining room or spare bedroom, where they can create a healing sanctuary. This space may have to double up, of course, if you have a dinner party or someone comes to stay, and that is fine. You can make your healing sanctuary 'come and go' if you need to do so.

So what makes an area special? No doubt you have gone into a room at some time and immediately found it inviting and comfortable. You will probably also remember the reverse: when you walked into a room and then could not wait to get out again. You know now that the energy you were tapping into in that room would be determined by whoever had been there before, the frame of mind they were in, the events that took place in that space, and also the geographical position of the place. You may remember this from discussions in Healing As Energy (see pages 25–40) about energy and places. So what can we do to create a healthy, healing environment?

Cleansing a room through visualisation

The first thing to do once we have chosen the space is to bless and cleanse the area. We want to imbue it with nothing but positive and loving vibrations. Choose the area you are going to use (avoid bathrooms and kitchens as they can have particularly strong energy levels which are difficult to disperse). If you are opting to use just a corner of one room, still go through and bless the entire room. If you work through this exercise on your chosen space and then decide to do the same with your whole home, that is wonderful. It can only enhance your healing work. There are many methods you can use to cleanse areas but here are just three. You can use all three on one room if you wish. Sometimes, a lot of cleansing is needed to release certain dominant energies from a space.

You need to have some time alone in the room when you will not be disturbed. Sit comfortably in the very centre of the room and close your eyes. Concentrate on your breathing. Feel heavy and relaxed in your chair. Feel the cosmic energy coming into the room from above. Feel it sweep all around and through you, but also feel it pouring down into the whole room. Picture it wiping away any stale energies from all the walls, the ceiling, the floor, all the furniture and furnishings within it. Feel yourself and the room being cleansed by the cosmic energy. Enjoy the process.

Now go back to concentrating on your breathing and feel your aura expanding. As you breathe in (remembering to keep your shoulders down and to let your ribcage expand fully outwards), feel your aura growing bigger in every direction. As you breathe out, feel your breath wafting your aura through to all the corners of the room. Feel it sweep around and through everything. As you do this, feel unconditional love for everything in the room and for the room itself. Visualise streamers coming from your heart or solar plexus. You may just sense a beautiful green or golden mist emanating from you and filling the room.

Now say a small prayer to bless the room. Ask the source of cosmic energy to let this room be used with love, light, beauty, purity and peace. Use the words that are appropriate for you. Mean what you say. Don't just utter words for the sake of it. What do you want to accomplish within this healing sanctuary? Ask for love and guidance always. Ask for protection. Make up your own affirmation which is powerful for you, something like 'My healing sanctuary exudes unconditional love, light and peace'. Say what is true for you.

How does the room feel now? Is there an area which still doesn't feel as perfect as it should? Go back and repeat the cleansing and blessing process. Wait until you know you are sitting in a holy place which resonates with everything you feel passionately about. Commit to promoting holistic health within this space.

When you're ready, withdraw from the exercise by focusing on your breathing again. Make sure you feel heavy in your chair and that your feet feel heavy and solid on the ground. Cleanse and close down. Wait a few minutes until you get up.

Cleansing a room through scent

There are many forms of incense you can buy inexpensively to cleanse a room. 'Smudging sticks' are common and available through health shops. They usually contain sage, a powerful cleansing herb. You may already have your own favourite incense which you burn. If not, spend a little time smelling the different incense sticks that are now freely available in so many shops. Which scent do you feel drawn to? Make sure you have a tin or large ashtray to use with the incense. (Try to avoid synthetic scents as they can clog an atmosphere. Check for natural ingredients.)

Now go into your room and stand in the centre of it. Spend a few minutes focusing on your breathing until you feel balanced and relaxed. Next light your incense and then blow out the flame. If it is a smudge stick, there will be quite a powerful, smoky atmosphere. Incense sticks are less smoky. (Whatever you choose, choose carefully as the smell will be strong.) Now wave the incense stick around and through every area in the room, right into each corner and up as high towards the ceiling as you can reach. Feel the smoky incense wafting around and through everything, cleansing and rejuvenating as it does so.

As you do this, offer a blessing which is right for you. It may come in the form of an affirmation which you can repeat on other occasions when you come into the room. You may simply ask the source of higher consciousness to bless each and every atom of energy within the room and to cleanse unwanted energies out through the smoky atmosphere.

When you have filled every corner of the room, return to the centre of the room and let the incense or smudge stick extinguish itself slowly on a safe surface which will not burn. Sit or stand in the centre of the room, close your eyes, and send out unconditional love through every pore of your being to all of the room. Commit to allowing only loving, healing vibrations to exist within this space.

When you're ready, withdraw by focusing on your breathing again. Make sure that your feet feel heavy and solid on the ground. You may find that the room feels very heavy and smoky now. You may want to leave the space and let it settle quietly. Make sure the incense or smudge stick is completely safe and cannot cause damage before you leave.

Cleansing a room through sound

You don't have to use any instruments at all to cleanse through sound. You can cleanse a room purely by clapping your hands. It is also a way to prove how energies have different sound patterns attached to them.

Go into the room you wish to cleanse. Make sure you are alone during this process. Now stand in the middle of the room. Clap your hands vigorously about ten times. Notice what that sounds like. Now move to a corner. Clap your hands again. Does it sound very different or exactly the same? Move to different areas of the room, clapping in each. When is the sound different? Does it sound hollow in one area and much thicker in another? Explore your room and keep clapping as you go. Tune in to which area sounds comfortable and which area sounds clogged or congested.

In the areas which feel thick or fuzzy, clap more vigorously and for longer periods. As you reach these congested areas and clap, also offer an affirmation, 'I release all blocked energies within this room'. Keep repeating this process.

Now return to the centre of the room and clap again. Does it sound quite empty and clear? There should be a distinctly sharper sound to the clapping now. If it still feels fuzzy and indistinct, you need to repeat the process again. Keep clapping until the whole room feels lighter and brighter.

If you want to add sound other than clapping your hands, you can use a rattle. It can be a baby's rattle or a homemade affair such as a jar of dried beans. The noise will be just as effective. Some people love to use Tibetan bowls (a specially made bowl whose rim resonates at different levels when the finger is run around the top of it). Other people may favour Shamanic instruments or drums. If nothing like that appeals to you or is available, do not worry. Clapping works just as well.

Once the room is cleansed, you may choose to then play a favourite piece of music. Make sure it feels appropriate and vibrates at a level which complements your own healing energies.

Afterwards you must remember to cleanse yourself thoroughly and then close down. It's quite possible you may have unwittingly absorbed some of the stale energies as you were clearing the room. You don't want them. Make sure you get rid of them. Focus and balance yourself before you finish.

You will probably be amazed at how different the space feels after cleansing and blessing it. We so often do not acknowledge what unwanted and unnecessary old energies are lurking around a room. It is not until we get rid of them that we realise just what an atmosphere they were causing in the first place. It is lovely just to sit quietly in a cleansed space and enjoy its fresh, pure energy.

Perfecting your healing sanctuary
Now you have practised some or all of the above techniques, you are ready to consider how you would like this healing sanctuary area to work. You need to consider the colours, shapes, sizes, sounds and smells you want within your space.

You may have already been aware, during the cleansing process, that you do not want certain objects or pieces of furniture within your healing sanctuary. It does not mean that these objects are harbouring a bad energy, it just means that they do not complement your own energies at this time.

A very important aspect to start with is just how much do you want in your healing sanctuary? Are you someone who responds well to clean, clear spaces which are mostly white, or do you enjoy having a variety of objects around you and a host of bright colours? Neither is right or wrong, incidentally, but you need to check which feels good for you. Start with how much you feel you want in your space and continue from there. If you know you are too cluttered and want to clear out, then work methodically through all your pieces and decide which is a positive and which is a negative influence for you. You can always move the objects into another room or store them in a loft or garage until you feel ready to make final decisions about their use. The only piece of furniture which you cannot do without is a comfortable, upright chair. It would also help you to include a second chair for yourself and a small table.

Now let us look at colours (remember you can work through your entire home at some stage and decide whether what you have around you is actually complementing your own energies. This is not just applicable for your healing sanctuary). What colours work well for you?

If white is the only right colour for you, then you need not spend a fortune on white walls and white rugs and so on. Bleach an old sheet white and lay it over your carpet or tack it against your walls. Do the same to cover your chair. The only warning note about everything being white is that it can remind some people of hospitals or doctors' surgeries. If you bring someone into your healing sanctuary and you can feel that they are uncomfortable, ask if they would like some colour or some changes made.

If you enjoy bright colours, then again choose carefully. If your room is too busy and too multicoloured, it may feel crowded and people may end up feeling slightly claustrophobic in it. Choose where you want your bright colours and where you will benefit from a soothing, neutral colour. The chair, for instance. If you paint it bright orange and the person you are healing hates that shade of colour, it will affect their ability to relax. It is a nice idea if you can have a white chair and then use different coloured cushions. Let your person choose which colour they would like to sit on.

If you want certain colours but have not got them immediately available, you do not have to repaint or drastically change the area. Spend a little time going through posters in a shop and see what colour attracts your eye. You may also find a soothing scene or image which you love. Then pin it to the wall during healing. You can always remove it at other times.

The shapes and sizes within your space are important, too. Do you prefer soft, rounded shapes or do you like strong, angular objects? Whatever you choose, keep the objects to a minimum. Remember every object carries its own vibrations and may affect the healing energies in the room. Many people love to have crystals around them as they work. If you opt for this, choose the size and shape carefully. A large crystal in a small space can overpower you. Choose a soft, polished crystal if you respond well to rounded objects. Consider the colour of the crystal carefully, too. Remember its colour will also impact on your space.

You may want your protective animal around you in physical form. If you see a picture or statue which represents your guardian animal and this is affordable, then find an appropriate place for it within your healing space.

If you appreciate the sense of touch, then have fabrics and objects which feel good to you. Have a small silk cover on the table or a print on the wall which you like to run your fingers over. Keep a little smooth stone in your pocket which you can stroke before you start healing. Wear a soft item of clothing or hang a suitable object around your neck which you can finger. Enjoy your appreciation of touch and use it constructively within your healing sanctuary.

Sounds are very important. Some people crave silence and find it hard to work with any noise. Others find different music deeply inspirational. The harp is often considered the most celestial of instruments and is good for higher consciousness. However, it is again a personal choice. You might find flute or cello music much more comfortable with your energies. You may prefer a tape of dolphin noises or the sea or birds singing. Avoid loud or discordant music which will not help balance your energies. You want to calm and focus your thoughts, not to have them jumping about energetically from one area to another. Loud, pulsing music is wonderful for dancing and releasing pent-up emotions, but it will not balance you for healing work. Also, what works well for you may not agree with the person you are healing. Try to keep a small selection of different types of music. Again, you need not spend a fortune in music shops. Second-hand and charity shops often carry a good stock of unwanted CDs. Spend some time browsing through and see what appeals to you or what you think might have a healing benefit for others.

Smells are also very relevant for healing purposes. Aromatherapy is an alternative healing form which uses the power of essential oils to balance and energise you. Although it works primarily on scent, it can be much more than that because the oils can also be massaged into the skin and thereby have a direct influence on the energy meridians in our body. (See Healing Through Massage in Part Three for further information on this subject.) You may already have discovered a new scent from cleansing your room with incense. You may feel you would like to work more with fragrances. Do this through experimenting. To begin with, you do not have to spend a lot of money on pure essential oils. Although they are wonderful and can be very powerful, you can explore what you like and do not like initially through cheaper means. Try having a bowl of oranges near you as you work. Do they make you feel good? Start paying more attention to flowers and their scents. Wander through parks and gardens and really observe what is there. Smell every flower, not just the obvious ones likes roses and jasmine. What do you like? If you have not got a patch of greenery near you, then wander around a florist and breathe deeply. Does anything appeal to you? Once you have developed a deeper relationship with the scents you like and do not like, then you can consider spending money on an essential oil which you know is right for you. Again, try to avoid cheaper imitations and items such as synthetic room sprays. Many artificial scents are full of chemicals which can actually damage the fine filtering fibres within our noses. That can again imbalance our energies.

You also want to consider lighting. Natural sunlight is always nurturing and energising. Even daylight coming through a window on a cloudy day can infuse the room with a soft light. If you do not have natural light in your healing sanctuary, you can always alter artificial light. Soft light is generally much more relaxing than a bare light bulb or fluorescent tubing. You could change your bulb to a lower wattage during healing and change it back again afterwards. Candlelight can be very restful on the eyes and soul, as long as it is safely placed out of harm's way. Scented candles are an option which can combine a pleasing smell and a peaceful, soft light. You can also buy lightbulbs which have just a hint of a soft colour in them which can change a harsh light into a more harmonious glow. Experiment as much as you can to discover the best way to enhance your setting.

There is one last point to be made regarding your healing sanctuary. Just as we made reference to your physical cleanliness and personal hygiene, so it is relevant with the space you create. Clean it. Keep it free from dust and cobwebs. Keeping your healing sanctuary clean and tidy demonstrates your love, respect and appreciation of all you can accomplish within this space.

Once you have looked at all these points and created a space that feels right for you, there is one other aspect of creating a healing sanctuary which is important. You now want to attract suitable people to heal into this environment. Let's look at how you can choose the right person.

CHOOSING SUITABLE PEOPLE TO HEAL

It may sound strange that you have to choose suitable people to heal. Surely anyone who needs healing will benefit from your spending some time with them? And, as you are rapidly learning, absolutely everyone needs healing on some level. So why should you have to discriminate and choose the 'right' person?

We are going to look at a fact which has not been acknowledged so far through this book, but it is important and you have to consider it in the light of helping to heal others. Any esoteric field of study, whether it be in the psychic, paranormal or spiritual realms, has the potential to attract people whose energies are deeply out of alignment. They can be described very much as lost souls who are completely out of their depth in their current physical body. They are not 'bad' people or souls, they are not harmful and they deserve our unconditional love and support.

However, they are also difficult to handle as far as spiritual healing is concerned. Their energies are vibrating on such a different level they will not necessarily respond well to the techniques you have so far learnt. They may require additional, deeper spiritual alignment which can only be offered by a highly experienced healer. In addition to this, their particularly discordant energies may affect you, no matter how much you try to close down, cleanse and protect yourself.

What all this is leading to is the understanding that there are energies around which you will find extremely difficult to deal with. Again, do not become alarmed into believing they are 'bad' energies which you have to avoid. They are not. They are simply more difficult to handle, and to give you confidence and nurture yourself you need to choose people whose energies are less complex and less intimidating. It is all too easy to meet someone socially and to immediately think that you can offer some help without stopping to think about whether you really want them within your own living space, how much you actually know about their energies and how they may react with you. Remember that you are in a vulnerable position once you invite someone into your own home. We are going to take a look at how you can avoid the pitfalls of choosing the wrong person.

First, make sure anyone you choose is either someone you know or who is known to you through a mutual friend or family member. If you meet a stranger at a large, lively party, it is not the place to delve into a deep conversation about spiritual healing and what you want to accomplish within it. Spiritual healing is not a subject which responds well to alcohol or drugs. You may be completely sober, of course, but how much do you know about the stranger's state? When you start to explore a new world which makes so much sense to you it can be so tempting to share it openly at any opportunity, but spiritual healing just does not respond well without some discrimination. As you start to discuss your beliefs, you will be expanding your aura and opening all your chakras quite unconsciously in an environment which may not be conducive for you. Crowded trains and buses are other areas which may adversely affect you if you start speaking passionately about your spiritual awareness. Naturally you want to share and it is good that you do so, but learn discretion and sensitivity before you open up. This will help you in the process of choosing someone suitable to heal. Under no circumstances should you ever advertise your interest in helping others in a shop window or in a local newspaper or magazine. You are leaving yourself in far too vulnerable a position.

Conversely, people to whom you are very close can also be hard for you to heal. If you are in some way connected to someone, whether it be a blood tie or emotional involvement, it is very difficult to sever those connections between you to allow unconditional healing to take place. Our auras intermingle and react to our close friends and family all the time. To heal effectively, you would have to cut all those ties and remain in neutral territory. It is not easy to do.

So who would be suitable? The first question to ask yourself is 'Would I feel comfortable alone in my home with this person?' It can startle you to discover what powerful reactions crop up when you ask this question. If your immediate response is uncertainty, followed by a slight nagging doubt, then dismiss them as a possible candidate. Whatever your initial reaction, there was a good reason for it. You can always ask yourself that question again about them on another occasion but always listen to your first, intuitive response. If there is some mistrust, then continue your search.

It could be a person whom you know in some capacity, whether it be a working environment or a social circle and to whom you feel an affinity. This does not mean a sexual attraction; it means someone whom you have quietly tuned in to on a number of occasions and with whom you felt a sense of connection. You need to have spent a little time with this person.

Their age is generally irrelevant, although it is suggested that you avoid teenagers or anyone younger. This is just because they may not yet have the skills to handle their own energies and to take responsibility for the healing process. We often are not ready to understand spiritual concepts until we are into our twenties and older.

If, when spending some time with this person, you have found yourself thrown off-balance and are left feeling uncomfortable in any way, avoid offering them spiritual healing until a later stage. You can always increase your degree of challenge in healing work after a period of time when you become more knowledgeable and confident. Keep going back to the question 'Would I feel comfortable alone in my home with this person?'

You may be fortunate enough to find suitable people straight away, but do not worry if this does not happen. Just continue with your own healing process until the right person comes into your life. When they do, you will know it without question. It feels rather as if a lightbulb has gone off over their head. You will look forward to working with them, because you know it will benefit both of you.

Of course, there is the question of how to approach the subject. Honesty is always best. Explain you are new and very much in the early learning stages. By all means explain why you believe spiritual healing is so important and beneficial. Do not be surprised if it comes out awkwardly in the beginning. You may find your thoughts are clear in your head but you cannot always find the right words to formulate how you feel. If you find speaking with others a challenge, then you might want to try writing down on a piece of paper how you view spiritual healing and the mechanics of how you think it works. Then practise saying it out loud before you approach someone.

The majority of people are always interested on some level. A few are sceptical and dismissive but you are unlikely to be drawn to those at this stage. Expect them to ask a lot of questions. They may be flattered that you are interested in healing them, but they are also likely to be slightly suspicious and possibly defensive. Expect reactions such as:

- Why? Is there something wrong with me?
- I'm not spiritual enough for something like that.
- Do I need healing that badly?
- Is this to do with ghosts and black magic?
- What would I have to do? I know nothing about spiritual things.
- Is it dangerous?
- Will it cost me?
- Are you qualified?

Be honest with the last question but go on to explain that you take spiritual healing very seriously. Say how long you have been working on your own healing and clarify why you want to heal others. Let them know that you understand your responsibilities and limitations and that whilst you cannot guarantee to transform them into wonderfully healthy human beings, you will also not hurt them in the process.

You also need to be clear about how much time you will require of them. Once a week is best but if they can only manage once every two weeks or even once a month, you can still offer to work with them. Be very clear about the fact that you will not charge them in any way. You may want to ask for an hour of their time. Although you will not necessarily be healing them for a full 60 minutes, it is very easy for that amount of time to slip by. It is taken up by their arrival, settling down, your relaxing and opening-up process, the healing itself, followed by your cleansing and closing down and then asking for their feedback.

Also let them know that they are not required to actively participate in any way. So many people fear that they have to 'get up and do something' or perform in some way. You need to let them know that all they have to do is relax! The more relaxed they are, the more you will be able to accomplish. Explain that you will be on your own in your healing space with them and that they will not be disturbed during the time you are together.

Once you have found the right person and arranged a mutually convenient time, you are ready for the process of learning how to heal others.

IN THE HEALING SANCTUARY

It is suggested that you read through this chapter several times and familiarise yourself with its contents before you actually bring someone else into your Healing Sanctuary and start working with them. It is not surprising that most people are very nervous before they first start, so the more conversant you are with the routine, the more confidence it will give you.

There are several steps you need to go through each time when you heal others. Although you may use different healing techniques as you progress and discover what works best for you, there are certain aspects of healing others which you must always follow. They are necessary to ensure the safety of both the person you are healing and yourself. They are as follows:

- *Settle the person you are going to heal and explain your limitations and the rule regarding orthodox medication. Allow them to relax.*
- *Relax yourself and then open up.*
- *Say a silent prayer/blessing/affirmation and ask permission to heal.*
- *Tune in to the other person's chakras and then heal as appropriate.*
- *Close and protect the other person's chakras and aura.*
- *Cleanse, close and protect yourself.*
- *Say a silent prayer/blessing/affirmation.*
- *Obtain feedback and ensure the person's state of well-being before finishing. Ensure you both drink a large glass of mineral water each.*
- *Cleanse the room afterwards.*

Now let's work through this list and see the implications of each step.
First, you want to put your chosen person at their ease. They

will probably be nervous and uncertain as to what is going to happen. Have them sit in the comfortable, upright chair and ask if they are too hot or cold. Offer them a drink of water or juice. (Alcohol, tea and coffee are all stimulants and should be avoided during healing.) Let them know where the toilet is should they need it before you start or after you have finished. Ask them if they would like any music and let them choose from your selection. Keep the music soft and unobtrusive. You want them to feel able to speak without having to raise their voice if they have something they need to say. If you want to use essential oils or incense, check first that they like the smell you are planning to use.

Now explain again what you are going to do. Tell them that you do not need to actually touch them but if you feel it might benefit them at any time, you will ask permission first. Explain that they only have to relax and that nothing else is required of them, except that they let you know at any time if they feel uncomfortable or if they are in any pain. Let them know that they can also offer positive feedback if they want, such as 'That feels nice!' Repeat your rule about any orthodox medication that they may be on and insist that they continue taking it until they speak to their doctor to discuss it further. Encourage them to realise that this healing process is meant to be a comforting, gentle experience and that you will do your utmost to ensure they have a pleasant time during the next hour. Remind them that you take a few minutes to open up and relax yourself, so they do not expect anything to happen straight away. Let them know they can close their own eyes if they wish and ask them to concentrate on their own breathing for the next little while.

You may or may not wish to ask them if there is a particular area or condition upon which they would like you to focus. Many people are not in tune enough with their own state of health to know what they want to look at. Some people feel too nervous to ask. Some simply do not wish to discuss areas of their life which they feel are not working or are causing them stress. Others will fall over themselves in their rush to tell you everything and bombard you with a long list of what they need to 'heal'. Either way, it can be off-putting and not necessarily helpful. It is always best if you can learn to tune in yourself to a particular person and their energies and work unconsciously with helping them, trusting that a source of knowledge higher than yours will do the required work to heal their energies. Of course, if someone has a major issue which they really want to address, you should listen and ask for guidance from above to help them during this healing session. Otherwise, trust that you will do what is right for them because you are being guided and led along the right path for them.

Preparing to heal others

Now you are ready to start stage one of your work in healing others. This involves preparing yourself.

You need to relax and focus yourself. You are not going to concentrate on yourself during the healing itself. However, in the preparation, you have to do so. Sit or stand a reasonable distance from the person you are about to heal. Take time to ground yourself, as your nerves will probably mean that you lose your sense of earthly gravity for a moment. Feel grounded and balanced. Remember to breathe deeply and comfortably. Cleanse if you are holding any unwanted sensations which may block your energies.

When you are ready, you are going to open your own chakras, one by one. Do this thoroughly and make sure you feel properly open and receptive before you continue. Check that your aura has expanded during this process. It should feel soft and puffed up and it should pulse gently around you. It should feel comfortable.

Now focus on the cosmic energy. Feel it pouring into the room and filling it with love and light. Feel it surround and filter through every pore of your own body. Feel it doing the same for the person you are going to heal. Become aware that your whole healing sanctuary is pulsating gently with this pure, white energy.

Now become aware of how the cosmic energy is flowing through your body. You are merely an empty vessel, receiving the energy and then letting it filter out again through you. Feel it filter down through your shoulders, arms and out through your hands and fingers. Become aware that the healing energy is coming from above and that you are acting as a conductor through which it can move and thereby intensify its power. Notice how your hands tingle and that your fingers feel as though they are pulsing with an energy of their own. You might have the sensation of static electricity in them or they may feel heavy. The sensation of knowing you are ready to heal is a personal one for each individual.

You will probably also experience a sensation in your solar plexus/navel area. Again, this feels as though it is intensifying in energy. It makes you feel strong and very centred. You might be aware of giving out energy through your solar plexus. You may also have strong fluttering sensations through your heart chakra. This is because you are expelling unconditional love as you heal.

What is very important is that you realise the healing power is not coming from your own energy. Healing energy comes from the cosmic energy and you are merely the transmitter through which it can work more effectively. If you use your own energy in healing, you are damaging yourself and not benefiting others. At all times during healing others, you must be aware of the cosmic energy flowing through every cell, every atom of your body and flowing freely through all of you. Never lose consciousness of where the healing energy originates. Don't be tempted into thinking you will add some of your own energies to the equation. It will help no one. Your power as a healer comes from acting as a conductor. The more open you are, the more your own energies are flowing freely and not blocked in any way, the more effective you will be. This also relates to the earliest discussion about your own ego. Your ego has no place in spiritually healing other people. You are not concerned with your own abilities in any sense because they are not important. You are simply offering yourself as a conductor for a higher source.

This is a very heady experience. If you are working properly, you are left feeling wonderful. Remember to keep grounding yourself with the grounding energy if you need to during the healing process and feel long roots coming out of the soles of your feet, anchoring you deep into the ground. Maintain a degree of feeling balanced, grounded and focused, whilst also acknowledging the pure, infinite supply of cosmic energy which is flowing through you. You may actually see white light or mist during this time or you may just tingle from the experience of feeling it. It will be personal for you.

When you know you are fully opened and receiving the cosmic energy through you as a filter, then offer your own silent and personal message to the source of this energy. This intensifies your connection with the energy. Give thanks for its divine presence. Ask that you be shown the way to help the person you are healing in the best manner possible for them. Ask for protection for both of you. Say an affirmation if it feels a positive move for you. Use something like 'I heal (person's name) in the most beneficial way for them'.

The healing routine

Now you are ready to turn to the person who you are going to heal. Ask if they are ready and ask for permission to help them heal. Wait until they say they are ready before you step into their aura and start to work.

You are going to start by tuning in to the person's chakras. You don't consciously have to open each one, simply place your hands a good 12 inches either side of their body and work slowly up through each chakra, starting with the base and working up to the crown. Do not spend much time with your hands over their heart or their crown chakras as these are particularly sensitive areas. Check whether your hands are far enough out in their aura. If they say you feel too close or they have a sensation of heat which isn't comfortable, then move a little further off. Work gently through each chakra, noticing if you have a different sensation for each one. Remember what sensitive energies you are dealing with. If you feel you are prying at any time by being too close to their energies and making them feel uneasy, move away without being asked. Remember to keep feeling the cosmic energy pouring through all of you and out of your hands while you continue this process. You are not using your own energy.

When you have opened their chakras, then let your hands be led back to the area which you most need to concentrate upon. If you have remembered to keep breathing deeply and are relaxed, if you have remained focused on the cosmic energy flowing through you, you will know which area to go to irrespective of what you might have discussed earlier with the person you are healing.

For example, they might have insisted that they had a pain in their shoulder but you might know that it's only caused by an anger which they are holding in their solar plexus chakra. They might say their stomach is aching but you will realise they are stopping themselves from saying something to someone which is important and therefore their throat chakra is blocked.

Half the time, you won't actually know why you are going to a particular area. This doesn't matter. Again, if you have left your ego behind and are enjoying the process of selflessly helping someone else, you won't need to know why you are healing which area. You will be trusting in a higher level of consciousness and not needing praise or acknowledgement or confirmation of doing something right. You'll simply trust and that will be enough.

You may move from one area to another slowly or you may find yourself suddenly switching as your hands feel called to another area. You might spend the whole session on one area because it feels right. Always be sure that you are maintaining a comfortable distance from them and that you are working with the cosmic energy. Do not lose awareness of it flowing freely through you.

If you have images or sensations which come to you as you're working, make a mental note of them but do not necessarily voice them (we will look at why later). If you pick up something unpleasant, remember to wash it away. If you start to feel affected by their aura, step out of it for a minute and cleanse before you return. Use your protective animal or shield or crystal if you need it.

You will also know when it is time to finish. You will feel your hands slowly losing their energy or tingling sensation. Now you need to consciously close the person's chakras, starting with the base and working up to the crown. Do this very slowly and gently. You may be surprised to tune in and realise how much they have opened.

Now step back out of their aura and visualise the cosmic energy sweeping through and cleansing every part of them. Mentally wash through all of their aura, too. Now give them a cloak of protection. Ask that what is correct for them be given. Visualise or sense whatever it is.

Ask your person to sit quietly in the chair. Ask that they remain with their eyes closed and concentrate on their breathing. Explain that you are going to close yourself down and that you'll be ready to chat in a few minutes.

Closing yourself after healing others

You need to take extra care to cleanse yourself properly. Step well out of the other person's aura and cleanse yourself in your cleansing sanctuary. Take your time. Then let the cosmic energy wash through you again, filtering out any unwanted residue from the healing session.

Now go back to your chakras and close them down, one by one. Do not rush the process. Feel your aura settle more

*closely around you as you do this. Are you properly grounded?
You may still feel heady from the experience of healing
someone else. It can feel very powerful. Wash the experience
away and concentrate on your feet. Feel their roots anchored
deep into the ground.*

*When you are balanced and ready, offer your silent prayer.
Give thanks for what has taken place and ask that the person
you have healed may go away richer for the experience. Ask
for continued protection for both of you. Make sure you feel
balanced and ready, before you open your eyes. Focus on
an object. Check you are properly grounded.*

Now you need to confirm that the person you have healed is
feeling all right. Ask them if they feel solid and heavy or if they
are feeling slightly light-headed. If they say they do not quite feel
grounded again, then ask permission to put your hands on their
shoulders. Then rest your hands gently but firmly on their shoulders
and ask them to concentrate on their feet. Use the technique of
telling them to imagine long roots coming out of their soles and
anchoring them deep into the ground. Tell them to concentrate
on how heavy their weight feels in the chair. Wait until they feel
better before you take your hands away.

Now encourage them to drink a glass of mineral water. Explain
it is a physical part of the cleansing process and can be helpful.
Make sure you always have at least one glass of water yourself.

Handling feedback

Next you want to get feedback from them. What sensations did they
have whilst they were being healed? What was their overall feeling?
Really listen to what they say in reply. Try to understand what it
was like for them. You may recognise some of their emotions from
your own experience of healing yourself. They may say they felt
uncomfortable sensations at some point, in which case you need
to encourage them to tell you that during the session next time, not
afterwards. People often have images come to them as they are
being healed. If they want to share them, that is fine. Sometimes,

they are personal and not something they feel happy to discuss.

People can also be unexpectedly emotional which may embarrass them or leave them feeling particularly vulnerable. It is up to you to let them know that tears are perfectly normal and for you to put them at their ease. Tears are just a release and can help to balance the energies.

You may find that some people are very curious; they know that something was going on inside and around them, without knowing quite what. They may start to ask lots of questions to try to understand what spiritual healing really entails. Even if you have already talked to them about it prior to your healing session, you often find they did not really listen and had not taken in the points you were trying to raise. It helps if you explain it in the simplest terms possible. Using words like 'cosmic energy', 'subtle bodies' and 'healing vibrations' can be very off-putting, until you understand healing at a deeper level. Initially, keep it as basic as you can, to give them more confidence and encourage them to ask further questions. You can make it as simple as:

'People are not just their physical body. Everyone gives off and receives energy all the time. Sometimes these energies make you feel wonderful. Sometimes they drain you and make you feel tired and unwell. With spiritual healing, you are really dealing with all the energies around you and helping to balance them so that you feel a positive benefit.'

If you really want to take it further, then go on to explain the human aura as their own personal energy that interacts with everyone and everything else. Just be aware of keeping the subject as basic as possible. Try to use examples which they can relate to, such as finding a person draining or feeling an atmosphere in a room as soon as they walk in. The more you demystify the spiritual healing process, the safer most people feel. Really concentrate on your language and ensure you do not alienate people.

There is also the important issue of how much you tell them about what you felt and sensed during the healing session. The problem here is twofold. First, people need to discover their energy imbalances for themselves and to work with them when the time is right for them. Secondly, you have to consider extremely carefully how you phrase information as it may be misconstrued or appear to be a criticism. Let us use some examples to highlight these points.

You are healing someone and realise that they have a blockage in their throat area. You are not certain where it is stemming from but you have an image of a parent nearby as you work. You then may offer something such as 'There is some blockage in your throat area. It may be connected to your mother or father'. Their initial reaction will often be that if something is wrong with their throat, do they have throat cancer? (It is a common fear amongst the Western population that cancer will strike them.) Or else they will think their mother or father has throat cancer. Or that any of the three of them is going to develop it. People are not usually familiar with the way their spiritual bodies work and will not understand how a throat blockage can be significant on a more esoteric level. Even if you go on to explain what you really meant in detail, it is quite possible that they will listen and then still go away thinking 'Yes, but what if I do have cancer?'

You may sense tension in the navel chakra and be tempted to ask them if they have a difficult time relating with other people or whether they might lack sexual drive. Anything like that is intensely personal and no matter what you may have picked up, it is not for you to pass judgment or even comment. Whilst you know how sensitive and informative these subtle energies can be, it does not mean that they are aware of this. It can be very unsettling to have personal information suddenly revealed. They may know it themselves anyway and not want to talk about it or they may not be ready to face those issues yet in their life.

You could feel the heart chakra is quite clogged with emotion and that there is a love interest in their life which is not going well. You might feel tempted to double as an agony aunt and discuss their difficulties with them and offer practical advice. This is not your role as a spiritual healer. If they wish to talk about it and need to unburden themselves, that is a different matter. It is not for you to initiate any personal issues. You know that you have enough trouble trying to sort out your own karmic path in life.

How can you be in a position to unravel someone else's?

The true essence of spiritual healing is to learn how to help yourself through a deeper understanding of your own spiritual path. When you work on healing others, you have to learn how to let higher consciousness work through you and to trust that whatever healing you give is coming from that higher source and it will be helpful and appropriate for that particular individual. Once you become personally involved yourself, you may let your own energies interfere and you will not necessarily be able to offer the most suitable advice. Everyone's spiritual path is unique and for you to interfere to the extent that you advise others what to do is dangerous territory.

What is wholly endorsed is for you to pass on the methods that you use to heal yourself during your own healing process. You do not have to pass judgment on their particular personal situation. Reverse the process to talking about how it has helped you. It will stop them from feeling threatened in any way and prevent them from being left with the impression that you are telling them something is wrong with them. Simply share whatever experiences have been powerful for you.

If you know affirmations have made a difference or if you believe they could help the other person, then pass on how they work. Make sure you are responsible and accurate in what you give out. For instance, ensure they make an affirmation simple, concise and always in the positive. Make sure they know to repeat it regularly throughout each day. If you know that you have been helped enormously through your awareness of breath, spend a little time discussing your Breathing into Stillness. Pass on the technique (see page 68). You might find it helpful to go back to your progress chart from earlier work and check through what helped you then. You may be using different techniques now from your early stages. Try to recall the different exercises you used. Reread chapters and discover them again. Share them and help to pass on the healing process.

You may instinctively realise that the person is generally far too vulnerable and that their chakras are wide open much of the time. You do not have to use the word 'chakra', which may be alien to them. Explain that you feel they are so open, loving and helpful to others that they do not always nurture themselves enough. Then discuss some visualisation techniques they might use to help protect themselves more. Share the fact that you have a cloak which you draw around you or a shield or crystal. You can make an enormous difference to someone's life by offering a small, simple technique.

Whatever you offer in the way of an exercise, make sure you have been clear in explaining how it works. It is a good idea to ask them to repeat what you have said and to make sure that they really understand what you mean. Remember you are always responsible for their well-being whilst they are with you. You need to ensure that they do not go away with misconstrued advice which does not help them.

You may have people you have healed tell you that nothing happened. They may be disappointed or angry. This is not important for you in the sense that you have to let your ego go and not take it on board as a personal insult. It is merely a learning process.

If this happens, ask yourself if you were letting yourself be used as an effective instrument for healing. Were you blocked in some way? Did you not call upon enough cosmic energy to help you and were you therefore trying to use your own? If you know honestly that this is not the case and you were working to the best of your ability with full awareness of the cosmic energy, then turn to how you felt during the healing session.

Did you feel resistance from them? Did you feel that you could not get too close, or that there was a wall around them? Some healers just sense this, others see it, some know it without seeing or sensing anything. Becoming aware of a defence mechanism around someone is a very tangible experience and you get to recognise how you feel when it happens. Sometimes it manifests itself as a sudden feeling of literally hitting a brick wall. Sometimes you feel the energy become strangely flat and cold. Others get a warning heat in their solar plexus. You will find your own sensation.

This does not mean that you then pass the onus over to the other person and accuse them of being unhelpful. You can, however, ask if they felt nervous or if they were wary of what was going on. It might be that you simply got too close throughout and they felt they had to wrap their aura tightly in to them to feel safe. If they refute any of those emotions, let it go. Suggest that you try again on the next session and say that you will concentrate on how you might be able to help them more in the meantime.

You might want to suggest some breathing technique if you feel they were tense and breathing in a shallow way. Show them how to put their hands on their ribcage and check their own deep breathing. Suggest they practise that before the next session. Make sure you leave them with the feeling that you want to work on it, too, because you have a commitment to learning and helping others. By responding to their scepticism or anger in a calm, warm and responsive manner, you will leave them feeling more confident. Showing them unconditional love can be a very powerful act which unconsciously helps their own healing process.

You may then discover that the next healing session involves a greater degree of trust and that will enable them to relax more. You have then created the possibility of a healing scenario which can continue and intensify in strength. If the situation remains at an impasse, then you can either choose to let the matter go and suggest that the energies between you have not provided a conducive atmosphere for healing. You might want to suggest that they try someone else.

Or you can opt to go deeper and to question their own beliefs about healing as an energy form as opposed to orthodox, physical healing. You may find that they do not want to open their mind to the possibility of anything other than what they know already. You will quickly learn that you cannot force anyone to take spiritual healing on board if they are determined not to do so. Everyone comes to every experience in their life when they are ready and you simply cannot force the issue.

It does not mean you cannot offer to discuss what you believe with them. It is good sometimes to have other people question you. It gives you a chance to really consolidate what you believe and to explain why you feel the way you do. You may find you have the ability to explain better than you realised. You may leave them with something to think about, a possibility that life contains more than they thought. It does not matter if they do not embrace all that you say. If you have opened even a small door for them, you have accomplished something in the way of their healing process.

The most important aspect is not to let anyone leave in an angry or upset state. You must ensure that you have explained and discussed everything to the best of your ability. If you know they are not ready to listen, there is not much more you can accomplish during that session, but you should still ensure that they have understood as much as they are capable of. Keeping asking for help from higher consciousness that you might be able to assist as much as possible. Know that you are being responsible. Keep letting unconditional love flow from your solar plexus/heart area.

Refuse to be drawn into a negative environment. Once you know you have done all you can, then let the matter go. Remember to really cleanse and refresh yourself when they have gone. Do you suddenly feel drained when they have left? You were using some of your own energies. You were letting them into your own aura and they were dragging some of your energy back into their own aura. Realise that you need to work more on your self-protection techniques.

It is also necessary for you to keep cleansing your healing sanctuary after people have been it. All sorts of stale energies can linger. Sometimes, the room feels wonderful after a powerful session. Other times, you may really want to clean and dust the room out, using your spiritual tools. Just remember to always do the same with your own aura. If you can feel an atmosphere in the room, then it is most likely that some of those vibrations will have infiltrated your own energies, too.

It is very frustrating when you send someone away and feel you wanted to do more but could not do so with them sitting in the room with you. There will also be occasions when you want to heal someone and they cannot physically get to you or vice versa. However, there is another form of positive action you can take in these instances. Both these situations can benefit from another form of healing others which can be extremely powerful despite its apparently distant nature. It is called absent healing.

You do not have to be in the same physical proximity as someone to give healing. You can be just as effective if you are next door, in the next country or even halfway around the world. It would no doubt work if you were on different planets as well, although it would appear that this has yet to be put to the test! This concept of absent healing may take a little time to get used to but once you break it down logically, it makes perfect sense.

Spiritual healing is all about using thought processes to access higher awareness and to then shift energy patterns around and through someone. If you know that thought is energy and energy is everywhere, why should we need a person to physically be in our room to be able to help them?

Of course, it is easier to heal someone if they are right in front of us. We can create a stronger, more focused energy. We feel psychologically better because we have the physical presence of the person we want to help right in front of us. We are programmed to respond automatically to what is physically available. So their very presence gives us added security and strength. But it is not necessary for them to be in front of us to heal them.

Absent healing is used frequently across the world. It takes different forms, of course. Religious groups meditate and chant for peace in different countries. All forms of prayers for others are a type of absent healing. Just sending a loving thought to someone has an effect. Well-known healers use the technique of absent healing when they simply cannot be in a dozen different countries at once.

Do you know the saying 'Be careful what you ask for, because you will get it'? It is another extension of affirmations. Whatever thought you send out will create an energy which then rebounds back at you. What you have to realise is that if you have not been specific in asking for what you want, then you may end up in a difficult learning pattern. For instance, take the common prayers of wanting to win the lottery or acquire fame through some means. How many people also ask for the wisdom to handle it wisely? How many famous, wealthy people do you know who are miserable and extremely unhealthy: physically, mentally, emotionally and spiritually?

Absent healing is relevant to this discussion. You send out powerful thoughts in absent healing. You therefore have to make sure that they are specific and focused in such a way as to provide the maximum positive, healing energy.

Use this as a quick example to demonstrate the point. Think of someone you know who has been or is very ill. What is the first image that comes into your mind of them? It is likely to be of them stretched out in bed or of them looking pale or upset. Just by having the thought of them in that condition, you are helping to perpetuate their unwell state. Your thought is one of illness; unconsciously, you are continuing to encourage the energy of their illness by your thoughts. It is not deliberate, but it is still unhelpful. Now imagine them smiling, happy, healthy, contented, energetic and enjoying life to the full. Now you are putting them into a healing environment.

What you create is what forms the possibility for their future. This is so important for you to embrace as the power behind absent healing. What we create forms the energy for it to take place. Create a loving, holistically healthy environment with everything you see and feel and think, and you create the possibility for change. It does not automatically follow that the energies will shift immediately, of course. It just opens the door for change.

A positive factor in absent healing is that you do not have to tell the other person you are carrying out this work on them. This carries with it another form of responsibility. It means you must be crystal clear about the purity of your intentions during the session. Any negative vibrations which you send out will only rebound karmically back at you. It is no good deciding to heal someone because you want them to change only to make your life easier. That action comes from selfishness and is full of conditions. You are trying to impose your own will on someone and that will prove detrimental for you. Not only will you not succeed in your task but your selfish behaviour will carry an unwanted energy which will adversely affect you at some stage in your life.

You must know that your intentions are pure. You must know that you are cleansed and ready. You must be sure that you are acting in a state of unconditional love. You must know that you are accessing higher consciousness and allowing it to flow through you just as you would if the person were in the room with you. Then whatever the other person receives through absent healing will come in the form of a gentle, comforting sensation. It will not jar them or change their energies suddenly, which would leave them feeling very imbalanced. Absent healing involves that much more sensitivity and commitment to truth and integrity.

Some people believe the process is heightened if the other person is aware of what is taking place. You could try both experiments. Try absent healing on a person without letting them know. Then contact them and ask if you could arrange a mutually suitable time for them to be alone and quiet somewhere. All they then have to do at the stipulated time is to sit or lie down, relax and do nothing while you work on their energies from a distance. This literally can mean another country. It makes no difference. Then compare the sessions between the person knowing you were healing and being completely unaware. It is possible that by the person being aware of what is going on, the energies are heightened and intensified. It is equally possible, however, that they actually strain to receive the healing, which leads to tension and blocks and stops the healing from being as effective as it would have been if they had been unaware of the situation.

Absent healing technique

So let's look at what absent healing involves. Again it is suggested that you read the following several times and absorb the contents before you practise the technique on someone.

The best place for this work to take place is in your healing sanctuary, although it's not essential. If someone asks you for some absent healing, you can carry it out anywhere if you have a private, undisturbed moment. However, your healing sanctuary will reverberate with your own unique energies by now. You will probably feel very relaxed and comfortable in there. The cosmic energy may feel stronger and more focused because you have been generating it in there over a period of time. You may also choose to have something from the person you are healing in the space with you. Again, this isn't necessary but it may make you feel closer to the person involved. You can use a variety of objects: a photo of them (provided they look happy and relaxed in it), a letter or postcard they have written, an item which they gave you or even an object which reminds you of them in a positive, nurturing way. If none of those is available, you may want to light a candle for them and have it in the room as you work. You may feel it's right to light a candle, anyway. Create the space as you would normally, paying attention to lighting, smells and sound.

Now sit in your comfortable chair and open up in the usual way. Cleanse yourself thoroughly and make sure you are ready to work. Then open your chakras, one by one, and expand your aura. Remember to keep yourself grounded and focused. Then call upon the cosmic energy and feel it flood into the room. See it as bright, infinite and unconditionally loving energy. Feel it going through every part of you, cleansing and rejuvenating.

Then offer the prayer or blessing which is right for you, acknowledging the presence of the divine energy and asking for guidance and protection at all times. Ask that what is right be given for the person you are healing.

Now create the image of the person you are healing in front of you. You may want to actually picture them in

*front of you in your healing sanctuary or you may choose
to use your inner eye and create a space for them within
your own mind. Both are equally powerful.*

*See this person as being happy and full of loving energy.
Make sure they are smiling or laughing or just looking deeply
contented. See every cell of their body enjoying perfect health.
Everything in, through and around them is vibrating with
joyous energy and vitality. Really see this picture unfolding.
If you sense better than you see, hear them laughing, feel their
joy, imagine hugging them. Use whatever means is most
powerful for you. The more you create this wonderful image,
the stronger your healing energy becomes.*

*Now see or sense the cosmic energy pouring down upon
them. See it surrounding and protecting them. Know it is
there. Realise it is intensifying their already healthy state.
See their physical body absorbing the healing rays through
every pore. Notice how it forms a protective aura around
them and strengthens their own defence mechanisms. If
colours come into the visualisation that is fine, but do not
create them in any way. Notice what they are and then let
them work in their own way. Do not try to create a colour
because you think it would help them. Let the cosmic energy
dictate their healing pattern.*

*Also remember that you are not using your own energy in
absent healing. You are visualising a healthy state and then
letting the cosmic energy work on it for you.* Do not use
your own energies and try to heal them yourself. *It will not
work. Create a wonderful image and then feel the cosmic
energy taking over and doing its pure, unconditionally
loving work.*

*You might want to create an affirmation if it helps make
the healing energy more powerful. Keep it simple.* '(Person's
name) vibrates with perfect health and joy.'

Don't be surprised if you also end up feeling wonderful as you work on absent healing. The energies you create can be so strong and so positive that it can feel as though they are rebounding back at you and making you feel equally good. It is not what you aim for but sometimes it's a pleasant by-product.

When you know you have filled the person with as much joy and healing energy as they can take for one session, slowly withdraw from the scenario. If they stay as a bright vision in front of your eyes or in the front of your mind, you may choose to visualise their physical form of perfect energy being lifted up into the rays of cosmic energy and see them slowly ascending into higher consciousness. It is a safe and healthy way for you to let them go from your aura.

Now you need to concentrate on yourself. Cleanse thoroughly. Ensure that, in your healing process, you haven't let any of their unwell state come into you. You often aren't aware of this happening, particularly with absent healing. Make sure you cleanse all of you.

Give thanks to the source of the cosmic energy and ask for continued healing for this person. Also ask that you remain protected and guided throughout all of your work.

Then close all seven of your chakras, one after the other. Cleanse through again. Ground yourself. Protect yourself with your cloak. Really make sure that you are focused again before you open your eyes and get up.

You may find that, despite your best efforts, the happy image of the person you have healed continues to play around your mind. Keep washing it away, but always do it lovingly and gently. Part of your discipline in healing is learning the ability to shut off when a session has finished. You can end up drained, having used your own energy, if you do not discipline yourself.

Remember to try this on different occasions, telling the other person and then not mentioning it, to see what effect it has had.

You should always remember your added responsibility with absent healing as opposed to hands-on healing. The person you are healing is much more vulnerable. They are not necessarily prepared for your work. You must be especially gentle, you need to have a particularly strong bond with your intuition and constantly ask for guidance and protection during the process. Always check that you are working from pure intentions of unconditional love and a genuine desire to help others. Make sure you have no hidden, personal agenda under the surface which will adversely affect you and the person you are healing.

When you feel more confident with your healing techniques, try increasing the number of people you work with. As everyone's energies are so different, you can gain a true appreciation of this by working personally with different energy fields. This is the means by which you can really tap into an individual soul and see what is required for that person. General healing is still very powerful but when you can properly appreciate everyone as unique, then you can start to work at a deeper level.

Keeping a healing diary

It would help you to keep a healing diary if you are working with several people at once. The best solution would be for you to ask the other person to contribute as well. Simply write the name and date of the healing session and then underneath write, first, how the healing session felt for you. As always, be very aware of what you write and how you phrase things. You might make it very simple, such as 'Heat around right leg. Tingle in my hands near heart. Too close near brow so moved out six inches. Felt churning sensation near solar plexus area.' Make sure it doesn't in any way imply that they have a problem. Then ask the person you have been working with if they would contribute themselves. You can do this with absent healing, as well. Just ask them to dictate what they felt over the phone or ask them to put it in a letter. Again, they can be very brief. They might just put 'Felt relaxed. Drifted off so cannot remember much.' Some may want to write reams about different sensations and emotions. It can also be an extra therapy for the person you were healing. They may find it difficult to talk about what they felt but prefer the relative safety of writing something down. Even if the person you were absent healing was unaware of what was taking place, ask them for feedback. Your healing diary can become an educational textbook for your personal learning experiences. You start to notice similar sensations and what they might mean. You realise that you are beginning to appreciate everyone's individual energy and to treat everyone differently. Some people will dislike you being too near them. Others will need that close proximity.

When you have worked at this level for a period of time, you may feel you are ready to work at a deeper level. You may be ready to consider some further healing techniques for others.

HEALING OTHERS AT A DEEPER LEVEL

Up until now, you will primarily have been working unconsciously in your healing of others. You have been trusting the wisdom of higher consciousness and cosmic energy and letting them guide you without question. This is exactly what you need to do at all times. However, we are now going to start to introduce another dimension, which is you using your own intuition to help you understand what is taking place within the aura and chakras of the person you are healing. *This doesn't mean you are going to use your own energies to heal others*. It means you use your own gifts of divine wisdom to work with higher consciousness and increase your perception and the subsequent power of the healing energies. *You don't use your own energies to heal*.

This means you have to increase your own perception. This will have partly been taking place without your realising as you continue to work on your own healing process and that of others, especially if you have been keeping a healing diary and noticing what different sensations and feelings mean personally to you. However, now you want to start delving deeper.

For instance, you may regularly get the sensations of hot and cold as you work with someone's aura. Perhaps it is sharp and dull sensations in your hands. You may sense it as a dense fog in some areas and as a bright, clear atmosphere in others. Whatever comes to you, start to question it more. What level of their aura are you working in? Do you feel physically uncomfortable with this feeling, or is it more emotional? Do you suddenly feel a little tearful or angry, or do you feel a metaphysical headache as though there is a mental stress going on?

You may see colours as you work. You may even see various shapes and movements within their aura itself or around their chakras. What exactly do you see taking place? Can you sense the movement of the chakras or do you even see colours around them? What do those colours mean to you, and is that relevant to this person's life at present?

Notice more and more if you have images as you work during your healing sessions. Many people have sudden flashes of a situation which is causing someone distress or even incidents from the past which may still be floating around their aura, causing blockages, tears or holes within their own energy field.

If you feel very little is happening as far as your own perception of healing is concerned, then you may be guilty of letting yourself be complacent. Do you feel that you have learned a great deal now and that you have reached a comfortable plateau of knowledge? Perhaps you believe that your relationship with the cosmic energy is strong enough and that you can work efficiently within the boundaries you have set up. Perhaps you do not see them as boundaries but merely you reaching the limit of your abilities. You can never reach a limit in your abilities because there are no limits. The only limits are those set by your own mind. The people who feel they know a great deal are the people who know the least. The richest, wisest people are those who realise that what they know is a minuscule percentage of an infinite supply of knowledge. If you feel you are reaching the end of your discovery, then you have barely even begun.

Using images as tools

Let's use some visual images to help you expand your thoughts about spiritual healing and what can be accomplished. All this relates to your own healing, but also applies to everyone else you come in contact with to heal. Bear in mind, before you start this section, that the visual images displayed are not an indication of how you should always see auras and chakras. Remember everyone's perception is unique and what one person sees on a spiritual level is not necessarily the same image that is perceived by someone else. Don't confuse the pictures with thinking that this is what you must strive to 'see' in someone's aura. These images are being used as tools to help you expand your thoughts and to encourage you to see with your own eyes so that you can discover for yourself what your spiritual reality 'looks' like. Do keep that in mind as you study the pictures and work with them.

Now look at the drawings of different auras opposite. They give a very small indication of the varying states of someone's aura. Remember an aura changes constantly. We are not trying to define people into particular groups and say that this aura represents this type of person. We are all capable of having our aura look like all six of these illustrations at different points in our life. Can you think of times when your aura may have looked like one of the drawings? What can you learn about yourself and others by observing them? If you are not a visual person it does not matter, as you can also just feel the sensations of these different auras.

Let's start with figure 1. What is your initial response to this person – what does this aura tell you about them? Perhaps it shows someone who is very self-contained and does not give much away. Can you think of strengths and weaknesses in this attitude? This person is likely to be very self-sufficient and capable. They probably function quite well within their own world. What would they miss out on; what opportunities and openings are they denying themselves by not reaching outwards? Where in your life is there an indication of you doing this? Maybe you have been healing someone who you think may have an aura similar to this at times. What were the sensations like working with them? Did you get any particular colours associated with this sort of behaviour? Perhaps you have had someone seem like this initially and then noticed a change through different healing sessions.

Now study figure 2. What is the feeling you get from looking at this aura? Is it restful or energised; would you feel calm or agitated in the company of someone radiating this auric energy? There certainly seems to be a lot of energy being expended but it appears sharp, distorted and possibly out of control. Perhaps you have had an occasion in your life when you have suddenly lost your temper or become hysterical. Have you been around someone else when they have exploded? What was the atmosphere like when that happened? Was it a tingly, electric feeling, or did it seem like shards of hot metal were shooting off them? Did you see bright colours or was it like shooting black darts? What might this do to your energies

Figure 1

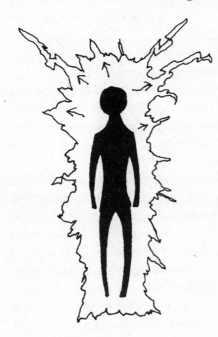

Figure 2

Figure 3

if you were standing near them? If you have a memory of losing control, can you remember how ungrounded you felt during that time? Sometimes people have absolutely no memory at all when they become hysterical or deeply distressed. They are so ungrounded and out of their actual physical body that they leave their memory behind for a while. If you have the opportunity to observe someone from a safe distance who is either very angry or upset, notice what is happening to their aura and watch the energy patterns around them. The vibrations can be very dramatic and it is easier to see such violent energy changes as they are so vivid.

Turn back to figure 3. What is the overriding sensation you feel? What do the turned-in arrows indicate to you? Notice the aura is still expanded, it is not sucked tightly in to the body. What do you think you would feel standing next to this person? Does it make you feel uncomfortable just to think about it? This person is not reaching out in any way, they seem totally involved with themselves. They are also not allowing anyone in their aura. Would you expect this person to be voluble or silent? It would indicate someone who is brooding over something and their intense, inward energy might make them appear as though they were a tightly-packed explosive ready to ignite. Do you know anyone who often sulks if they do not get their own way? Perhaps you are someone who turns inwards when upset. What do your energies feel like when this happens? What is it like to be in the presence of someone like this?

Move on to figure 4 (page 266). What do these spindly arrows mean to you? How does it make you feel when you think about standing next to this person? Notice how the arrows seem to turn back in to their own aura. What does this tell you about them? This aura comes across very much as someone who is constantly reaching out to others and then sucking what they want of others back into themselves again. Notice that they do not seem able to give much of themselves in this equation. Do you know people who seem to do this? Perhaps you were healing someone and felt your own energies being sucked away from you. It can happen without you realising it, unless you are well focused and aware of the energies around you. This is where your crystal, shield and mirror can be so helpful. Are you aware that you too can treat others like this on occasion? Do you sometimes feel that your own needs are so great that others should simply be there for you without question? People can often do this to family members who respond by giving their own energies, often through guilt or out of sheer habit. Have you drained a friend or family member without realising it? Observe, too, how the energies contained in this aura seem to disappear into the ground, as though they are not truly being fed or nurtured by their grasping behaviour. Consciously sucking other people's energies seems to have little or no benefit to our well-being. We need to embrace what is available for us through a loving, open exchange of give and take. That is what makes positive karmic energy.

Now look at figure 5. What is going on with this person – what do all those sharp points make you feel? Have you people around you who you would describe as prickly? Are you guilty of this yourself at times, and how does it affect the ability of someone to get close to you? If you try to move into the aura of this person, what is the sensation you would experience? Have you already had this feeling before with others and, if so, did you know before you went to step into their aura that it would be difficult? Were you surprised by the sudden sharp feeling as you tried to approach? What experiences in life would make someone create this prickly shield around them and how would you help to break down these defences? Can you think of occasions when creating this form of protection could actually be a positive action? Maybe you can think of something you could choose to create which might be more powerful or beneficial. What would happen if you stayed too long in the presence of someone like this? You would probably end up feeling so pricked and bruised that you would either want to retreat or have to create a strong shell around yourself to cope. Sometimes this sort of person can be so frustrating, especially if you can 'see' that the person inside is so tender and loving, and you want desperately to shed them of their prickles. However, they have to shed them in their own time and when they feel safe to do so. Unconditional love can dissolve many prickly shields.

Lastly, look at figure 6. What is happening with this person? Their aura seems to be almost beside them and not surrounding their physical body. What does this indicate to you? How do you think

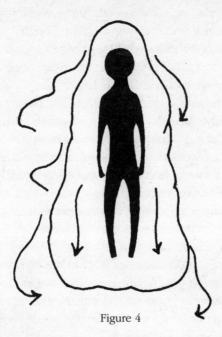

Figure 4

Figure 5

Figure 6

this person would feel while in this state? Have you ever felt that your body was not quite balanced with the rest of you? It might be when you had a particularly clumsy day or when you were not feeling well and so shut yourself off from your physical being. Try to imagine your aura just being to one side of you and leaving the other part of your body unaided. How does this make you feel? Perhaps you have healed someone who felt as though one side of their aura was empty and the other was distorted in some way. Did you notice if the person seemed properly grounded through the healing session? How often has someone's aura felt well balanced? Have you often noticed that one side seems different from the other? Have a quick check of your own aura right now. Is one side giving off or receiving more energy than the other? If this is the case, take a moment to balance yourself.

Is this making you appreciate all over again just how complex and fascinating the human aura is? Do not forget that the drawings only depict the entirety of the human aura with its seven layers meshed together as one. How much more complicated would the drawings become and how three dimensional would they need to be to encompass all the different layers and the individual activities within each layer? You will notice there is no drawing of what a 'perfect' aura should look like. What you see and feel as vibrating with perfect health will be a very personal experience. You might feel you have yet to experience that state.

Drawing your aura
Now have a pen and paper nearby (use coloured pencils if you like) and when you are ready, try the following exercise which will help you to access deeper levels of spiritual healing.

Sit in your comfortable chair and relax. Close your eyes. Cleanse through. Then focus on your breathing and when you feel relaxed and comfortable, open up your chakras, one by one.

Now concentrate on your aura. How is it feeling today? Are you starting to become aware of the different layers? Is one layer feeling stronger and brighter today? Perhaps you feel undercharged and lacking in vitality? What is happening with the cosmic energy from above? How strong does it feel today? Notice if your feet feel properly anchored to the ground and what sort of energy flow is going into the earth from you. Notice if you feel expanded evenly on either side and do not forget to focus on the back and front of you. Really tune in to how your aura is feeling at this moment.

Then when you're ready, open your eyes and pick up your pen and paper. You might want to visualise the cosmic energy coming through your crown and down your arms and into your fingers and hands before you start drawing. Now draw what is happening with your aura. Don't worry if you think you're not artistic. Just draw a stick figure and then draw the clouds of energy around you. You might want to do two sketches, one from a side view and one from the front view, so that you can get a more three-dimensional overview. Don't just draw one line representing all of your aura. If the seven layers feel too complex, then at least draw four levels and mark them as physical, emotional, mental and spiritual.

Really tune in to your aura and see what is happening on these different levels. Draw how you see the cosmic energy around you. How strong is it? Are you using the grounding energy? How do you want to draw the interaction between you and this energy? Use your colour pencils if you are clear about what colours feel right.

Are there breaks or rips in your aura anywhere? Are there any holes? Do some areas feel darker and more clogged than others? Perhaps certain areas feel wonderfully alive and pulsating. Mark this just as 'dark' and 'light' if you do not want to shade it in. Do some areas feel much warmer or colder than others? Write the appropriate words down. If feelings attach themselves to certain areas, put that down, too. Use anything to express clearly and vividly how your aura is at this moment in time. Draw for as long as you like.

When you feel ready, put down your pen and paper. Cleanse thoroughly in your cleansing sanctuary. Then close down your chakras, one by one, and protect and ground yourself before you continue.

Now look at what you have drawn. What does it say about how you think and feel and the level of energy you have at present? Notice if you have further insights. Try the exercise at different times and observe how your aura varies.

Do you want to try drawing other people's auras as you heal them? If you find it helpful for yourself, you might find that other people feel it is beneficial to actually have a pictorial image of how you see them. Again, this carries the responsibility of not alarming anyone with what you draw. If you show dark masses and sharp lines, it is possible someone could be unnerved and think it is indicating illness or problems. Try tuning in to the person beforehand and decide if it is right for them. Explain that you are not an artist so it is not meant to be visually pleasing, but more of a tool through which they can learn something more about themselves.

You may also discover that as you tune in to other people's chakras you have the urge to draw one of them. You may know instinctively that this is an area they could benefit from looking at and that they are ready to do so. Always think carefully about what you draw and how you explain what you see. They may find it helpful to go away with an actual image of their aura, or part of it. Remember that their healing will continue in different forms after they have left their session with you. A pictorial image may further help that process.

Reading your inner signs

So how else can you use your intuition to help you heal? So far we have been looking at healing others whilst always being guided by the power of cosmic energy. This should never change. However, you can work at a deeper level with the cosmic energy and higher consciousness to learn how you may help others at a deeper level. This of course requires even greater sensitivity and awareness. You also have to be crystal clear that when you work at this level, you truly are working with your higher consciousness and not with your own imagination or personal ego. Let's look at how this works.

We discussed earlier how, during certain exercises, you delve into the area where you 'know' something without needing further explanation or proof. It can be likened to entering that state of Breathing into Stillness (see page 68) where you are aware you are in a different realm and ready to work at a different level. You also may have experienced it during the I am a Hologram and Embracing Life exercises (pages 102 and 181). You obtain a sudden flash of insight into a higher order of life, a greater significance about why you are here on Earth and what you and others can accomplish. You may have found it happening quite often during your reading of Our Individual Spiritual Path in Part One (pages 173–84). However that moment of intuition happens for you, you need to acknowledge it and to know when it is happening.

Often a physical sensation will occur at the same time. It may be a light tickle in the stomach area, or a flutter around your heart. Some people see a particular colour of light. Others feel a buzzing around their head. Some feel nothing but sense it deep inside on another level. How does it work for you? If you know you have experienced this altered state of consciousness and are ready to work more with it, then you are ready for this form of healing others. The more you have found quiet time for yourself and worked through various meditations and exercises, the more honest you have been with yourself and the greater your quest for learning, the more ready you will be for this challenge. You might choose to share what you are doing with the person you are healing. You might like to explain that you are going to try working at a deeper level. Reassure them that nothing is required on their part.

Healing at a deeper level
Try this next exercise only when you know you are ready. Read through it first to determine whether it is right for you at this

stage. You can always come back to it later if you wish.

Deal with the person you are healing in exactly the same manner as before at first. Always ensure they are comfortable and explain that they should continue any orthodox treatment they may be undergoing. Let them relax and then open yourself as usual. Offer your personal prayer and then ask if the person is ready for healing.

Now when you start running your hands over their aura, ask higher consciousness for more information about what is happening. Ask if there is anything more you can do to help this person. Start this process by working your way through the person's chakras, from the base upwards.

At each chakra, ask if there is healing needed. Ask that you be shown what is most helpful. This might mean that you are told to imagine heat or cool air from your hands; it might be that you are told something which the person could do to help themselves. It might be that you are told a particular colour in healing would help them. You may also be told the time is not right yet and to let the situation alone.

Whatever information you are given, make sure that you know you are in an altered state of consciousness when you are working. You don't want to interfere with your own personality or thoughts in any way. This could prove detrimental to the person involved. Don't let your own thought processes come into the healing session. You are relying solely on your true intuition, which is basically guidance given by a higher source. Always check that you are working on this higher level. If you have any doubt, don't pass on whatever information you are given. Wait until you know it is right.

You also need to know that the way the information is passed on to you may not always be as discreet and sensitive as it needs to be. Always rephrase anything you are told that might be construed as worrying or alarming. By now, you should know your different healing subjects quite well and you should know those who panic or worry more than others. Gauge each healing session at a different pitch, according to the needs of the individual you are working with.

Work through all the chakras and then let your hands return to whichever area feels right. Again, ask for more information as you work. Continually request that you be given more detail, as long as it is helpful. Always ask that it be appropriate for the individual and always ensure it comes from the highest source of awareness.

You will soon discover you can work at a much deeper level this way. The more you trust and the more open you are to the powers behind spiritual healing, the more you can accomplish. There will be sessions when you will completely remove your own energy and ego from the situation and you will be able to offer truly insightful and helpful healing. The more you leave yourself behind, the more powerful this deeper healing will be.

When you work at this deeper level, you must always ensure that you close the person's chakras with extra care. Add extra protection for them. They may unconsciously have opened up even more than usual during this gentle session. Always cleanse and close down thoroughly yourself. Always offer a personal prayer of thanks for this powerful guidance and love, and always ensure you get proper feedback from the person you are healing before you finish. Make sure you both drink plenty of mineral water. Don't let them leave being more open and vulnerable than usual. Cleanse your healing sanctuary afterwards.

Once you have worked at this deeper level, you may find it difficult to return to the earlier methods, where you relied solely on guidance from the cosmic energy and never questioned what was happening. There is nothing wrong with working at this deeper level, as long as you always remember your responsibility to the person you are healing. Some people are simply not ready for certain levels of healing. You always need to consider the level they are at first and foremost, before you think about which healing you will use.

In Part Three you will be looking at further tools for healing, some or all of which you may want to use when healing others. However, before we delve into these areas, we are going to take a separate look at healing when children and animals are involved. Although spiritual healing works on every level with any life force, both children and animals require a slightly different approach.

Up to this stage, you have been encouraged not to practise any spiritual healing on children, including teenagers. The reason for this is because their energies are much more delicate and vulnerable. We all know that children are very impressionable and easily influenced. This happens because their energy systems are not fully developed. They are wavering, as the lines of energy are not as powerfully connected or resonating as clearly as ours. This is why it is so easy to corrupt and imbalance a child's energy. The work we do with healing children needs to be particularly sensitive and gentle.

Generally speaking, a well-balanced child will need little healing. They are good at balancing their own energy systems because they have not yet learnt to create blockages and tears. But there will be occasions when you can see that a child does need help on some level and you will know that you can help them. It might be on a practical level, like a sort throat, or they may feel worried over an issue in their life. We are going to look at how we can accomplish this healing safely.

So often, all that is needed is the will and ability to communicate properly with a child. Encourage the child to discuss what is going on in their world. Once you clarify a problem for them, they can often go away and balance their energies themselves. Never rush in to heal a child, convinced you know best. Children are so much wiser and more capable than we give them credit for.

Let us take a brief look at what happens with a child's chakras and auras from the time of birth through to adulthood. This will help you to appreciate their vulnerability to spiritual healing.

The changing chakras

Start by having a closer look at the illustration of a young baby's chakras on the previous page. What do you notice from studying the picture? Notice the long, narrow funnel of the base chakra.

Observe how wide open the crown chakra is in relation to the rest of the chakras. What does this imply? Think about our earlier discussion of reincarnation and karma and how the spiritual soul is brought down into a physical body for the purposes of learning and following one's karmic route. This diagram of a baby's chakras suggests that the entering of a soul occurs through the crown chakra.

Babies are born very much in touch with their spiritual selves. In fact, they are often more in contact with spiritual entities than they are with earthly, physical reality. What adults sometimes laughingly refer to as a child's fertile imagination is often no more than the child communicating with spiritual energies that many adults cannot see. So many children have what is called imaginary playmates who seem very real to them. They often hold conversations with them and want a place set at the table for them or play endless games with them. You may have had the experience yourself but forgotten it. You may have a memory of

The chakras of a baby.

being told by a parent or guardian not to be 'so stupid'. Adults ridicule it usually because they are unnerved by the experience of a child having a comfortable conversation apparently with thin air. In fact, they are usually spiritual friends for the child. They are often thought to be helpers to assist the child in earthly living. They usually disappear as the child gets older, when they are no longer needed.

The narrow funnel for the base chakra indicates the child's need to root itself in physical reality. Often this is a struggle. The chakra needs to be more open and active than the others to assist this process. Babies are not used to dealing with earthly reality. They have to be taught all the practical, physical aspects of life in order to be able to survive.

Notice how small and rounded the other chakras seem and how spindly their lines of energy connecting them all seem to be. Now look at the adult and baby's chakras illustrations below and compare the two. You can see how delicate the child's chakra seems in comparison. It only learns how to open into a cone-like

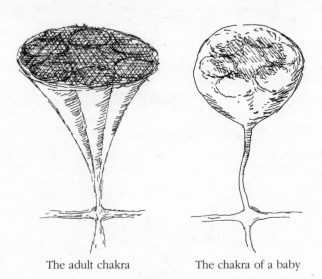

The adult chakra   The chakra of a baby

A comparison of adult and baby chakras.

shape as it develops into maturity. Also, the cloak of protection we talk about creating as adults, which is also known as etheric protection and can cover the chakras (it can manifest psychically as a sort of film-like cover), is not available to young children. They have no means of closing and protecting their chakras when young. They only develop this ability as they mature.

It is also interesting to note that babies are not born with fully developed, full-coloured auras. Most babies are born with a soft, light blue energy field around them. As they grow, colours are added into their aura, each adding to the child's earthly experiences and remaining within their aura as they grow.

They also develop in a certain order, through their chakras. First come the reddish hues of the base chakra as the child becomes rooted in physical reality and forms a relationship with everything physically around them. It is no wonder that children often form deep attachments to certain stuffed animals and other objects when they are very young. They are learning to grasp reality – literally! They also feel very threatened when the objects are suddenly taken away from them. They need to increase their connection with all physical things, not have them taken away and therefore weaken their relationship with them. Most people are familiar with a baby's screams when a favourite toy is taken away.

Next, the navel chakra starts to expand and orange enters the child's aura. Here they develop a relationship with their emotions and how they feel about others. They are often very voluble in their emotional expression, laughing and crying easily as they explore these new sensations.

At around the age of seven, children develop the ability to protect their chakras. Now they are sturdier, more certain of themselves and what is around them and they gradually start to assert their independence.

Now they start to further develop their mental faculties. The solar plexus chakra starts to strengthen and become more active. Yellow enters into the child's aura. Their ability to concentrate increases and their perception of the mind and thought processes start to mature.

As they approach adolescence and puberty, the heart chakra starts to open and make itself felt. That is swiftly followed by activity in the throat, brow and crown chakras. Varying shades of green, blue, purple and white now enter their aura. This time of enormous change – as a child prepares for adulthood and sudden responsibilities, and as the chakra activity changes from the very tangible, earthly emotions through into the spiritual realm – is deeply confusing and unsettling. Anyone who remembers their adolescence would no doubt acknowledge how difficult it is. Mood swings are prevalent as your chakras suddenly open themselves and you experience a wonderful rush of pure energy. The next moment you feel in a state of confusion as they suddenly close and block off energy and communication. You can go from euphoria to deep depression within minutes. Conditional love suddenly seems much more important than unconditional love as you swing from an emotional high to a terrible low.

The aura and chakras are in furious, constant states of change throughout this time. The subtle bodies of energy always reflect the physical reality of what someone is going through. If you ever have the opportunity to watch a young adolescent and their mood swings, it can be vivid and revealing. You can see a black cloud of depression lift from their shoulders in a single second as they feel wonderfully uplifted by something such as a long-awaited phone call from a potential love. That black cloud can then descend again just as suddenly a few minutes later. No wonder the majority of parents find their children's teenage years totally exhausting! Do not forget that as a parent you are unconsciously absorbing all those energy changes and trying to adjust to them yourself. It is very hard to remain impartial and unaffected as a parent.

As the adolescent enters adulthood, the shape of their chakras and aura start to balance out. This is when many human beings make a major choice. They may decide to settle for a very simple life without resorting to curiosity about why they are here on Earth. They may marry and have children and decide that their lives will revolve around material and familial matters, without questioning their own spirituality in any way. This is not to say that they are wrong or bad people for opting to do this. It simply means they do not wish to explore a deeper part of their lives and they live quite contentedly in a sphere which suits them without completely fulfiling them as spiritual beings. Many others spend their lives in a search for understanding life and the meaning of their presence here. Some people find meaning through religion, others through hermit-like solitude. Others seem to be perpetually in a state of change and unrest, striving intently for something without ever discovering quite what it is they want. Here in the West we are finally beginning to return to our spiritual roots and discover our true selves.

Natural-born healers

However, to return to a child's development. Has gaining an appreciation of how a child's chakras and aura develop made you realise how vulnerable and delicate they are? It is difficult to give appropriate healing in this sphere because most of us have forgotten what it is like to be a child. We keep approaching children from an adult's perspective and that is not necessarily helpful. We forget just how open and easily influenced we were as children. We forget how confused we felt over so many issues and how we struggled to learn a great number of lessons in life.

The upside of this situation is that children are naturally such spiritual beings that if you introduce methods through which they can help themselves, this is the greatest gift you can offer them, as far as healing is concerned. Rather than trying to influence their energy system with hands-on healing or absent healing, offer them a means through which they can help themselves.

For instance, take an example where a child has been having stomach aches (a common childhood complaint). If it is your child or you know the child well, you can always gently rub the child's stomach or just place your hand gently on the area and offer unconditional love as a healing tool. That is often very effective. Children respond wonderfully to a sudden flow of love from the heart or solar plexus area. But you can go further to help. Ask the child to ask its tummy what is wrong. Most children will think this is a completely normal request. If they should question you, simply explain that the different parts of our body know why they are ill and if we ask them nicely, they might tell us what is wrong. You can even say it is like a silent little voice inside the head that helps you when you need a friend. They might like to hold their stomach themselves as they ask their stomach the question 'What is wrong?' They might ask the question out loud or they may do it silently to the inside of their stomach. Let them take their time and do it their own way. In most cases, they will find an answer.

Sometimes, of course, they use their imagination and make up a reply. More often, they simply listen to their inner voice and let it tell them what is going on. They do not have the same system of doubt and confusion over spiritual awareness which we have. They will trust their inner voice because they have not yet built up all these barriers to stop themselves from listening.

Encourage your child to listen to different parts of their body. Is their throat sore? Ask them to ask what would help it. Are they tearful and you do not know why? Ask them to ask their heart or their tummy what is going on. Have they got a headache? What caused the headache? Ask them to speak to their head and talk about it.

Of course, you have to strike a balance here. You do not want your child carrying on conversations with parts of their body throughout the day or at inopportune moments. You can deal with this by explaining that our bodies like to help us but they like us to only ask them when we really need it. Our bodies also want some peace and quiet when we talk to them, so it is best to wait until you have a quiet moment at home before starting to ask questions.

At all times, encourage children to feel free to talk to you and tell you what they are thinking and feeling. This is so easy when they are young and becomes progressively more difficult as they enter adolescence. Always try to keep those lines of communication open and let children know you are there for them when they want to talk to you and discuss problems. If you take the time to really stop and listen to what children have to say, you will find out that they have so much more spiritual knowledge inside of them. They can often end up teaching you things you had not considered before. Again, make sure you use language that makes them feel comfortable. Try not to get caught up in using words like 'cosmic energy', 'chakras' and 'auras'. Use the word 'energy' as much as possible and simplify concepts so that they are easily grasped. Your work healing others should have prepared you for this process.

Healing a child

If you feel that there is an occasion when you want to do hands-on or absent healing, because you know it is right, then you must do so with great sensitivity and gentleness. Below is a guide to help you through this, but again it should be stressed that you should not do this unless you know intuitively that it is right to do so. Your primary concern should be that the child is not frightened in any way.

You need to start by explaining energy to the child and telling them that you are just trying to help them balance themselves again. Let them know that you will not touch them in any way and that they need to do nothing at all except close their eyes and relax. Then open yourself in the normal way and say a prayer which relates specifically to the child, asking for help to be particularly sensitive and intuitive.

Ask the child if they are ready and then make sure you start your healing at a greater distance than you would from an adult's body. If you normally start about a foot away from an adult, then make it nearly two feet away from the child. Now ask that you be given the right flow of cosmic energy which is appropriate for this child. You may notice a sudden slowing of energy or a sudden, lighter feeling as the energy changes as it flows through you. You may just feel vaguely different or you may tingle at a lower frequency. Keep asking that you be given the guidance to be sensitive and gentle in all areas of their aura and their chakras.

Start as usual with the base and work your way through the seven chakras, but this time do not linger over any of them. Just tune in and feel their energy and then move on. Remember to keep a good distance away from their body at all times. You should notice a great deal of difference as you run your hands over their energy centres. The energy will feel lighter, less focused and less sharp. Remember that they cannot take the same rush of energy into their systems as an adult.

You don't need to ask for higher guidance to give instructions for the child, although you may find that the child is receiving information for themselves. They will probably be much quicker to tell you whether something feels good or whether it feels uncomfortable. Ideally, you should know this before they do, if you are tuned in properly. They will probably give you information about colours they see and sensations they have. To them it will be quite natural and a pleasant experience. If they say they feel uncomfortable or in pain at any time, tell them to imagine standing under a wonderfully warm shower and get them to cleanse themselves thoroughly.

Let your hands move naturally to other areas you know need healing, but always keep your distance and remember to pay attention to the energy as it flows through you. Keep it at the intensity which is right for the child.

Don't spend as much time healing a child as you would an adult; they don't need it. Make sure you close and protect each one of their chakras in turn. Then give them an extra thick layer of protection and unconditional love.

Step well back and cleanse and close yourself down. Give a prayer of thanks and then turn your attention to the child and check on their well-being. Most children will still be up in the clouds somewhere after healing. You should be able to feel this in them. Spend some time getting them to concentrate on their feet. Tell them about the roots of a tree and to imagine these coming from the soles of their feet. Tell them to notice how heavy their bottom feels in the chair. Make sure they are grounded and balanced again before you ask for any further feedback. Before they go, make sure that they are well earthed again.

You will notice that you get different feedback from a child. Children often simplify what we try to make very complicated! If something feels good, they will tell you so. If they didn't like it, they'll let you know. They often have very vivid images and sensations as they are being healed. They usually feel much more open about sharing their experiences. Make sure the child knows that spiritual healing is not something all children are suited to and that it is not good for them to go away and practise on others. Explain it is fundamentally an adult experience and something they can look forward to more when they are older.

The same sensitivity is needed if you are healing an adolescent. Generally speaking, an adolescent will not let you come within a mile of their aura and they are quite right to feel that way! They are struggling enough with their own energies without having someone else interfere. However, if for some reason it becomes appropriate, again keep a large distance between you and the other person. Again make sure you temper the cosmic energy flow through you so that they are not bombarded with too much energy. It is very difficult to work with the energy of an adolescent and it is really not recommended that you do so, unless you are told intuitively that it is right in an exceptional circumstance.

Whenever you are in danger of forgetting about the delicacy of a child's aura and chakras, go back and study the illustrations on pages 275 and 276. Learn to fully appreciate their very vulnerable, unique qualities and remember to love them unconditionally, whilst allowing them to grow and learn at their own personal level.

Animals heal us in so many ways that perhaps this chapter should be called 'How Animals Heal Us'. It is impossible to heal an animal without receiving so much back in return. It is a uniquely humbling and profound experience.

Of course healing animals differs in that their energy systems are not the same as ours. No one is quite sure where the chakras of different animals are located, or how many major chakras animals possess. That they respond to spiritual healing techniques is beyond doubt. They respond instinctively to energies around them and lack the cynicism humans often find difficult to shed.

There have been many different experiments carried out on animals which seem to prove that they possess what we would call telepathic abilities, or spiritual awareness of others. Do you have an animal to whom you are very close? Try a few experiments to see how attuned you are to each other. They can be simple tests such as the following:

- *Are you waiting for your cat to return from its daily stroll? Start thinking about the cat coming back to you. Imagine it trotting through the cat-flap or waiting at the door. Even imagine having its favourite treat waiting for it in the kitchen! Visualise your cat, see it and smell it, imagine stroking it and loving it. If you focus for a little while, you will often find your cat walking back in to you. They have picked up your energies and returned to the fold.*

- *See whether your dog is telepathic. Think about taking your dog for a walk, at a time other than the usual hour. Think about getting the lead and walking out the front door together. Imagine your dog's pleasure. Keep visualising the scenario, but do not actually say anything to your dog. After a few minutes, it is quite likely it will come up and wag its tail expectantly. It will have sensed the energies around you which indicate going for a walk.*

- *Do you own a bird? Try imagining that your bird is tweeting at you, or if it is flying free, imagine it landing on your head. Feel it being contented, enjoying itself in an act such as studying its reflection in glass. Choose just one option and focus on it. Notice what happens after a few minutes; it may be imitating what you were creating in your mind.*

- *If you own a rabbit or hamster, imagine it playing with its favourite toy, nuzzling your hand or involved in any activity it enjoys. Again, just focus on one image at a time and take a few minutes to relax and concentrate. See how it responds after a little while. Is it copying your thought patterns?*

- *If you own a horse and it is grazing loose in a field out of your sight, try standing quietly by the fence and sending your vibrations out to the horse. Have a carrot or imagine having one, think about stroking the horse, but do not call out to it in any way. Keep concentrating. Notice if the horse then trots up to you, suddenly finding you when previously you were out of sight.*

If you conduct these experiments more than once and at different times of the day or week, you will soon be able to eliminate coincidence from the equation. Animals really do respond to the individual energies around them.

Animals instinctively feel different emotions. Have you witnessed an animal cowering away from people shouting at each other, or trying to comfort someone who is upset? Have you noticed a creature sharing a human's joy? Animals also smell danger and fear. Life forces give out different odours with different emotions and animals such as dogs and elephants can actually tap into the different odours and react accordingly.

If you are scared of dogs, for example, every time you are near one you will give off the scent of fear. This in turn will unnerve the dog which will often respond nervously or aggressively, simply through your fear having made them feel uncertain. Humans who say animals do not like them just mean that they are nervous around animals and that, in turn, creates an unhealthy energy cycle. You have to break the pattern of fear to be able to move on.

So how can one safely heal animals? The answer is similar to that for children: with great sensitivity and gentleness! Most animals are very trusting and their auras are generally quite open and vulnerable, particularly those of domesticated animals.

Feeling an animal's aura

The best way to start the process is simply to feel an animal's aura before you attempt any form of healing. You need to tune in and develop a relationship with their different energy system before you can learn to work effectively with them.

Provided you can safely move within an animal's aura without fear of attack, you can experience the aura of whatever animal you want to tune in to. This applies to your pet snake, cat, dog, horse, spider, pig, hamster or whatever. Every living creature has its own personal aura. Some are more difficult to tap in to than others. Whatever animal you choose, try the following exercise.

Wait until your pet is relaxed and preferably somewhat sleepy. You don't need to consciously open up and expand your aura for this exercise, but make sure you are relaxed and focused. Sit or stand comfortably near your animal but do not actually touch it or stroke it in any way.

Start with a small prayer. Ask that you be shown this animal's aura in a way that will help you to heal in the future. Ask that you be allowed to enter their world and their experiences for a short while. Ask for protection, love and guidance during this time.

Place your hands quite a way from the animal. Relax and take a few deep breaths. Now start with the head area. Keep your hands a good 12 inches or so from the animal.

What is your first sensation? Let your hands drift slowly over the animal's body. Linger where it feels right and notice where you feel a stronger energy activity. Is there a chakra in the vicinity? As no one is quite sure where animal chakras are, you can explore these possibilities for yourself.

Breathe in their unique animal scent as you work. Imagine what it would feel like to be their shape and size. How would the world seem to them? How do they move? What limbs do they possess? What about their eyes and ears? Do they have teeth and a tongue like humans; have they a tail? Imagine what it would feel like to have four legs or a tail or to only slither as a snake. Enjoy the exploratory process.

You will find yourself opening up as you work, without having to try. If you are really relaxed and focused, you may find yourself actually feeling as though you are inside the skin of the animal you are tuning in to. You may find yourself going into a deeper meditation about the animal and its abilities and personality. All animals have their own group spirit to which they belong, a sort of sphere of energy in which they resonate and interact. They, too, are following their own karmic path in life. You may have an insight into this as you work. Remember to keep asking for more information and a deeper sense of understanding as you work. Don't be afraid to silently ask questions and see what you are given back in reply.

You may notice that your animal relaxes into a deeper sleep as you do this. If you are relaxed as you carry out your investigation, your loving vibrations will relax your animal even more. You will find you can spend quite a bit of time doing this without disturbing them. Just make sure you keep a reasonable distance from your animal's body and keep sending out your gentle love.

When you finish, make sure you put a protective cloak of colour or light around your animal's aura. Withdraw yourself and make sure you cleanse and close down. Balance and focus yourself.

You may then choose to actually draw a diagram of how you saw your animal's energy system, showing which areas felt stronger and brighter than others. Make a note of any sensations and images that cropped up for you. Then try this on another occasion and notice any differences. Always send your animal some loving thoughts when you finish and say a small prayer. Ask for protection and guidance for both of you.

It is fascinating to do this with different animals and really experience how they all operate. They all feel so different! If you love animals and feel very drawn to them, try compiling an animal diary and make notes about how they all vary. See if you can determine where their different chakras are and how their auras feel. Do some animals have much wider auras than others? Pay particular attention to the different images and sensations which they create in you. Are there similarities within each group spirit? You may realise that you start to have the same sensation every time you approach a cat or a dog. It will be personal to you.

Spend some time increasing your relationship to all animals before you start to move into the realm of healing them in some way. Start noticing animals everywhere you go. Sit in the park for a while and watch different dogs as they play and chase around. You can try going to a zoo and observing animals there, but so often they are not behaving instinctively because they are in unnatural surroundings; it can be a sad experience. Sit and watch birds by a water fountain or study ants, spiders or bees as they go about their daily activities in a garden. Try to become an open book and absorb all these different species and their relationship to man. The more you study, the more you can begin to truly appreciate, respect and, ultimately, tune in to all these very different life forces.

Healing an animal

When you have spent some time in this new world, and when you feel you have increased your understanding for these creatures, then you can try your first healing experiment with an animal. You might simply want to imbue your animal's aura with some extra love during your first time; it does not necessarily follow that your animal has to be ill for you to work with their energies. Whatever you decide to do, make sure you are gentle and sensitive throughout.

Try to have the animal in comfortable and relaxed surroundings. If they are asleep, it will help the process. Stand well clear of their aura as you open yourself up in the usual way. Offer a prayer relating to the animal and ask for help from the group spirit of that animal. You may find you have a powerful image or sensation which you identify as having connected with that animal's energy. Don't rush your relaxing process. Ask that you be allowed to give the level of healing which is appropriate for that animal. As with healing children, you may find the energy rush suddenly change as it goes through you. Animal healing is on a different vibration again.

When you feel ready, move into the animal's aura and place your hands in the area which feels right for you. If you have felt where their chakras are, go over each one, gently, and tune in to each area. Keep asking for guidance from above.

Always keep checking that you are giving the right level of healing energy.

Don't worry if you find yourself drifting into a different state of awareness as you work. Because animals are on a different level of consciousness, their energy is so different and the images, sensations and feelings you have during the healing session may be unlike anything you have experienced before.

If the animal responds in any way as you are working which might indicate it is unnerved, then move out of their aura for a moment, speak softly and soothingly to them and picture them being cleansed under the pure white cosmic energy. After a moment, they will probably settle again. Wait a minute before you move back in again. Adjust your healing energy accordingly.

If you believe the animal is in good health, then simply send unconditional love into their energy field and imbue them with divine protection and support.

When you're ready to withdraw, follow the usual system. Close down the animal's chakras and give them a form of protection which feels right for them. Then stand back and cleanse thoroughly. Close down yourself and then offer a prayer of thanks whilst asking for continued protection for both of you.

If you are keeping an animal diary, make a note of how the healing session felt and how the animal responded, both during the healing and in the days which follow.

Of course, you can also offer absent healing on animals. You follow the same procedure as for human beings and remember to always imagine the animal as well and happy, full of energy and appreciation of life. Imagine them occupied with their favourite toy or activity in the most comfortable surroundings. As animals do not possess human cynicism, they often respond very well to spiritual healing. You may want to compare your human healing diary with your animal diary and note the effects that your healing has had.

There is a flip side to healing animals. As mentioned earlier, animals also heal us with their very special and unique energies. It is interesting to note that many hospitals are now openly advocating the presence of animals in wards where children are unwell. Of course, the animals have to be specially vetted for health and hygiene standards and psychological suitability for the task of being petted by a wealth of different children every day. However, positive improvements are being uncovered in children's conditions through the appearance of these animals. Why should this be?

Spiritually, one could explain it using the unique, unconditionally loving energies animals exude. They do not question or feel repelled by illness. Anyone who is feeling depressed or unwell only has to experience a gentle nudge from an animal's nose and to succumb to the subsequent rhythmic, gentle stroking of a fur coat, to know how wonderfully comforting it can be. Further tests are also being carried out in nursing homes for the elderly to test their responses to animals allowed into their environment. Lowered blood pressure and reduced states of stress are being recorded in these instances. Obviously, this clinical testing is still in its early stages, but initial reports are very encouraging and only seem to demonstrate what spiritually aware people have always known: animals play a large part in healing humans.

PART THREE:

FURTHER HEALING TOOLS

There are, of course, additional non-living instruments one can use to aid spiritual healing, irrespective of whether you are working on yourself, other adults, children or animals – and even plants! In this part of the book we are going to take a look at the extra tools available and encourage experimentation. The more time you have spent on Parts One and Two and dealing with your inner awareness of healing, the more effective you are likely to be when using these other tools. There is a section at the end of the book which gives you space to record your experiences with some of these healing tools.

PENDULUMS

Although pendulums are popular in Western society and have been used for thousands of years, you may not have seen them before or know how they work. The pendulums referred to in this chapter are not the sort you find on clocks; these pendulums consist of a variety of pointed objects that dangle from the end of a piece of string. They are held in the hand and different movements occur which are interpreted in various ways. Each healer has a personal relationship with their pendulum. Some find them more helpful than others. Many find that a pendulum will respond vigorously to their requests; a few find it remains completely motionless despite their focus and willpower. Before you spend money on a professional pendulum, consider making one of your own – it's quite simple.

All you really need is a small object which can be balanced at the end of a piece of thin string. Have a look at what is available around your home. A ring, small key, thick screw, or nail will do. Some of the examples shown overleaf will give you inspiration! Choose whatever you feel drawn to and tie it securely to a piece of thin string, no longer than 10 inches in length. Don't double the string, as you might when using a sewing needle.

Now try holding your homemade pendulum by the top of the string between your first finger and thumb. Your chosen object will hang motionless at the bottom of the string. Take a couple of deep breaths and try to relax your arm, hand and fingers. Now, without thinking too much about it, ask your pendulum to swing in any direction for you. Do not consciously move any part of your arm or hand as you do this; use your thoughts alone to make the movement. It does not matter if it swings back and forth, from side to side or in a clockwise or anti-clockwise circular movement. It does not matter if it just trembles slightly and then goes still. All you want is to create a slight movement. Give yourself a good five minutes or so for this experiment. Is anything happening? You may find it takes a while or it may take more than one occasion for this to work. Some will find the pendulum moves quite quickly and then becomes motionless again just as quickly. For a few the pendulum seems to take on a life of its own and starts swinging violently in a number of directions, despite the fact that their hand and arm are completely still.

Whatever you accomplish in this early stage, there is one thing you need to know. The pendulum itself possesses no mystical, unearthly power and has no direct energy of its own. No matter if you are using a beautifully cut crystal or a piece of polished beech wood, the pendulum itself is not powerful. It is the energy you flow into the object itself which creates the movement. In fact, you are imperceptibly moving your hands and fingers in a way that allows the pendulum to move. You are not experiencing a mystical phenomenon, no matter how much it may feel that way. Unless the pendulum is in your hands, it will not move of its own accord.

To test this out, hang your homemade pendulum from a door frame or a handle. Now command the pendulum to move in some way without your touching it. No matter how long you may try, it is virtually impossible for the pendulum to move in any direction at all.

The connection between you and your pendulum is a personal one. Another person using your pendulum will find it moves in differently or may not work for them at all. Different substances work well for different people. If you experimented with your homemade pendulum and it did move in some direction, then you might consider purchasing or making a more sophisticated version.

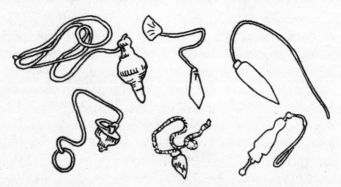

A selection of different types of pendulum.

There are plenty on the market you can buy, from small crystals to a variety of different woods. There are also brass, silver, gold and copper ones. Spend a little time deciding what feels right for you. Are you naturally drawn to trees? Do different woods seem to have different energies? Or do you love having silver or other metals around you? Perhaps you have stones and crystals around you because they resonate well with your energies. Pick up different objects and see which feels right. You might be walking in a park or by the seashore and find a beautiful shell, stone or piece of wood which feels perfect. Explore and find out for yourself what you like.

Once you start creating your own personal pendulum, you really need the object to be symmetrical and to have only one pointed end because, as you work with your pendulum moving in different directions, a pointed end and a balanced pendulum will make diagnosis easier and clearer. You may not want to use string or thread either. You might prefer a chain of some sort or a fine strip of leather. Let your intuition guide you towards what is right.

Getting to know your pendulum

When you have created a pendulum which is right for you, then you need to develop a closer relationship to it. If you acknowledge that the pendulum is only powerful when you are touching and guiding it, then it makes sense that you need to create a powerful energy between the two of you to increase your spiritual awareness. Remember this pendulum is only a tool to help you increase your own healing abilities. It is only powerful when you work well together.

First, you want to know how to get information from your pendulum. It works uniquely for everyone so you need to discover what the each swinging sensation means. Take three separate pieces of A4 paper. Draw 'yes' in large letters on one, 'no' on the second piece of paper and 'neutral' on the third.

Put the paper saying 'neutral' in front of you on a table. Now pick up your pendulum. You might like to relax and focus your thoughts. You might want to open your chakras and practise some deep breathing before you start. You may feel so confident with your pendulum that you feel you are already open and ready to work with it.

Now place your pendulum about 2–3 inches above the piece of paper. Try to relax your hand and arm. Rest your elbow on the table top to help balance you. Use your other hand to steady the pendulum before you start. Then breathe deeply and relax. When you're ready, ask your pendulum to move in the direction indicating neutral. This means the starting position of the pendulum or the position into which it will move if it is unable to provide the answer to any question. This movement will be personal between you and your pendulum. The pendulum may remain motionless, it may swing back and forth or go in a circle. Whatever happens, note its movement and then remove the piece of paper.

Now place the paper saying 'yes' in front of you. Repeat the procedure, asking the pendulum to show you which movement indicates a positive response. It must be different from the neutral position. If it's the same, refuse to accept it. Say firmly 'no' and request a different movement. Take your time and remember to keep breathing deeply.

When you are satisfied, move on to the 'no' sheet of paper. Again, elicit a firm response of movement, which must again be different from the 'neutral' and 'yes' positions.

When you have completed this, you should have three firm movements with which you can work. For instance, 'neutral' may be motionless, 'yes' may be a clockwise circle and 'no' could be a back and forth swing. Are you clear about which movement means which response?

Then you need to test your pendulum's truthfulness. Ask a simple and direct question such as 'Am I sitting down at this moment?' with the only possible answer as 'yes'. Note the response. Is it the right one? Go on to test the 'no' and 'neutral' positions. If it is not clear, then return to the three pieces of

*paper and work through the responses again. These three
pendulum movements should never vary. You need to be very
clear about what the directions mean. They will never change.*

*It is then helpful to imbue the pendulum with your own energy
to increase the vibrations between you. You can do this in many
ways. You might cleanse it and carry it with you while you visit
your cleansing sanctuary. You might just want to sit and close
it in the palm of your hand whilst sending it loving thoughts.
You may choose to 'smudge' it with incense. You might even
want to visualise the cosmic energy pouring down onto it and
surrounding it with positive vibrations. Carry it with you for a
while, perhaps in a pocket or in a small pouch in your bag. Sleep
with it under your pillow. It can be what feels right for you and
you don't have to tell anyone else what you are doing.*

So you now understand that you can determine the answers to
questions which require 'yes', 'no' or 'don't know' responses.
Let's look at small ways in which this can be helpful, and then
we will look at the deeper levels at which pendulums can work.

We are going to start with working on yourself with pendulum
responses, but these situations can also apply to healing others. Try
it on yourself first to test how effectively your pendulum is working.

There are many areas in spiritual healing where you may
sometimes feel rather lost, no matter how hard you are trying to
increase your awareness on other levels. For instance, you may
be aware that you are still trying to tackle a particular problem on
your personal healing chart but you seem to have become very
stuck on the issue and cannot see your way forward. What question
might help ease your confusion and light your way forward?

A good starting point would be to understand which chakra is
affected by a particular situation. You can go through your chakras,
one by one, starting with the base, and ask your pendulum 'Is my
base chakra being affected by this situation?' Remember to relax, focus
and open up before you start working. You know you are using the
pendulum as a tool to access higher awareness and so unless you
are breathing deeply and remaining open to the possibilities of

knowledge in the universe and your own ability to tap into that knowledge, you are unlikely to get many revealing insights.

Once you have ascertained which area is affected (and there may be more than one chakra involved) you may want to ask further questions such as 'Is this fundamentally an emotional issue from childhood?' or 'Is there someone presently around me who I am letting affect my energies?' You will find the right questions and phraseology which are personally helpful to you.

You may be feeling unwell physically and want to understand what has created the illness. Again, you can use your pendulum to help you delve further. You could start by questioning whether the origin stems from a mental process or an emotional upset or a spiritual factor. You may find that you have a physical illness to learn a lesson about physical energy and how you are not pacing yourself properly. As long as you phrase a question requiring a 'yes' or 'no' answer, you are open to the possibility of learning more about the situation.

You can also use the pendulum to guide you on practical matters such as allergies. Do particular foods agree/disagree with you? Try placing your pendulum over particular foods if you suspect you may be allergic to them. You can also just write down the name of the food on a piece of paper and place the pendulum over that. There are so many confusing factors which contribute to allergies and it is very helpful to be able to narrow down the field.

You might also be trying to decide which crystal or which healing remedy might work best for you. Try placing your pendulum over a series of crystals and see which would be best for you. (New Age and health shops are quite accustomed to this behaviour so it is unlikely to cause concern or amusement.) Check which bottle your pendulum is drawn to. It is equally possible that you already know what is right for you simply by looking at it.

Just a word of warning here. It is easy to become obsessed with your pendulum in the early stages. A person has even swung a pendulum over a box of oranges in a supermarket to determine exactly which orange is the right one for them! Try to use your pendulum only in cases where you really need to enhance your awareness.

It is difficult to use the pendulum as a diagnostic tool for future events. It can be tempting to use it as though it were a fortune-telling tool and to get caught up with questions such as 'Will I meet the person of my dreams?' or 'Will I make lots of money?' Remember that the pendulum does not possess magical powers. You are only using it to help you delve deeper into your own subconscious knowledge. Acceptance of your world in its present state and complete trust in the future is the only healthy state for you. If you need to question your future experiences, you need to spend more time concentrating on your holistic health and spiritual path.

Having looked at some of the lighter implications of pendulum work, let's now delve into the deeper levels at which the pendulum can be very useful. We are now going to relate pendulum work to healing others and see how it may be both useful and revealing.

Chakra analysis through pendulum work

You have already used the pendulum to focus on your own chakras. Now let's look at how the pendulum might help diagnose other people's chakras. For this, you need a willing participant.

Ask your participant to lie flat on a comfortable surface. Ask them to lie on their back first of all. (As five of the seven chakras open both front and back, you will want to explore both openings at some stage.) Ask them simply to lie as still as possible, close their eyes and completely relax. It doesn't matter if they drift off during this exercise. They might enjoy some soft music to listen to while you work.

You want to open up your own chakras and prepare yourself to work in as relaxed and focused a manner as possible. Always offer your personal prayer and ask that you deal with the person using as much sensitivity and gentleness as possible.

When you are ready, approach the person, holding your pendulum in whichever hand feels comfortable. Now start by placing the pendulum above their base chakra. This has only one opening and is just below the base of the spine. Place the pendulum as close as feels suitable to the person concerned. If they say they feel uncomfortable, move the pendulum slightly higher. Check they feel all right before you continue.

Now, you don't have to consciously open up their chakra or even tune in to it. Simply place the pendulum over their base chakra and steady it with your other hand. Now wait until the pendulum starts to move. At this stage, it's not necessary to ask any questions. Simply let the pendulum move of its own accord. During this time, free your mind of any preconceived notions about this person. That's hard to do, but unless you are free from bias, you will let your own thought processes affect your work. When the pendulum has settled into a movement (or no movement even), make a note of it and move on. You might want to draw a figure of the seven chakras and fill in the movement of each chakra as you work, to help you remember.

Slowly work your way through the seven chakras, noting each movement. You may find many are the same. Some may not react at all and some may prompt vigorous movement. If your friend notices this, reassure them that it is not unusual. Let them know it does not indicate that anything is wrong. They may be feeling more vulnerable than usual from lying down.

When you have worked out the movement of all seven chakras, put down your pendulum and have a quick cleanse. Pull down some cosmic energy into and through your own energy system and then work your way systematically back over the seven chakras using your hands, keeping a distance of at least 6 inches from the participant's physical body. Ask that you give healing in the most appropriate way for them. You may feel more drawn to one chakra than another.

Now ask your participant to turn over and repeat the process whilst concentrating on the back of the energy centres. You may be surprised to note they respond differently. It is possible for the front of a chakra to be open and the back completely closed, and vice versa. Again, make a note of all the movements and offer healing to the chakra(s) which feel appropriate.

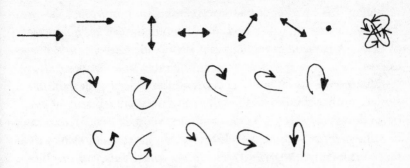

The pendulum can move in many different ways.
Here is a selection of its movements.

When you've finished, go back and gently close their chakras and offer each a film of gentle protection. Then ask them to turn over onto their back and repeat the gentle closing and protective process. When all their chakras feel closed, step back and cover them in a cloak of protective light.

Ask them to lie quietly for a few minutes while you cleanse and close yourself down. Protect yourself properly. Offer a prayer of thanks and ask for continued protection. Check that your friend is feeling all right and that they are grounded again. Then ask for their feedback while you drink your water.

If you experience this pendulum work over a period of time with the same person, you will be able to make comparisons. You will soon discover that the chakras move differently according to the person's moods and experiences. A few may remain constant. You will gradually realise what the different chakra movements indicate.

This again becomes a personal journey of discovery. You and your pendulum will work differently from other healers. Try to be specific about the pendulum movements. You may notice that suddenly there are wide, oblong swings, or sharp, tiny little circles occurring. It becomes more complex than just a back and forward swing or a neat circle. The more specifically you notice the differences, the more you can chart the comparisons. Working out the pendulum movements can become very complex and extremely revealing. Take a look at the movements shown opposite. Can you see how diverse they are? Each movement indicates a different state of being. A pendulum moving in a circle with a 2-inch diameter as opposed to a 6-inch diameter means different states of being.

When you work with the pendulum, notice the different sensations that come with the different movements. If you are wary of working on others, you can work on yourself first. In this case, use drawings of your chakras from Delving Deeper into Chakras in Part One (see pages 185–94). Place your pendulum over each one to check out your own situation. Build up your confidence this way before working with someone else.

An experienced healer who works well with their pendulum will be able to determine, from slightly different movements, what is going on within each chakra. This hints at the psychological state of the person. It is not a quick journey to get to this level of awareness but it does show how powerful a tool the pendulum can be when used with dedication and enthusiasm.

You may find the pendulum opens a lot of spiritual doors and rely quite heavily upon its guidance and strength. You may continue this relationship for the rest of your life. There are several well-known homeopaths and practitioners of alternative medicine who always use the pendulum to determine which remedy is suitable

It is also possible, after a period of time, that you do not use your pendulum quite so much. You may realise your own spiritual awareness has accelerated to a level where the necessary knowledge will come to you without using the pendulum.

You may stop using the pendulum for years and suddenly want to pick it up again one day. It does not matter what relationship you form with your pendulum, as long as you use it wisely and lovingly.

If you found using a pendulum was a powerful experience for you, you may find you are the kind of person who benefits from using additional tools on a regular basis. Often very grounded people, who are very physical in expression, find the comfort of a physical object enhances their spiritual well-being. Whatever your response to the pendulum, let us now take a look at your relationship with crystals and see whether they may benefit you.

CRYSTALS

Crystals are extraordinary objects of nature. The more you understand about them, the more fascinating and powerful they become. They have a perfect molecular structure and are commonly used in many modern appliances as transmitters. They are used to amplify sound waves in radio and light waves in televisions.

However, during their work in spiritual healing, we are not so concerned with their literal, physical properties but more with their less definable, subtler energies. Crystals at their most powerful are said to be transmitters of all the knowledge stored within the Earth's core. One could expand that to include all universal knowledge. This is not as fanciful as it might first sound. Think about the practical use of crystals in appliances. They are simply being used to accentuate the energy waves in an object. As we have now reduced human and cosmic powers into streams of energy, why should a crystal not also be effective in tapping into and accentuating those fields?

Crystals are used to help spiritually in so many ways. They can clear stagnant energy from a room by absorbing negative rays. They are particularly useful placed on or by appliances such as computers, televisions and microwaves to absorb potentially harmful rays. They can help when a room has had a powerful, negative influence in it and needs to be cleansed. They are used to accentuate wonderful, positive energies and to direct energy into different areas of a room. If you have a particularly dark or airless part of a building, they can change the energies dramatically within that area.

They are often worn by people for protection or enhancement of a particular area in their life. This does not just mean at their throats or heart as necklaces, but also as rings, bracelets, anklets, toe rings and belts. They can be sewn onto different areas of clothing or kept in a pocket. They can be put under your pillow at night, or kept on a desk in front of you at work. They can be part of a mobile which tinkles gently in the breeze in your garden, or in a room in your house where every time a door or window is opened, the draught creates a movement in the mobile.

Many healers use crystals either in their healing sanctuary or in their hands as they work on themselves or someone else. Sometimes people are asked to hold certain crystals in their own hands as the healer works on them. Sometimes they are placed on different chakras to help aid healing processes. We will discuss how all this works later on.

Of course, some crystals are more powerful than others. Likewise, some people work more powerfully with crystals than others. You need to start experimenting to discover your own personal relationship with them. As with pendulum work, this does not have to be expensive, especially in the early stages.

Start by simply taking a walk in a forest or a park or stroll by a seashore. Pick up any stone or small rock you see. Hold it in your hand for a minute. Do you get any vibrations from it? If you feel nothing, that is fine. You might have to conduct a number of experiments before you may get any results. Notice what colour stones you are drawn to, what shape and what texture.

Next time you are passing a New Age shop, go in and look for crystals. So many shops now stock a variety of stones. Pick different ones up, feel their energies. You can do the same in jewellery shops or craft shops. It is becoming increasingly common for gift shops to sell different, small stones set into necklaces which are quite often accompanied by a small leaflet explaining the stone and its inherent properties. Often they are grouped into headings such as 'love', 'protection', 'fertility' or 'knowledge'. Next time you see one of these craft stands, stop and explore them. Do you feel drawn to one crystal in particular? Why? What information is available about it? Can you relate it to any situation within your current healing chart?

Whenever you do find a stone or crystal and decide to take it home, you have to do one thing straight away. Cleanse it. Your crystal will have absorbed whatever was around it before you got hold of it. Of course, that could be lovely forces such as waves pounding on a seashore or being part of nature's energies in a garden. However, as you cannot be sure what the past influences have been, you need to imbue each crystal with a fresh energy.

Always cleanse any stone or gem you buy or find.

You can cleanse crystals in a number of ways. Try any of the following and see what feels best for you. You might find some stones respond better to different techniques.

- *Dissolve approximately a quarter teaspoon of sea salt in a pint of filtered water. Use sea salt as opposed to table salt because it is purer. Place the crystal in the water/salt mixture. Leave it for several hours or overnight.*
- *Place the crystal in full sunlight for several hours.*
- *Smudge the crystal with your favourite incense or smudge stick.*
- *Hold the crystal in your hand and go into your sacred cleansing sanctuary. Feel the stone being cleansed.*
- *Open up as you hold the crystal in your hand. Then imagine the beautiful cosmic energy coming down and cleansing your crystal. Imagine it increasing its energies and powers through direct contact with the cosmic energy. Remember to close down afterwards.*

Never forget the cleansing when you bring a crystal into your home or workspace. Until you have worked with crystals for a while, you may not fully appreciate how powerful they can be. Remember they can also transmit negative energies if they are not cared for and cleansed regularly. If you have stones within your healing sanctuary or if you use them to absorb negative energy rays, they must regularly be cleansed using one of the methods described above.

When people start working with crystals, they want to learn all about which crystal contains which healing elements and what they should get for themselves and others. However, it is difficult and often misleading to always group crystals into particular uses and powers, because each is individual and each has its own distinct properties and uses, according to who owns it or uses it. Also, as you read above, crystals can be used in such a wide variety of ways. Before you read more about general qualities attributed to certain crystals, try to let your own intuition lead you first. Start developing your relationship with crystals based on instinct, not on what any written guide tells you should do. Let us look at different scenarios when you might want crystals around you, or others. We will start with simple examples and work towards the more complex.

Would you like a crystal around your workspace or home environment? Is there an area within your space that you feel could benefit from healing? Perhaps you spend a lot of time sitting at your desk or standing by the kitchen sink or ironing board. What crystal would help you in those tasks? You do not have to go out and buy an expensive stone. Choose a small one or find one from nature around you. You could even go through old jewellery boxes. So often we already own gems but have forgotten about them. Place the stone in your chosen place and leave it there for several days. Has the energy changed within that area? If you are not sure, try changing the crystal to somewhere else. Put it under your pillow, place it by the bath or shower. Put it in your jacket or sweater pocket and finger it at different times during the day. You might want to give it to someone else. Place it by a photo of someone. Does that feel better? Put it in your dog's basket or animal's cage. Do they seem to benefit from it?

You see, we all need different crystals at different times. It is good to change the location of your crystals. Do not become stuck in thinking one crystal can only stand in one place. That creates another form of stagnant energy. You want to be growing and evolving in your spiritual awareness, not standing still in the same energy all the time.

Notice where else and when else you could benefit from crystal energy. The possibilities are endless. Experiment all the time to see what works for you and those around you. Place one in your fruit bowl. Does the fruit taste any different? Put a small clear crystal in your drinking water. Place one by an ailing house plant. Keep noticing any changes.

Tuning in to a crystal

Have you someone around you who is unwell at present? You may be doing absent healing on them, but give them a small crystal to hold in their hand or to keep near them. However, you do need to tune in to the crystal first and see if it is suitable for them. Once you start thinking about others, you want to take responsibility for them and exercise as much sensitivity as possible. Do not just assume you are getting it right. Use your intuition to find out. This is a good time for you to consider how you can tune in to your crystal and check what is the most beneficial place or purpose for that stone. Try the following exercise with any crystal.

Make sure the crystal has been cleansed first. Always cleanse every crystal as soon as you take ownership of it. Never tune in to an uncleansed stone. It may prove to be an unpleasant experience.

Sit in your healing sanctuary and take your time to relax, open up and cleanse yourself. When you feel focused and ready, pick up the crystal and hold it in your hand. Hold it in both hands or cup your fingers over the crystal if you wish. It may increase its vibrations for you.

First, appreciate the weight, shape and texture of the crystal. Keep your eyes closed as you run your fingers over it. What are the first sensations you have. Cool? Heat? Does it pulse gently or does it feel almost static with crackling energy under your fingers? Do you feel invigorated or soothed by its presence in your hands? Maybe your heart has started to beat more quickly. Perhaps your fingers are tingling. Or have your shoulders dropped and your neck muscles softened as you hold it? Is it making a particular chakra open or causing activity in a certain area of your body? Do you feel comfortable holding it or are you feeling slightly off-balance? Keep questioning how you feel. Wash away any sensation you don't like.

You will probably know quite quickly whether the crystal is right for you and your environment. It doesn't take long for you to either bond with or to feel alienated from the crystal.

If you feel comfortable with the crystal, you will want to know how best to use it. Continue holding it in your hands with your eyes closed. Now silently ask that you be shown how it will best benefit you. Sit quietly whilst you wait for a response. It may come in different ways. Some people have a silent conversation whereby they are told what would be a good solution. It sometimes feels as though they are talking to themselves or sometimes as though a distant, outside voice is guiding them. Others will simply see the crystal in the location where it belongs, such as on a chain around their neck or by a certain object. Sometimes you just know where it belongs without any words, images or sensations. You will be given information in the way which is right for you.

If you know that the crystal is not meant for you, then ask to whom it should go. You obviously came into contact with it because you are meant to pass it on to someone who would not otherwise have found it. Again, the answer to this will come in different ways. Often an image of the person will flash in front of your inner eye. You may be given their name. You may suddenly feel their presence or see an object which you immediately identify as belonging to that person.

When you think you know to whom it belongs, then say their name silently to yourself as you hold the crystal. How does the crystal respond? Is there a sense of recognition? Do you feel right about it? Or perhaps you have been putting your own interpretation on things and not listening clearly to your own higher sense of intuition.

When you know you have tuned in to the right person, ask if you can have any information about how this person can best use this crystal. You may receive nothing in response now, because it may be right for the other person to work it out for themselves. You may not need to know it because the other person may already realise its purpose. If you receive nothing, that's fine.

Offer a blessing for the crystal. Bless the other person as well, if you are going to give it away. If you are keeping it, ask that both you and the crystal learn from each other. Ask for protection for the crystal and yourself.

When you've finished, take the stone with you into your cleansing sanctuary. Feel both you and the crystal being washed and re-energised. Then step out of your cleansing space and put the crystal down, outside of your aura.

Now close your eyes and cleanse again, on your own. Give thanks for what you have received and then close down in your own personal way and protect yourself thoroughly. Make sure you feel focused and grounded before you continue.

If you have realised that you are meant to give the crystal away, make sure you explain to the person why you are giving it to them. Let them know that you are sure it is right for them. Suggest that they simply hold it and feel its energy. Ask them to let you know how it feels. Ask them to let you know where they decide to keep it and how it affects them. Hopefully it will be in a positive, nurturing fashion.

You might want to start a crystal diary, if you find it difficult to remember all your experiments. It will also clarify for you when a crystal worked and when it did not. Make sure you make a note of which crystal you have used. Notice if you have more success when you pass the crystal on to someone else.

Sometimes people can be very good 'finders' for others but not necessarily choose the best crystals for themselves. This can also mirror their ability to help others in a powerful and beneficial way, whilst often ignoring their own needs and spiritual path. Do you fall into that category? Always remember that if you do not nurture yourself you cannot be a truly effective healer. If you keep finding crystals and then passing them on to others without retaining any for yourself, then stop and reassess your situation. How much of a natural giver are you? Do you find it hard to receive still? Then you must promise yourself a crystal for yourself. Go looking for one that is right for you. Treat yourself to it and keep it in a spot which will constantly remind you how important it is to nurture yourself, as well as others.

Do you know someone who is in hospital or very ill? You may know someone who is terminally ill and not know what to do for the best. You might want to take a small gift in to them but cannot imagine what would help. Offer them a small, smooth stone which you know resonates gently and in tune with their depleted energies. You may find people are sceptical as to its beneficial qualities, but at least holding onto a smooth, cool object can be comforting for them. You might want to place it by their bedside and let its delicate vibrations clear a healing space around their bed.

Once you have tuned in to different crystals and their energies, you might want to take a look at individual stones and what is considered their most powerful qualities. If you have discovered something different in your studies, that is quite acceptable. Always trust your instinct and higher intuition. You may realise that you have already discovered what is generally accepted about the different stones. Let us take a brief look at different healing needs and see which stones might help. Remember, what follows is just a guide. There are always exceptions and personal preferences which take priority.

- *Do you know someone who has trouble being grounded? Do they spend all their time with their head in the clouds, not acknowledging physical reality? Then smoky quartz would be a good choice. It is also helpful to have someone holding a piece of this as you heal them as it encourages them to remain in their physical body and receive maximum benefit from the healing session. This is a good stone for the base chakra.*

- *Are you or is someone you know guilty of rushing around all the time, living life at a fast pace and not being good about taking the time to slow down and relax? Then having rose quartz around might be very calming. This is generally an excellent stone for all states of agitation.*

It calms, soothes, balances and quietens the mind. It is also very good for the heart chakra and to encourage a sense of universal love and understanding.

- *Are you in need of extra protection at the moment? Are you or is someone you know being bombarded by different energies, some of them difficult to handle? This could apply to a psychiatric nurse or a prison warden or a police officer. Extra protection could help them in the form of black jade, jet or amber. Tiger's-eye is also commonly used for spiritual protection, although it also adds the dimension of understanding and inner awareness. Tourmaline also provides a protective shield around someone. It is best to wear these stones actually on or around you at all times. If someone does not like wearing jewellery, they can always keep it hidden in a pocket or bag.*

- *Do you feel someone needs a good cleansing at present? Do you have an area which needs cleansing and re-energising? Try using some amber. Wear it or place some within the energy field of the room. Amber is very effective at drawing out negativity and purifying the atmosphere.*

- *If you meditate and want some inspiration, then you can place lapis lazuli, fluorite or sodalite within your aura while you concentrate. You could even try lying down and placing a small stone on your brow chakra. Can you feel it pulsing as you focus on the chakra?*

- *Do you feel you are suffering from a negative attitude yourself? Do you feel that you need clearing out and that you need to let go of some old patterns and habits and pave the way for change? You may know someone around you who seems in this state. Try the beautiful green stone malachite for this task. Just a small piece can help shift old energy patterns which have become stuck.*

- *Are you working on a group project at present? Are you concerned about creating trust within the group and would you like to encourage everyone to aspire to similar goals with a unified energy? Try having hematite at your group meetings, which will help ground, focus and create like-mindedness amongst the group.*

- *Lastly, are you as a healer guilty of letting yourself burn out by giving too much to others and never knowing when to stop? Do you feel that you have so many directions in which you need to give of yourself and there is little left to nurture you? Then acquire a peridot crystal (a yellowy-green gem) and keep it close to you at all times. Let its calming and nurturing energies help re-balance you. In addition, physically find some time to relax and unwind. Learn to be gentle on yourself.*

Chakra awareness through crystals

Certain stones are connected to the chakras as well. They are often connected colour-wise. Here is a guide to what you might find useful for each chakra:

Base: smoky quartz, ruby, garnet
Navel: carnelian, topaz
Solar plexus: citrine, yellow sapphire
Heart: rose quartz, emerald, jade
Throat: blue sapphire, turquoise
Brow: lapis lazuli, sodalite, fluorite
Crown: amethyst

You can work with these stones and the chakras in different ways. Some people find that simply holding the relevant crystal in their hand whilst focusing on the chakra concerned can really help to unblock energies and repair tears and holes in the aura. Others like to actually have the stone in contact with the chakra itself. Try working through the next exercise.

Start off by lying down on a comfortable, flat surface and placing the chosen crystal over the chakra area. Secure it in place if it feels as though it will slip off your body. Now close your eyes, relax and open up in your own time. Go through each chakra to open them up, not just the area you want to work on. When you feel balanced and ready, then continue.

Bring your focus to the crystal on your body. Every time you breathe in, feel the energy from the crystal being absorbed through your chakra and into your body. Every time you breathe out, feel any unwanted, stale, blocked energy seeping out through all the pores in your body and disappearing into the air. Bring your attention to nothing but the crystal and your chakra. Nothing else is relevant at this time in your life.

As you breathe in the energy of the stone, notice how its energy pulses. Is your chakra in tune with the crystal's energy or are you out of sync with each other? Which way does the energy move in the crystal – is it a deep clockwise sweep or anti-clockwise in flow? Does it match your chakra? If you have spent time working with pendulums, you may already know which movement your chakra favours. How is the crystal now able to effect change in this?

If you are experiencing a blockage within your chakra, you may feel uncomfortable during the healing process. You might feel tearful or suddenly angry towards someone. You may be forced to confront an issue you hadn't looked at before. Crystal healing can be very powerful and for that reason you shouldn't try it until you have spent some time working alone on your own subtle energy fields. It 's fine for you to feel different emotions. Whatever sensations or feelings you have that you don't want, wash them away in your cleansing sanctuary. By now you should have learnt how to be in control of your own energies so that you can let go of anything you don't want and can't deal with at present.

It's not always unpleasant. Often you may only have wonderful sensations of strength and loving energies being all around you. Your crystal may simply revive and energise you, leaving your chakra feeling nicely healthy and balanced. Remember, if you're dealing with the navel, solar plexus, heart, throat or brow chakras that they all have energy centres front and back. You may want to experience lying on your stomach and attaching a crystal to the back opening of the chakra to feel the difference in energy.

Lie there and enjoy the crystal's energy for as long as it feels right for you. You may have insights into areas of your life which have been troubling you. You may simply be imbued with a wonderful sensation of comfort and perspective about life in general.

When you're ready, you want to cleanse and get rid of any unwanted energies which may still be lingering around the crystal's energy field. Leave the crystal where it is and place yourself in your cleansing sanctuary. Feel the crystal being cleansed with you. Feel both yourself and the crystal tingling with additional energy as you finish the cleansing process. When you're ready, step out of your cleansing sanctuary. Take the crystal from your chakra area and place it outside your own aura.

Now lie down again and concentrate on cleansing again, closing your chakras and protecting yourself. Remember always to give thanks for the insights you have been given during your work. Be particularly careful to close down whichever chakra you have been working on, and protect it with an additional layer of loving light. Make sure you are well closed down and grounded, before you get up and continue your day.

You may want to keep separate notes of your own chakra healing with crystals and see for yourself which stones work best for you. It is very important you go through the process of working with crystals and your own chakras before you try using crystals to work with others. When you feel you have gained a certain, deeper understanding of the powers of crystals, then you may want to take the process even deeper and use crystals to help increase your own healing work.

This is a very sensitive area. The fact is that some people simply are not suited to crystals being used on them. They may find them too powerful or too intrusive for their own subtle energy fields. They may have got used to your own gentle energy and the additional effects of a crystal being used can literally make them feel as though they have had an electric shock. It can be very unsettling.

Of course, not everyone is that sensitive. Some people find them wonderfully helpful and just feel an additional sense of well-being when they are used. So the secret is to introduce any crystal work slowly and gently, constantly checking how the person you are healing feels about the experience. If it makes them feel uncomfortable or nervous in any way, stop the process. Be very aware through each stage of how they are responding. Never push them to accept something they are not happy with.

The best way to start introducing crystals into your healing sanctuary is just to place one somewhere within it before you start a session. Do not place it too near your healing chair in case it makes the person feel uncomfortable. When they arrive, show them the crystal and ask them if they like the new addition to the room. If they are intrigued and respond favourably, ask them if they would like to hold it. Then ask them for feedback. If they immediately say it feels good, ask if they would like to hold a crystal during a healing session.

If they like the prospect, then your best option is to have a small dish of different crystals from which they can choose one. Ask them to tune in to the crystals and decide which one feels right or which one seems to leap out at them. Try to have a variety of colours, shapes and sizes. By letting them choose themselves, it often makes them feel comfortable and in charge of the situation. It does not really matter whether this first stone is the most beneficial for them. It is simply paving the way for the future. Make a note of which stone they chose in your healing diary.

There is one note of caution here. If you know the person you are healing has cancer or a tumour of any kind, do not let them choose a green stone. The difficulty with green is that it is often used for growth in different aspects of life. You do not want to unwittingly encourage growth of a cancerous condition. Of course, it does not follow that you necessarily will, but it is best to be safe in these circumstances.

Once they have chosen, suggest they hold the crystal in their hand whilst you heal. They may prefer to let it rest in their lap or, if they are lying down, to let the crystal lie somewhere near their body. Let them use it in a way that they feel comfortable. During that first healing session, do not work with the crystal yourself. Simply ask them at various times if the crystal feels different – hot or cold, for example, or pulsing or still, and listen to what they say. Notice which chakra you are near when they comment. Let them feel safe with this new tool and follow the same procedure for the next few sessions, always letting them choose their own crystal. You may soon notice a pattern from their behaviour and their choice alone may help you in determining their healing progress.

Once they have accepted the presence and effect of crystals, you can try to take it a stage further. For this, your best choice is a clear crystal that is small and held comfortably in your hand. Ideally, it should have one pointed end through which you can direct and focus energy. You may already have one in your collection and know it is right for you. You may want to spend some time finding the right crystal. There is no rush because you will find what is suitable when you are ready. Now you want to enhance your relationship with this crystal such that it becomes a more powerful focus for you.

Crystal energy

To do this, you need to spend some time increasing your energies with the crystal. Again, cleanse it thoroughly, carry it with you, hold it in your hand whenever you meditate. After a few weeks, you may feel sufficiently bonded to work at a deeper level. Try the effect of this on your own body first before experimenting on anyone else.

Hold the crystal in your hand as you open up in your usual way. Focus and balance yourself. Ask for help from above in your work. Concentrate on feeling the cosmic energy above and all around you and then flowing through you. Feel your own personal reaction as the cosmic energy sweeps down your arm and into the hand that holds the crystal. Now feel the energy as it flows through the crystal and out through the tip, which should be pointing away from you.

Notice what you feel as the energy surges through from your hand and into the crystal. Is it a different sensation from your normal healing responses? Does your hand feel hotter or cooler suddenly? Perhaps you have a different tingling or tickly sensation in your hand. What do you feel happening as you focus the energy through the crystal itself?

If you see auras quite easily and often see colours around people as you are healing, you might notice a stream of light coming from the tip of the crystal in your hand. Now, very gently, place the crystal's end so that it points at the back of your other hand. Keep it a good 2 feet or so away. Can you feel the energy in a finely focused line, as it hits the back of your other hand? If you can't feel anything, then bring the crystal a little closer to your hand. When do you start to feel something? Now concentrate on the flow of cosmic energy through you and into the crystal. Can you feel a sudden increased surge? Put the crystal down in your lap for a moment and concentrate on sending healing energy from one hand to the other. Is there a sudden drop in energy flow? Pick up the crystal and compare it again.

Experiment with this energy through the crystal. Try focusing it at different points on your body. Are some areas more sensitive than others? When does the crystal flow feel more powerful than others? Remember to keep your awareness of the cosmic energy. Is there a part of your body which you want to heal in some way? Try pointing the crystal at the area affected. You might

even want to try letting the end of the crystal gently touch your
skin. Is that too strong or do you find the sensation pleasant?
Do you have a plant which needs healing? Try focusing the
beam on the plant and see what you feel. Can you see any light
or any energy activity taking place?

When you've finished, remember to cleanse both yourself and
the crystal. Close down thoroughly and protect yourself. Wait
for a few minutes before you get up and continue your day.

Were you surprised by how powerful the beam of energy from the crystal felt? The more you work with your crystal the more powerful the focus of energy becomes and the deeper the levels of healing you can achieve. With that also comes added responsibility for the increasing complex levels of energy which you are tapping into. Work slowly and gently with your crystal awareness, especially if dealing with others.

Of course, you might also have felt nothing! If you felt very little, then ask if someone you are healing would be prepared to experiment with crystals. You can then try using the crystal focus on them, once you have opened up and balanced yourself. Of course, you need to start at a large distance from their aura. You can always work your way slowly into the body, but notice when the person says they feel something. Ask if they feel comfortable. You may find they really enjoy the whole process and find it soothing and yet powerful. If they are someone who does not respond well, cease using crystals when working with them and return to the healing energy from your own hands.

If you and the person you are healing both feel comfortable with crystals, then experiment together with the process. Ask them to hold different crystals in their hand. Ask them to change hands, too. Ask if they mind having different crystals placed over different chakras and see how they respond.

There are also some very deep techniques for working with crystals when healing. Some experienced healers actually use them to 'dig out' blockages within people's energy fields. They can be used to repair rips in the aura or to help open chakras.

Work at this level requires a great deal of knowledge as it can be dangerous, so it is not suggested you try any of these techniques for yourself. However, it is good for you to know that the potential benefits of crystal therapy are a never-ending powerhouse of positive energy.

Your relationship with crystals can be a gradual, ever-growing process of discovery. There are so many different types of crystals. Once you are comfortable with them, you may even choose to buy larger and more powerful stones which can literally resonate throughout a space. You may find certain crystals work well in your bath or placed near it. Others are right for your working environment. Then try swapping them over and notice the effect it has on you. Always remember to keep cleansing your crystals, particularly if you use certain ones regularly in healing.

If you develop a close relationship with a number of your own crystals, then do not let others touch them. By all means, have a selection for the person you are healing to use and always cleanse those afterwards. But if you have a particular favourite with which you heal, it can be quite damaging for another person to touch it and imbue it with their energy. It is a bit like having two radio stations suddenly blaring forth at the same time. It is confusing! It does not mean anyone else has a 'bad' energy. It is just different from yours and creating a powerful healing crystal is a very personal experience that does not benefit from interference.

Through working with crystals, you will start to notice that different coloured stones seem to respond well to different people and to different situations. It is a natural progression, therefore, to now look at colour healing and its potential benefits.

COLOUR HEALING

Colour therapy works on many different levels. Whilst it can be very powerful, it can also be fraught with some pitfalls and hazards. It is important that you read through this chapter carefully before trying to put any colour healing to the test. There is one general rule which is always safe: when in doubt during colour healing, you can always visualise bright, clean white as a colour. Pulsating white is always cleansing and gentle enough not to cause harm to any part of the aura.

Let's look at why colour healing is important and how it can possibly work. Did you know that different colours actually vibrate at different frequencies? Just as different levels of our aura pulsate differently, so do colours. This also explains why certain colours will help to restore energy balance and others may actually add to the imbalance in some way.

We also respond to certain colours instinctively. When you think of the colour red do you think of it as warm and invigorating or as cool and soothing? The majority would have to say they think of red as a warm and energetic colour. Is light blue a warming colour? Most would say it is cooling and calming. We also use colour in our everyday language without realising it. 'I was green with envy.' (This, incidentally, refers to a sludge green not the beautiful grass green of the heart chakra.) 'I was in a black mood.' 'I'm feeling blue today.' 'He went ashen grey at the shock.'

You have already been increasing your own personal relationships with colour through some of the healing work you have done so far. The drawings you have done of your chakras are of particular interest. Go back and look through your seven chakra drawings from Delving Deeper into Chakras (see pages 185–94). Do you notice certain colours dominate? Even more importantly, what colours appear to be missing from most of your drawings? What colours are you not drawn to? Look through your wardrobe, walk around your house, study paintings you like and do not like. What are the colours you feel most drawn to? What are the colours you avoid?

Often, the colours we avoid are the ones we most need to help heal areas within our energy field. The reason we ignore them is because to focus upon them, or to have them regularly around us, might activate certain memories or niggling reminders of areas of our life we have yet to deal with. We would rather sweep many emotions or problems out of our mind than actually face them. Yet, until we face them and sort them out, we are no doubt creating various energy blockages and tears within our own energy system. In other words, we are denying ourselves true holistic health by our refusal to deal with this area in our lives. Let us look at some common statements people make about colours.

- *'Red and orange are tarty colours. Only common people wear them.' People who often say things like that are the very people who are denying their own sexuality and/or sensuality on some level. The reasons for this can be various: fear, childhood upbringing, past abuse, feelings of inadequacy or lack of love and so on. It can be as simple as being told as a child or adolescent that they are ugly. They then close down part of the energy surrounding their navel chakra. It is a short step to then continuing into adulthood with the belief that no one could ever want them.*

- *'Oh no, I can't wear yellow. It makes me look jaundiced.' Jaundiced in what sense? It may not reflect the physical condition of jaundice but may indicate that this person has deeper issues involving jealousy, bitterness or envy over some situation in their life. They avoid yellow because they do not want to face these areas.*

- *'I always wear black. It's so chic. You can't go wrong with black.' Black as a colour has its uses just as every colour has. Black can protect and ground you. It can help you feel safe when you are particularly vulnerable.*

This is why black is traditionally worn at funerals. Sadness makes people feel very delicate and black helps offer protection. However, always wearing black will often lead to you shutting yourself off from others. It can drain energy and other colours from your aura, too. Unless it is balanced with plenty of white, it may ultimately prove to depress you.

- *'Blue and green should never be seen.' This refers to the two colours being unharmonious together. Yet consider what in nature is blue and green. Just about everything! Yet do people feel that green trees against a blue sky is unattractive? Do green palm trees by a blue ocean look ugly together?*

The more you think of people's attitudes to colour, the more you start to question what is actually right and wrong, colour-wise. The truth is, nothing is good or bad. As everyone's aura is unique, so everyone's need for colours is a unique experience. You discover what is right for you, and others, only through practice.

Although there are rough guidelines set out for the different colours and they are a good starting point for a beginner, you will gradually develop your own personal relationship with colour, just as you did with crystal therapy. It is important you know a few basics before you start practising, but after that, only gentle experiments and time will show you the way to work with colours.

Colour testing

We are going to start off with an experiment and see how you personally respond to different colours on a spiritual level. Before you start, you need seven pieces of identically shaped and sized paper. Each piece needs to be a different colour: red, orange, yellow, green, blue, purple and white. You should be able to find inexpensive, multicoloured writing pads in stationery shops. Do not worry if you cannot find the exact shade of blue, green, purple and so on that you want. A reasonable proximity is enough for this experiment. If you prefer to use small pieces of fabric in different colours, that is also fine, but make sure the fabric is identical in size and feel.

Start by laying the seven pieces of paper or fabric out in front of you. Without concentrating too much, just run your hands gently over the tops of the colours. Do they feel different? Do your hands tingle more on some than others? Do you feel different temperatures? You might find some colours don't feel very comfortable and others you want to linger over. If you feel very little difference during this, it does not matter, but spend a little time exploring how you feel about these colours. The more you notice your different reactions, the easier the experiment becomes. Wash away any sensations you don't like.

Now close your eyes. You want to keep your eyes closed throughout, right until the end. Pick up the seven papers or fabrics and shuffle them in your hands. Keeping your eyes closed, lay them out again in random order. With your eyes still shut, take a moment to focus your thoughts. Concentrate on your breathing, open up your chakras and ask for help during the exercise.

When you're ready, and still keeping your eyes closed, feel for one of the pieces of paper or fabric and either let your hand rest over it, or pick it up and hold it. What is the first colour which comes into your head? (Don't open your eyes and check on any until you have finished the whole exercise.) This isn't a guessing exercise where you play a game for fun. This is testing your own individual response to colour. You don't need to see a colour to respond to it. Each colour vibrates at a different level and you can feel the difference through sensory awareness alone. This exercise is to help appreciate that. Try not to rush the process. When you feel you know which colour you are holding, then put it down, cleanse quickly, and pick up another piece. Again, tune in to the colour and see what it feels like. Go through all seven pieces and decide what they may be, before you then open your eyes.

How many did you choose correctly? What is your relationship
with the ones you guessed right? Are they colours you are
particularly fond of, or ones you do not like having around
all the time? You might start keeping a colour diary and
noticing your changing response to different colours.

Make sure you cleanse thoroughly and close down. Check
you are focused and balanced before you get up again.

Don't worry if this experiment has little effect on you. You might go
back to it again at a later stage and find it more effective. It doesn't
mean you can't work well with colours now. You may simply want
to work with them in a visual way to appreciate their true power.

Let's progress our relationship with colours by studying some
established guidelines with the seven chakra colours with which
we are already familiar. We are also going to add several others
which may be useful. Some of what you read may be familiar from
your present understanding of the chakras and their functions. You
may also find a few insights that help you appreciate why you
personally like certain colours and dislike others. Always
remember that these are guidelines to help you in the early stages
of colour appreciation. They are not strict rules to which every
colour healer will adhere. It is important, however, that you have
some degree of understanding so you can practise safely.

The seven chakra colours

Red is used to stimulate and recharge energies. It helps increase
your relationship with the physical world – both appreciation of it
and your will to remain earth-bound. It warms cold areas and
activates sluggish systems.

It can help with colds, poor circulation, anaemia and multiple
sclerosis. It can offer a surge of pure physical vitality. It affects all
areas related to the base chakra such as the lower part of the body,
the spinal column, the adrenals (endocrine organs which produce
hormones) and the kidneys.

Do not use red with high-blood pressure problems. It can generally overexcite and aggravate conditions if used too intensely.

Use **orange** to strengthen the immune system and to increase sexual energy. It is helpful after illness to build up the physical body again. Orange also helps to increase your ambition and to promote emotional stability.

It can assist with sexual complaints, pneumonia and multiple sclerosis. It affects all areas within the navel chakra, such as the reproductive system (ovaries in women, testes in men) and our immune system.

Orange, if overused, can agitate mental conditions.
If sexual intimacy is a major issue, use orange sparingly.

Yellow helps clear the mind and promote mental agility and clarity. If the head feels 'foggy', yellow can help shift the stagnant energy. It can give more confidence and help learning processes. It also assists with mental depression.

Yellow is good for stomach complaints, indigestion, bladder problems, loss of appetite and kidney malfunctions. It relates to the solar plexus chakra which covers the stomach, liver, gall bladder, pancreas, spleen and nervous system.

If yellow is overused, it can lead to anxiety with troubled thoughts. Whilst it can help eradicate headaches, if used too vigorously it could actually create the sensation of a headache.

Green is extremely important in healing as it flows from the heart and gives wonderful unconditional love. It gives a sense of everything being all right with your life. It promotes peace, truth and quiet calm. It offers hope and balances energies, giving a good sense of perspective. It helps growth in all areas of life.

It can be useful in treating overactive thyroids, high blood pressure, ulcers and nervous disorders. It relates to the heart chakra and therefore the heart, circulatory system, upper back, thymus gland and vagus nerve, which supplies the heart, lungs and other major organs.

However, never use green when dealing with cancer or any other condition with tumours or malignancy because it may encourage growth, rather than shrinkage.

Blue promotes a sense of calm. It is cooling and peaceful. It soothes agitated conditions. It can help people to speak with truth and clarity, whilst encouraging their sensitivity to spiritual issues. It encourages inspiration and creativity. It is also considered a good antiseptic colour. It is used a great deal with healing children. (You may remember from Healing Children (pages 274–83) that a young child's energy field is predominately blue. Other colours come into their aura as they grow.)

Blue is helpful for underactive thyroids, feverish conditions, abscesses, burns and nausea. It is related to the throat chakra which governs the thyroid gland (which secretes hormones that regulate body growth and metabolism), bronchi (passages leading into your lungs), lungs and alimentary canal (where food is digested). The ears can also be affected.

Whilst blue is one of the safest colours to work with, too much blue may create a lack of physical energy and vitality.

Purple (which also veers into indigo and violet in hue) is used to help balance and harmonise the different levels of energy in the aura and brings you to greater understanding of spiritual concepts. It is good for purifying the body and also detoxifying.

It helps in cases of cancer, infection, leukaemia and diabetes. It is related to the brow chakra and connects to the lower brain, left eye, ears, nose, nervous system and pituitary gland. Most head and face conditions respond to this colour.

Too much purple can promote depression and/or headaches. It is a colour which vibrates at a high frequency and is therefore quite powerful, so use it gently and carefully.

White is purifying and cleansing. It also eases pain. It helps expand the aura. It will increase your connection with others on a spiritual level. It offers peace and comfort.

It is connected to the crown chakra and therefore relates to the upper brain and right eye.

It is always used both in the beginning and ending of a healing colour session. Used at the beginning, it increases the intensity of any colours which are then used. At the conclusion, white is cleansing and energising. White light is never harmful.

Remember, none of these guidelines is definitive. You will have to experiment and learn for yourself what works best for you and the individuals to whom you offer healing. Don't be misled into thinking only one colour is used for treating an ailment. As you now know, physical conditions are usually the result of a past experience which has not yet been cleared from our energy field.

To say, for instance, that a cold simply needs red to cure it is oversimplifying the case. What caused the cold to manifest itself in the first place? Is there an underlying sense of feeling unloved or unappreciated, or stress from a past or present situation which has not yet cleared from their aura? To heal with colours you constantly have to keep digging deeper into spiritual awareness and ask for help in using appropriate colours.

Other useful colours

As beneficial as the seven chakra colours can be, other colours are also useful during healing as they perform additional functions. Let's have a look, in slightly less detail, at the powers of pink, silver, gold, brown and black.

Pink is very good for generating a soft, generous love for others. It is soothing in emotion. It is useful for releasing anger or feelings of neglect. It does not just work on the emotional level as it can also help with skin inflammations and disorders. A deeper pink hue, going towards rose, can release a stronger sense of love for others and is helpful for heart and lung conditions.

Silver has similar qualities to white, in that it can help amplify and accentuate the healing process. It is also used, however, as a means of purging energy fields of unwanted debris and can work effectively in cauterising torn areas of an aura after healing. Silver is a useful aid in increasing meditative concentration as it speeds up vibrations and aids communication with spiritual energies. It has a high vibrational frequency and therefore should be used with more caution than white.

Gold is powerful in enhancing higher awareness and increasing your own power to work effectively. It helps you to connect with the true source of cosmic energy and allows you greater spiritual expression. It works at a very fine frequency as it resonates with the energy in the seventh layer of your aura. Gold is always recommended in the treatment of cancerous conditions, as indications are that cancer creates a rip in the seventh layer of the aura.

Many people have a dislike of **brown** but it is a powerful and useful colour when handled correctly. It aids deep appreciation of, and connection to, the Earth. It will ground people and stabilise them if they are in an over-excited condition. It can leave people with a renewed sense of perspective and bring them back down to Earth in a comfortable, controlled manner. Too much brown, however, could be depressing.

Black is another colour with which many people struggle and in truth it is difficult to handle well. It must always be balanced with white, to avoid overuse. When used well, black can help lead you within, spiritually, and show you deep peace and an unearthly calm which nurtures and educates. A very soft, smooth, deep, velvet black can be uplifting and provide a heavenly, safe womb for meditation and higher states of awareness. It can also help you come to terms with death and truly understand its process. Black will help to heal bones.

> *However, excessive use of black can lead to depression and a sense of being cut off from everyone and everything. If you, or the person you are healing, have a tendency towards 'black moods', then avoid using this colour until you are more experienced and confident with your understanding of colour healing.*

Do you feel you are developing a clearer understanding of some of the benefits of working with colours? You need to study the different indications of each colour and have a good working relationship with them before you try healing others with colour. You also have to learn how to create colour and to offer it in a healing way.

Colour-charging the aura

To simply imagine a colour, and then picture it coming out of your hands or solar plexus area, will not necessarily create a right colour. When you *think* of a colour, do you know what colour is created by the process of thought? Yellow. Yellow is the colour of thought, of mental images and energies. Therefore, if you just *think* pink, you will give out yellow. If you think red or green or blue, the same thing will happen. Thought creates yellow. This may sound confusing to you. If you do not think the colour into being, what else are you supposed to do? How can you possibly give out a colour without thinking it first?

You perform colour healing by *becoming* a colour, not by thinking about the colour. There is a subtle difference in this action. If you think it, you are using your own energy, your own thoughts, your own ego, in creation of the colour. If you simply become the colour, then you are not actively involved in the process. Remember how we never use our own energy to heal others. Colour healing is no different. We simply become the colour and then let the Cosmic Energy flow through us and impart that colour into someone else's aura at the level at which it is most beneficial for them. So how can we possibly become a colour without thinking it? To help you work your way onto this new level of understanding, you can use the physical exercise below as a stepping stone. Try this when you have some time alone, so you do not feel self-conscious as you work your way through the mechanics of it.

First look at the illustrations on page 333 which demonstrate the movement needed. Practise the movement on its own first of all, before you add colour to it.

Start by standing with your feet about 12 inches apart and your hands by your side. Bend your knees and breathe out (keep your feet flat on the floor). Now straighten your legs and breathe in (feet remain flat on the floor). Repeat several times until you feel comfortable with the rhythm. When you're ready, add the arm movements. Raise your arms, elbows bent so your hands are in front of your chest, palms towards the ground. Now, as you bend your knees, let your arms sweep down in front of you and then straighten your arms as you start to straighten your legs. Let your arm movement continue up in a sweeping movement in front of you and then return back to the starting position. Then continue the movement so it becomes one continuous circular expression. Practise this for a few minutes. Check you are breathing out as you bend your knees and in again as you straighten them. When you are happy with the physical movement, move on to the colour work.

You now want to breathe in a colour every time you breathe in during the exercise. You want to start with red and work through all the chakra colours. You feel the colour filling every part of you. You pull the colour up from the ground through your feet and hands. It fills the air around you; you pull it in through every pore of your body. Remember, you are not visualising the colour, you are not thinking the colour, you are becoming the colour and accepting its

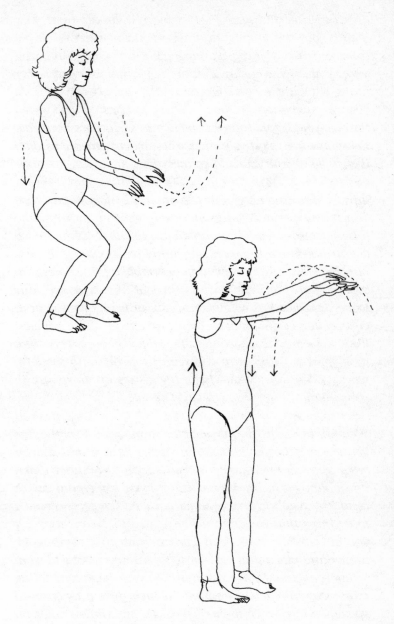

The movement for colour-charging the aura.

presence and strength. Every time you breathe out, you breathe out the same colour. Can you see the red coming from your aura? Keep working with the colour until you know you are the colour. You are not thinking about red or trying to create it, you simply are *the colour red. Wait until you have experienced the pulsating, energising flow of red through you, before you move on to orange. Always remember to breathe the colour out after you have breathed it in. Feel the whole of your aura filled with the colour, not just your physical body. You have totally* become *the colour.*

You may experience odd sensations or emotions as you do this. As you increase your relationship with colour, so each colour will come to mean something personal to you. You may have an image or emotion or symbol which comes with each colour. You may have an insight as to how you may work best with this colour. You will probably find certain colours more difficult to become than others. Those are most likely to be the colours you most need for your own personal development. Make sure you return to work with them on several occasions. Write down the results of your work in your Colour Diary for further reference.

When you have worked through all seven colours, make sure you cleanse thoroughly with the white light. Stand still for a few minutes and make sure you are properly closed down and balanced before you move off to do something else. It would be helpful for you to write down the seven colours and your initial reaction to them in your colour diary. If you feel confident, you can work through pink, silver, gold, brown and black and see how those colours react with you. Whatever colours you want to use in your healing sessions, make sure you have experienced them first and charged your own aura with them, before you practise on others.

You don't have to go through this physical exercise as you heal others. This is being used as a means for you to open your spiritual awareness to colours and experience them for yourself. The more you bond with the different energies of different colours the more quickly and effectively you can use them when healing others. Remember, you are working towards *becoming* a colour, not visualising it. If you only visualise colours and therefore give off nothing but yellow around you, you and the people you are healing are liable to end up with hefty headaches! Practise and practise again charging your aura with different colours. When you know you are ready, slowly introduce colours into your healing sessions.

Colour healing technique

As with all new techniques, check how the people you are healing feel about colour healing. Talk to them first about their relationship with colours and what they like best. You might choose to have different coloured fabric, sheets of paper or coloured pens and ask them what colours they like most. Ask them what they like least. Make a note of them in their healing diary and see how their preferences change over the different sessions. Always make it clear that you can stop using colours if they want to or if they find it uncomfortable. Let us look at how you can heal others using colour.

As always, you want the person you are healing to be comfortable and relaxed. Ask them to let you know if they notice anything different during or after the healing session.

You want to open up in the usual way. Relax and focus your thoughts. As usual, offer your short prayer and ask for guidance that you may use the right colours. Have the cosmic energy sweep through you and around you. Now step forward in their aura and start the healing session in your usual way. Tune in to each of their chakras but notice this time whether the colour seems bright and energetic enough for each centre. Don't offer colour healing at this stage, just notice what you sense is happening colour-wise in each chakra.

When you have worked through all seven chakras, then stand back and feel white light pouring through and around all of you. Transfer that white light into all of the other person's aura. Let it cascade round and through them. Let it be as powerful and pulsate as vividly as possible. When you have charged both your aura and theirs with beautiful, white light, move back and concentrate on their chakras again, starting at the base.

Is the base chakra vibrating with rich, warm red? Is their navel chakra bright orange both front and back? You now want to start colour healing through their chakras, but make sure you offer this gently. Keep a good distance from their physical body and when you know you need to offer a colour to help them, concentrate on becoming that colour first. Feel your body and aura swell with that colour. Ask that the appropriate level be released through your hands or solar plexus into that area. Make sure you are not lost in the pleasurable experience of becoming different colours and ignoring the other person's individual needs. Remember, too much of any colour can damage. Be responsible and loving in your actions. Keep asking for guidance all the time. Work through each chakra slowly and carefully, maintaining a reasonable distance all the time.

Step back and observe the person's aura. Can you now see colours emanating from different areas of their body? (Once you work at a deeper level with colours, it becomes quite normal and comfortable to see colours around others.) Can you see dark areas or brightly pulsing spots that you had not noticed before? If it feels appropriate, go towards those areas and use whatever colour you are told will help that particular area. If in doubt at all, use soft white light to help the healing process.

When you know you have done enough, step back and cleanse and energise them with the white light. Gently close their chakras and protect them. Is the cloak of protection which you offer them a different colour this time?

Then cleanse, close, ground and protect yourself. Notice if your own cloak has changed in colour or texture through your colour healing. Make sure you get proper feedback from the person and see how different, if at all, they found the whole experience. Ensure both of you drink some mineral water. Make sure you work with colour on different occasions and note any changes that take place.

Colour healing can be extremely intricate and complex. It is possible to perform certain 'surgical techniques' on a spiritual level, using colours to help the healing process. Many experienced healers can use a colour to completely cleanse a level of the aura, then use another to sterilise this operation, another to cauterise or 'sew' any rips and a final colour to protect and aid healing. It is not suggested that you will work at this level, but the more you understand colour therapy and its benefits, the deeper the level at which you can work. Only time and gentle, constant practice will help your personal development in this area.

HEALING THROUGH SOUND

We have already discussed healing through sound in a number of exercises such as Verbally Releasing Anger (see page 145) and also Cleansing a Room Through Sound (see page 226). However, these are just tiny manifestations of what is a much more powerful healing tool. We have talked about how music can be of great benefit while healing and you have been encouraged to use appropriate music whilst healing and to ask the person you are working with what they would prefer. All these experiments may have now increased your awareness of how certain types of music can be extremely helpful. You may have added additional sounds from nature such as bird song, dolphins and waterfalls to test their usefulness and found they, too, can work at quite a deep level. A purring cat resting on your chest is another wonderful example of healing sound.

So why are some sounds so helpful to us, whilst others are very discordant and disturbing to our energies? Just as colours all vibrate at different frequencies, so do sounds. The vibrations of sound are affected by a number of conditions: resonance, rhythm, melody, harmony, pitch and timbre. Different vibrations will affect different chakras; specific sounds can actually activate and heal each chakra and enable it to spin at a faster frequency. We are going to look at this in more detail later.

However, to start with we are going to look briefly at some research done by a Swiss scientist, physician and musician, Dr Hans Jening. He studied the relationship between sound and form (known as cymatics) and the results of his work actually help clarify what physically happens when sound occurs. One of his tests consisted of placing very fine grains of sand upon a metal plate. He then sent different, unbroken streams of sound through the plate. What he discovered was that every sound created a different pattern of sand on the plate. Not only that, but the shapes remained consistent. For instance, if he started with one sound, moved on to another and then returned to the first, the grains of sand would form one pattern and then another before reforming exactly into the first pattern again. Certain sounds created harmonious, symmetrical shapes; others produced chaotic, disjointed formations.

It was a British osteopath, Dr Guy Manners, who took this one step further by trying to create a three-dimensional form from sound. Working with Dr Jening, he used more than one frequency, simultaneously directed through the metal plate, to encourage three-dimensional imagery. They discovered that two, three or four combined frequencies made no difference. However, as soon as five were used at the same time, three-dimensional images began to form. Dr Manners went on to create a machine which reproduced these different combined sounds. This machine is now recognised and used throughout the world. Tests show it has a dramatic effect upon human energy fields and can help realign and charge energy systems.

This work with cymatics has helped move the power of sound healing into a more readily understandable and acceptable healing tool. Of course, we can look back to ancient eras to appreciate that sound has always been important. Every spiritual movement in history has been associated with sound, whether it be through chanting, mantric repetition or the use of ancient instruments such as drums and rattles. Early spiritual civilisations were very aware and utterly in tune with the rhythm of nature and its very life force.

There are Egyptian medical notes on papyri dating back over 2,600 years which talk about certain incantations being cures for ailments such as infertility and insect bites. Alexander the Great, in approximately 324BC, was said to have had his sanity restored by music from the lyre. Great composers through the years paid great attention to the therapeutic use of their compositions. Handel apparently said that he did not want to amuse his audience with his music; he wanted to 'make them better'. Many singers through history are reputed to have cured people of their ills through their singing, including Philip V of

Spain who was serenaded by a famous operatic performer of the 18th century, Farinelli, and was thereby discovered to be cured of a chronic illness. Of course, the accuracy of some of these events is difficult to prove nowadays.

What we can do, is work constructively with sound ourselves and see what effect it has on us. We are going to look at how different pitches of musical notes are affiliated to different chakras and see how their sound affects us.

There is also the aspect of different musical instruments being more in tune with certain chakras. For instance, the drums are very good for grounding and therefore useful for both the base and navel chakras. Percussion instruments also come into this category. The solar plexus and heart chakras respond well to the flute and woodwind section. The throat, brow and crown are more susceptible to the harp and also to wind chimes. Certain instruments such as the piano, when played in different ways, can benefit all the chakras. These are not rigid rules to which you should adhere; they are simply guidelines from which you can start your own exploration.

You can make a start to appreciate the differences just by humming two very different notes. Take a good, deep breath and then hum any low note, it does not matter which. What can you feel vibrating? How does it make you feel? Do you feel secure and well-grounded? Now take another deep breath and hum any high note you choose. How do you feel now? Are you grounded? What part of you is vibrating? Notice what different images or colours you experience. Whatever happened, you will appreciate that there is a vast difference between a very high and a very low note. Your whole physical body and auric field react very differently to each. Now we have to work on a more individual basis and see how your own energy responds.

Below is a list of the chakras and the musical note which is generally attributed to each one:

Base	Middle C
Navel	D
Solar plexus	E

Heart	F
Throat	G
Brow	A
Crown	B

Remember that these notes are guidelines only. You now need to experiment to see how you personally respond to these notes.

Healing yourself through sound

It would help if you have a piano or other musical instrument which offers the musical scale. A cheap recorder would be sufficient to start with, or a child's musical keyboard. If you can sing in pitch yourself, use the scale to help you pitch the right note. (It is often useful to think of 'Doh, Re, Mi' from *The Sound of Music* to help you get the right note.) Through the following exercise, it would make it easier if you recorded the seven different sounds on your phone or computer which you then played as you relaxed.

Start off by sitting comfortably and relaxing. Concentrate on your breathing. Open up your chakras and focus on the cosmic energy.

Now start by playing the note of Middle C. Focus on the sound as it vibrates and gradually fades into the distance. Can you feel any activity in your base chakra area? Play the note again. Sustain it for a longer period of time. Is anything happening to you? Now try humming the pitch yourself. Often it takes your own sound to activate the chakra's energy. Let the vibration of the sound fade away into the distance. Notice if the chakra movement continues. What did you feel was happening?

Now move up to the navel chakra and experience the sound of D above Middle C. Go through the same process and notice how you feel. Work your way, one by one, through to the crown chakra and the note of B. Notice all the changes which occur.

Now try skipping from Middle C up to B and then back again. (If you can only do it octave by octave, do not worry. Skip up to C and then back to Middle C.) What effect does this have on you? Try going from note to note more quickly. Skip notes, slide up and down the scale. Change from a hum to an 'ah' sound. Then use an 'oh' sound. Lastly move to an 'um' sound. Be aware of any sounds which feel uncomfortable.

When you've finished, cleanse thoroughly and close down. Pull your cloak of protection securely around you. Wait for a few minutes before you get up.

You may have been surprised by the effect of the notes on you. If you already have a close affinity to, and appreciation of, music and sound you may have responded quickly and favourably to the different notes. You may feel your chakras tingling pleasantly afterwards. If you felt very little and perhaps felt rather silly during the exercise, you might want to repeat the experience on another occasion, but this time use a piece of music which has been written in the key of the note. Below are a few suggestions for each chakra:

Base	Schubert's *March Militaire*
	Holst's *Mars Music*
	Brahms's *Symphony No. 1 in C Minor*
Navel	Mozart's *Divertimento in D*
	Brahms's *Hungarian Dance No. 5*
	Pachelbel's *Canon in D*
	Mahler's *Symphony No. 1 in D Major*
Solar plexus	Mozart's *Symphony No. 39 in E-flat Major*
	Chopin's *Tristesse Etude in E Major*
	Mozart's *Piano Concerto No. 26*
	Mozart's *Horn Concerto in E-flat*

Heart	Bach's *Brandenburg Concerto in F Major*
	Debussy's *Clair de Lune*
	Scriabin's *Piano Concerto in F Sharp Minor*
	Beethoven's *Symphony No. 8 in F*
Throat	Bach's *Brandenburg Concerto in G Major*
	Schubert's *Ave Maria*
	Rossini's *String Sonata No. 1 in G*
Brow	Mendelssohn's *String Quartet in A Major*
	Schubert's *Piano Quintet in A Major*
	Beethoven's *Piano Sonata No. 28 in A Major*
	Schumann's *Piano Concerto in A Minor*
Crown	Dvorak's *Cello Concerto in B Minor*
	Tchaikovsky's *Symphony No. 6 in B Minor*
	Schubert's *Unfinished Symphony No. 8 in B Minor*
	Brahms's *Clarinet Quintet in B Minor*

Of course, there are many other appropriate pieces of music and you need to experiment to see what works best for you. It is also possible to find your own chakras responding to slightly different notes. It is interesting to realise that the highly respected American healer Barbara Ann Brennan works with sound using different notes for each chakra. She has experienced positive healing results by using the following:

Base	G (below Middle C)
Navel	D
Solar plexus	F
Heart	G
Throat	A
Brow	D
Crown	G

You can see there is a difference between the way Barbara Ann Brennan works and the methlods used by some other healers.

Yet neither is right or wrong. You can only work with what is right for you. To find what is individually true for you, you need to experiment with the different notes.

The same is also true, of course, when you work with others. Once you have developed some confidence through working on yourself with sound, it would help increase your understanding of the power of healing in this field if you start practising on others. Choose someone who you know is already fond of music and enjoys having different music playing during the healing session.

If you feel unsure of yourself, you can start off simply by playing a piece of music which you know is in a certain key and testing their response to the music afterwards. While you are healing them, spend a little extra time over the particular chakra involved and see what additional sensations you can pick up this time. If you know that a person needs special attention to a certain chakra, you can put on appropriate music for them during the healing. Once you have experimented with different music, you will get to know how different chakras are affected. Remember, also, that what works for you will not necessarily work for someone else. Always tune in to the individual needs of the person you are healing. Ask for help from above if you are not sure what is best for them.

Healing others through sound

To work more specifically on someone else's chakra, you might try recording the seven different notes together, letting each sound last for a good few seconds, and then try working in the following way. You may feel embarrassed initially by the closeness of this exercise but if you can get over that stage, you may find it very powerful as a healing tool.

Ask the person you are healing to sit or lie comfortably (lying is preferable, but only if they feel happy with that position). Explain you will be using sound to help balance their energies and ask them to give feedback as you work with them. Then open up as usual, relax and call upon the cosmic energy.

Again, feel it working through you at all times. Go through the chakras of the person you are healing and tune in to each.

Now put on the music and let the first note play (Middle C). Place your hands over the base chakra (not too near!) and feel any response. Also look and see whether there is any activity in their aura. Often you will see colours during sound healing.

As the note dies away on the tape, hum the note yourself, concentrating to let the cosmic energy work through you. Notice any difference through vocalising the sound yourself. Ask them if they feel anything themselves.

Now ask them to hum the note with you. Again see if there is further activity in the area of the chakra. (If you feel really confident and are very comfortable with the person you are healing, you can try moving your mouth closer to their chakra and actually humming into the energy centre itself. Only do this if both of you feel comfortable. Stop immediately if they experience any discomfort.)

Now go through all seven of their chakras and repeat the same procedure with each subsequent note. There may be areas which the person finds too sensitive or uncomfortable. Simply cleanse, close and protect that chakra with an extra beam of pure, white light and then move on.

To help the healing process, ask the person to also visualise the colour associated with each chakra during the sound healing. An interesting situation often develops. If there is an imbalance in a chakra, they often find it difficult to visualise that colour. If sound has helped to restore the balance, they suddenly find it easier to see the colour in their mind's eye. Any difficulty with a particular colour usually means they would benefit from healing on the related chakra. (This also applies to your own energy system, of course.)

Always practise with your usual sensitivity during this healing. You may be amazed at the effect sound has on someone's chakras. It is often a tangible sensation which you can appreciate, as well as the person you are healing.

As it can be so powerful, you must make an extra effort to cleanse and close down their chakras when you have finished. Protect them with extra light. Give them an extra cloak of protection afterwards. Thank them for their willingness to participate in the experiment. Make sure you cleanse and close down properly yourself. Protect yourself thoroughly before you finish. Discuss your results as you drink your mineral water and make sure you clean your space afterwards.

If you found the results to be disappointing during the sound healing session, try using a different note for each chakra (trying using Barbara Ann Brennan's notes and see if the person responds more to those). Don't be afraid to experiment and keep practising continually with different sounds.

Work with different New Age recordings and spend time absorbing the sounds of nature and see how your own chakras respond. Then notice how someone else may feel totally differently about something which you find wonderful. Some people find dolphin noises, for instance, to be soothing and spiritually uplifting; others actually liken the sound to nails scratching across a blackboard!

If you feel you work well with sound and would like to try enhancing the quality of and power of sound healing, you can also add a particular vowel sound to each chakra's note. The actual tone of the sound you release, as well as the pitch, can assist the healing process. Below is the chart showing each related sound:

Base	Middle C	Ooo
Navel	D	Oh
Solar plexus	E	Ah
Heart	F	Ay
Throat	G	Eh
Brow	A	Ee
Crown	B	Ee
To balance all chakras together (use any comfortable note):		Om

Working with these additional sounds does intensify the healing process and can be an emotional experience. Ensure that you experiment with these vowel sounds on your own first of all, before working with others. In particular, the sound of 'Om' is often used as a mantra in deep meditation. Work with this sound by yourself and understand its hidden depths before you encourage others to do the same.

As always, ask for guidance and love during sound healing sessions. Ask that you always be shown how to use the appropriate level of sound for each person, including yourself. Keep a sound healing diary to record your findings so that you can compare different responses and remember how to work individually for each person you heal.

Strictly speaking, massage itself does not have to come under the realms of spiritual healing because it can also be a very pleasant physical relaxation, without necessarily having spiritual benefits attributed to it. There are also a number of situations in which some massage techniques are inadvisable, such as after a recent operation or during pregnancy. It is important that medical advice is sought before embarking on treatment. However, provided you are in a position to enjoy it, massage can be wonderfully beneficial, If you are tense or your muscles are aching, a basic massage can help relax you. Good, deep muscle massage can be enhanced by various means, which then move it into the realms of a deeply spiritual experience.

To start our appreciation of massage on a deeper level, it is helpful to refer back for a moment to our discussion of the Hologram theory in Our Individual Spiritual Path (pages 173–84). Do you remember the concept that each part of us actually contains the memory or subtle energy of all of us? (Refer back to page 180 for these details.) If you start to look into different forms of massage, we find this theory can also be applied successfully.

The best known form of this is reflexology. Reflexology is the massage of both feet to promote health throughout the entire body. The way this works is that each part of each foot is representative of different sections of the human body. If you look at the illustrations on page 350 you will see how comprehensive this is. Everything in the body can be felt through a point in the foot. Apart from this being an interesting analogy with the Hologram Theory, it is also connected to the energy meridians which run through all our body and with which acupuncturists and shiatsu practitioners work. We are reputed to have more than 72,000 energy meridians throughout our body and many of these are said to end in points of the feet. In dealing with all aspects of holistic health, we are constantly being reminded how each and every part of us is connected to something else. Therefore when we damage one part of ourselves, another part is often affected.

Reflexology is not a technique you can learn overnight. It takes considerable study and practice before you can identify the different areas during massage and learn how best to massage and to manipulate them. There is also more than one form of reflexology. The Metamorphic Technique, for example, is very different from more orthodox approaches.

A basic foot massage will remind us that we often neglect this very important part of our body. We spend so much time on our feet and often cram them into unsuitable and restrictive attire, yet how often do we ever pamper, acknowledge and appreciate them? Many of us have negative attitudes to feet and associate them as unsavoury, often smelly, parts of our body, which we need to keep hidden. Reflexology can create a shift in awareness and appreciation of feet. If you feel drawn to foot massage and can see it as a powerful healing tool, then do make sure you seek the services of a good teacher.

Similar healing can be carried out on both the hands (in Kirlian photography, each part of the hand is also representative of different parts of the body), although the practice of hand massage is not so widely used. General consensus seems to be that more energy meridians can be found in the feet than the hands.

There are also all-over body massages which deal very much with the energies of the subtle bodies. Shiatsu is gaining popularity in the Western world and many people have had great benefits from it. It is an ancient Japanese technique which works on the basis of contact with various pressure points in the body. These are again related to the energy meridians. The word shiatsu itself is Japanese and comes from 'shi' meaning finger and 'atsu' meaning pressure. Therapists often will use more than their fingers: thumbs, whole hands, elbows, knees and feet are all common tools. Shiatsu is also very much a spiritual art in that it acknowledges the need for the healer to be focused, grounded and in tune with the person they are working on. They need to

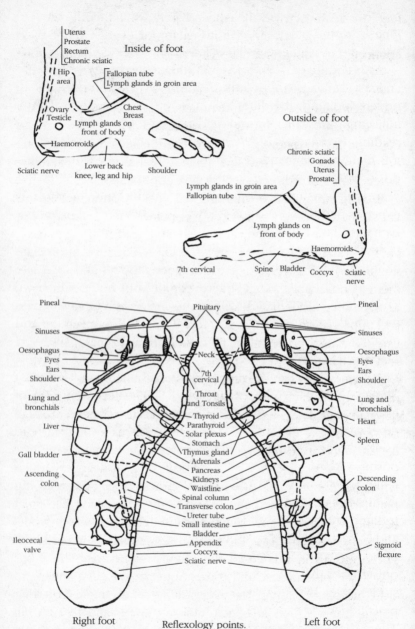

Reflexology points.

practise centring and balancing their own energies, they need to tune in to the other person's breathing pattern and work with awareness of their energy meridians at all times.

As it requires a good working knowledge of the position of at least 14 main meridians through the body and also an understanding of the different ways to apply pressure, it is not a healing form which lends itself to practise after a few pages of reading. However, it is certainly a holistic form of massage and it is highly recommended as an experience. If you can afford to do so, treat yourself to a shiatsu massage and see how it makes you feel. Ensure you find a reputable practitioner. By experiencing it for yourself, you will be able to decide if it is a path you would like to go down and study further.

Lesser-known techniques which are linked under massage, although they work differently, are Rolfing and Pulsing. Rolfing is a relatively recent practice, developed in the 1930s by Ida Rolf. The treatment is a form of deep massage which focuses on an individual's relationship to gravity. Great emphasis is placed on creating a structurally balanced body with parts of the body placed vertically over the other: knees over ankles, hip joints over knees, shoulders over hip joints and ears over shoulders. The concept is that these misalignments occur from energy imbalances, often the result of earlier traumatic experiences. In other words, an emotional or mental upset can actually manifest itself physically within our body by altering our very structural posture. Rolfing seeks to re-create a healthy energy flow by realigning the body. This is done by a very deep massage which manipulates the muscles, ligaments and soft organs of the body. It differs from other well-known techniques such as osteopathy and chiropractic treatment, which concentrate on the realignment of bones and joints. Rolfing can sometimes be painful and it is only something which can be practised after a certain level of study. Again, if you have the means, visit an established Rolfing practitioner and experience the deep tissue massage for yourself. There is much evidence to show that the mental, emotional and spiritual bodies are positively affected by Rolfing.

Pulsing uses another technique but still comes under the auspices of spiritual healing. It is again a more recent holistic treatment, devised by Dr Milton Trager in Hawaii. The practitioner basically uses a gentle rocking motion on the body's skeletal system to help free tense muscles. It is then possible to affect different levels of the human energy field which can release blockages and increase flow. Again, this technique works on the basis that humans often hold negative experiences and images within their own body. The rocking motion encourages them to loosen and to let go of these traumas. An experienced practitioner will move around the body, rocking from the feet or head or any area which they intuitively feel is appropriate. Great emphasis is placed on breathing deeply and being as relaxed as possible. The pulser is encouraged to tune in to the energy and needs of the person they are rocking. The rocking itself can go from being gentle to being so slight that it appears as though nothing is happening. The healing process continues after the session has finished as energies within the person have been set in motion. It is not recommended that you practise this without professional tuition. Again, experience Pulsing for yourself if you can and decide what effect it has upon you.

More traditional forms of massage can also transcend into a spiritual healing process, often through the awareness of the masseur themselves. Many masseurs are natural healers and they instinctively work with the energies of the person they are massaging. A good masseur will know where you ache and where you need extra massage, without you having to tell them. Try massaging a friend or relative and while you do so, let your intuition guide you to the areas which most need work.

Traditional massage can also be taken into the realms of spiritual healing by adding the benefits of essential oils. Aromatherapy is rapidly becoming more and more recognised in the West as a powerful technique for balancing energies. We have already talked briefly about essential oils and how they can be useful for energising and clearing atmospheres from rooms. They have also been mentioned as being uplifting and invigorating when used during healing sessions. However, they can be even more powerful when used during a massage.

It is important to know the potential hazards of certain oils (for instance, during pregnancy it is important that you avoid certain oils such as basil, myrrh, sage and thyme) and children should always be given smaller doses. Never imbibe any essential oil and they should also be heavily diluted in a suitable carrier oil before being applied to the skin. Essential oils can be extremely powerful and their benefits are derived by using them in appropriate quantities.

When used wisely, aromatherapy is a truly wonderful enhancement to a massage and it is strongly recommended that you experience the benefits for yourself. Most good health shops will have testers of different oils which you can try. Just purchase one oil to begin with and gradually increase your collection. Good starters are lavender (excellent for relaxation), rosemary (good for re-energising), peppermint (cooling and good for nausea or headaches), marjoram (helps depression) and eucalyptus (helps with colds and other sinus-related conditions).

If you want to use it as a massage oil, place just a few drops of the essential oil into an inexpensive carrier oil such as sweet almond oil and shake vigorously. Then apply the oil sparingly over the body and massage gently. The scent can be a wonderfully uplifting experience both for the masseur and recipient, although it is the latter who benefits most as the oils actually penetrate through the layers of skin and into the body itself. If you are practising reflexology, add essential oils to the session and enjoy the added dimension of healing which occurs.

Any form of massage is basically the opportunity to effect healing through touch. The more balanced, focused, loving and aware you are, the more effective you can be in your healing through massage. Always ask for guidance from above to help show you the best way forward.

FINDING YOUR OWN SPIRITUAL HELPERS

As you work at ever deeper levels of spiritual consciousness, you may feel that some of the healing you do is not actually coming from you but is guided and aided by someone else. In fact, this is exactly what is happening. When we talk about leaving your ego behind during healing work and when you are reminded that the best way to become a healer is to make yourself into an empty vessel through which the cosmic energy can flow, these are all euphemisms for learning to let yourself be guided by and through, not only your own spiritual self, but other spiritual entities as well.

You may not find this concept surprising if you have already been working diligently at healing yourself and others. You may already know that when you do your 'best' healing, it is on the occasions when you actually do nothing at all but trust completely in a higher source. The more you work through your different healing experiences, the more sense this makes. If you still struggle with this as a concept, it may simply mean that you need to spend more time healing to fully understand and appreciate the energies with which you are working.

People often talk of wanting to find their spirit guides and this is all part of the same thing. When you were working through the exercise Finding Your Protective Animal (see page 214), you were learning to tap in to some of the protective energies around you. However, the individual energies which surround each and every one of us are not just protective. They can also be enlightening, nurturing and unconditionally loving. We each have many different, wonderful energies around us that we can always call upon when we need them. They are often there when we do not realise it. They are wiser souls than we and each is there because they serve a purpose in our life.

Some people actually believe that whilst they feel their guides around them and know that they are there to help, they do not need to actually visualise them or get to know them better. In other words, as long as they trust and work with them, they do not need to know who they are and what they do. Many people have an excellent relationship with their guides which works on this level of unconditional love and trust without needing to know more. For others, whether it be curiosity or a need to work more closely with their guides, they simply have to know. They may work best if they have 'proof' that these energies exist.

Getting to know your spiritual helpers is not necessarily a quick process. It can also be frustrating when you sense that some energy is near you but it will not reveal itself in more detail. The reason for this is simply because your spiritual guides are much wiser than you are. They know when it is right to make themselves known and when they need to stay in the background. They are only with us to perform a certain, designated function, as laid out by a higher consciousness or by God, if you prefer. It is important that they do not needlessly interfere on any level of our own spiritual development. We have to learn in our own time and at our own pace. The guides are still there with us, loving and supporting us, but they may not actively be involved in all our learning processes. Therefore, if you call upon them and they do not answer or come forward into your conscious thought, it does not mean that you are not 'doing it right' or that you cannot contact your spirit guides. It may mean that the time is not right yet.

It is also important to realise that spiritual guides always, always have an uplifting and loving energy when they come into your aura. If you ever feel uncomfortable or unhappy when calling upon your spirit guides, you have not brought a genuine guide or helper to you. Wash it away immediately. If it returns, keep washing it away. You should never feel anything other than wonderfully nurtured and completely safe with your guides. Do not let any other energies into your aura.

Connecting with your spiritual guides

It is also not possible for you to come in closer contact with your true guides without being in a state of deep relaxation and full of unconditional love. You may need to spend a little time getting yourself into a deeper state of meditation before you can connect with these lighter and finer vibrations. Make sure you are not interrupted at all during this work.

Start off by sitting or lying in a comfortable space. Have uplifting scents and objects around you. Essences which may help are rosewood, sandalwood, myrrh, angelica or frankincense. Crystals such as celestine, jasper and milky quartz are also conducive for spiritual connections. Appropriate music includes anything with the harp. There are also many New Age recordings which, although produced on synthesisers, can open your chakras to higher levels of consciousness. Dim the electric lights, place a lit candle in front of you. Sit on or wear soft, dark velvet. Colours which also help are those in the purple spectrum: indigo, violet and lavender. Experiment and see what has the greatest effect on you.

Now close your eyes and relax. Experience the Breathing into Stillness exercise on page 68. Take your time. Let every inconsequential thought evaporate into the air. Become aware only of your breath. In. Out. In. Out. In. Out. Feel all your chakras opening like beautiful flowers and pulsing gently. Notice how all the energy flows smoothly and freely between all your interconnecting energy centres. Feel at one with your physical, emotional, mental and spiritual bodies. You are complete. Whole. Acknowledge the cosmic energy above you. Let it come down and fill all of you. Breathe it in through every pore of your body. Feel your aura expand to encompass the unconditional love which it brings. Feel bathed and nurtured by the pure white energy.

Spend several moments appreciating your oneness with everything and everyone in the universe. Feel gratitude for the spiritual lessons you are now learning and the new awareness which you are embracing. Feel unconditional love spreading from your aura and reaching out into the universe as a whole. Sit in this state of thankfulness and love for a few minutes. Feel each breath coming in and going out of your body. Feel your heart beating gently and feel it connecting with the universal beat of the cosmos.

When you're ready, silently ask your spiritual guides to come closer to you. Tell them that you know they are there and that you would like to get to know them better. Gently ask them to come into your aura. Ask them to show themselves in the most appropriate way for you. Sit quietly and wait for them to approach. Don't rush the process. Let them come in their time. Remain in a state of trust and love.

After a moment, if you are relaxed and focused, you will experience something which is personal for you. You might have an image of a face flash in front of you. You may see a particular colour or smell a certain essence. You might suddenly have goose bumps as you feel a host of beautiful, disparate energies gently enter your aura. You could sense twinkling stars all around you. You may have a tickly sensation in your stomach or experience a sudden well of love from your heart chakra. You might feel a prickle of tears or a lump in your throat. You may sense a very light breeze float across your face. Some people simply enter a state of knowing, where words and images are unnecessary.

This is often an extremely emotional experience. Don't worry if tears well up in your eyes. Smile broadly if you want to. Take in a big breath and then let out a deep sigh of relief. You never feel alone when you establish contact with your spiritual guides. It is love and nourishment on a profound level. Entering this state is a very moving experience.

When you have adjusted to this new level of awareness,

continue your contact with these energies. Thank them for coming to you. Ask that they let themselves be known to you as and when the time is right. Ask if there is someone there who can make their presence known to you now. Is there a guide with whom you can start to work who will assist you on your spiritual path?

As you progress deeper, you may find words coming into your throat or into your head. You may be told a name. You may be given a shower of golden light and love to help heal you. Whatever you feel will be loving and comforting. Always acknowledge their divine love and guidance with thanks and love.

Don't worry if you see nothing and have no pictorial images at all during this time. Spiritual guides work on a different energy. They place little significance on seeing physical bodies, although they will manifest themselves into an image if it's important or necessary for your own growth. Concentrate on what you sense, feel and hear during this time. Keep asking questions of your guides if you need more help.

Don't be surprised if they don't answer everything as completely as you would like. Remember they are there to guide and nurture you, not to live your life for you! Often guides speak in what initially appears as a guarded or veiled manner which you may find frustrating. It is simply that you have to put in some work, too. All spiritual awareness comes through practice and continued meditation. You will have to return to connecting with your guides on many occasions to forge a strong bond with them.

They will let you know when you have had enough of their time. Although your guides may be more evolved than you, they are also working on their own spiritual paths. They have to get on with their own work, too. You probably won't think of this during your first communication and it's likely you will not want it to end. It is such a loving, comforting, nurturing state in which to rest, that it is very hard to leave sometimes. You will want to stay in that deeply tender, safe sphere for as long as possible. However, you can return at another time and they will still be there for you.

Send them love and thanks as they gently move out of your aura again. You may intuitively feel some staying closer to you than others. Some spirits work on such high vibrations that they can feel very far away sometimes. Others work nearer to Earth itself.

Now cleanse and close down. Closing down is particularly important. You have been working at such high vibrational levels that it's possible you may feel very disconnected from your physical body. Go through your grounding techniques and pull the grounding energy up into your body. Protect yourself with your cloak of light. Now focus on your breathing. Do you feel centred again? Open your eyes. Does the room still feel light and bright and rather far away? Close your eyes again. Go through each chakra and close them down, one by one. Protect each one. Put another cloak of protection around you. Open your eyes. Now sit quietly for a few minutes. Drink a glass of mineral water. Then get up and walk around, checking you are well-grounded as you do so.

Of all the exercises you have done so far, this one particularly needs grounding afterwards. You will have 'flown' to higher levels in your spiritual body and it can make you feel very disconnected from Earth afterwards if you do not concentrate on grounding and focusing yourself. Always have a few quiet minutes to readjust after this meditation.

Return to this exercise whenever you need help and guidance. The more you work at this deeper level, the easier it is to access. It also becomes very private and personal. You do not ever have to discuss with others how you work with your guides. You will find that you develop your own way of communicating which works well for you. You may only ever sense them around you with a loving, warm energy. You might always have the same sensation, like a flicker of light in the corner of your eye or a warm tingle in your solar plexus, and that will let you know some spiritual helper is at hand. Some people go on to have clear visual images of their guides through their brow chakra, their 'third eye', which is where clairvoyant experiences take place. Some will also carry on silent, protracted conversations with their guides in which an exchange of spiritual information takes place. The throat chakra is very active during that process.

The process of actually seeing your guides is a slightly contentious one. It has often been commented by sceptics (and fairly so) that whenever people talk about their spiritual guides they always seem to have a Native American, an Egyptian god or a Chinese sage with a long white beard! In fact, as each soul goes through many reincarnations and spiritual guides are wise souls who have experienced a great deal, they are likely to have been a host of other people during their lifetimes. They could just as easily have been a potato farmer or a drains inspector! The guides have no interest in their physical appearance; gender is also unimportant to them. It is we as humans who put great faith into a physical countenance. A guide may show itself to you as a native American in full headdress and war paint simply because it will create a stronger energy for you. If it showed itself as a rough, hunched farmer in dirty old trousers and boots, you might be less impressed! In fact, it is all irrelevant because it is the soul we connect with and are taught by. The outer, physical appearance has no importance in spiritual awareness. It is also a helpful analogy to make us consider how we respond to physical appearances and what we could learn from our reactions.

Always remember that your guide approaching you should be a wonderful experience. If you are not happy with what comes to you, you must always cleanse it away. Just as there are loving and nurturing souls who are there to help, there are also mischievous, troublesome energies who love to meddle and cause mayhem. This does not mean that they are evil or bad, they are often simply misguided. Their own energies are not balanced and they are working through their own difficulties. If you draw one of these towards you, you must also take responsibility for bidding it goodbye. After experiencing the joy of spiritual guides, you will always know if an energy is not helpful. Refuse to let any energy affect you unless it is pure and unconditionally loving. This does not mean to say that spiritual guides are without humour. They can often be very amusing in their speech and actions, but their behaviour should always come from a state of unconditional loving and not cause upset or hurt to anyone else.

A great deal has also been written lately about angels and fairies and the possible existence of either. Angels, in particular, have received a resurgence of attention and enthusiasm in the past few years. Many respected healers and psychics often hold angel workshops, which are geared to you attuning with your own personal angel. This is basically yet another method through which you can contact your spiritual guides. If your guide manifests itself as an angel and this works well with your own energies, it can be a powerful introduction to communicating with your guides. If you know a reputable, established healer or psychic who is holding one of these workshops, you could try attending one and see whether accessing angel energies is a way for you to increase your spiritual perceptions. Trying different methods can be helpful and enlightening, provided you always work from a state of unconditional love and gratitude.

CUTTING TIES

This is really the reverse of finding our spiritual helpers. Tie-cutting is an additional and very powerful tool which we can use to separate ourselves from other people or from other energies which we know we are holding on to for the wrong reasons. These reasons can be various and all are relevant.

You may have lost a loved one and are still struggling with your sadness. You may have finished a relationship but still feel irresistibly drawn to the other person, although you know it is unhealthy. You may feel dominated by someone. You may be frightened of someone around you now or from your past. You may feel guilt or overprotective love towards someone else. Of course, you will already have worked at releasing some of these unwanted connections and emotions through the exercises in Part One, such as Releasing Resentment (page 130), Physically/Verbally/Emotionally/Mentally Releasing Anger (pages 143–51) and Releasing Blocks Through Visualisation (page 166). They are all excellent exercises to help you deal with emotions. However, tie-cutting is different in that it works at a much deeper spiritual level. It is extremely powerful. It can also be an overwhelming experience because it operates at such a high level of consciousness. Tie-cutting is not recommended for everyone but if you feel up to the experience, it can be wonderfully liberating.

It is also important to look at what tie-cutting means. It is about letting go of unwanted, unhelpful, unnecessary and unhealthy ties between people. It is about letting go so you can take responsibility for yourself. It is about releasing negative emotions. It is also about continuing to love unconditionally. Tie-cutting is not about shutting yourself off or shutting the other person off. It is energy restored to the perfect balance of unconditional love.

In the case of people mourning someone who has died, tie-cutting is doubly important. You may have experienced, or know someone else who has experienced, the sensation of a person who has died still being near and around all the time. Close relatives and friends who pass on often come back to us in spirit form. Sometimes this is just as loving protection and they come and go as necessary. On other occasions, it can be because they are loathe to physically leave the person on Earth with whom they formed such a strong bond.

There is a clear distinction between these two situations. It is one thing to have a loved one periodically keeping an eye on us and sending us love. It is quite another to have a disembodied soul who is not moving forward on their spiritual plane because they are still too connected to the Earth plane, possibly by a cord connecting them with the person who is still alive. Remember, when we die, our souls pass on to other spheres for further learning processes. If we spend too much time grieving needlessly over the loss of a loved one, we can inadvertently hinder the other soul from moving on. It is rather as though an invisible thread were still connecting you to the person you have lost to the other side. If you know that you still have a powerful bond with someone who has died and you feel it is an unhealthy sadness and longing which has stayed with you, then you might consider looking at how you can let go. Remember, this does not stop unconditional love from flowing between you.

Cutting ties technique

This following exercise will work on both the levels we have been discussing. It will help you to let go of someone who has died with whom you still feel too strong a connection. It will also help you if you do this exercise with someone who is still alive but whose energies you feel are unhealthily tangled with your own.

You want to be relaxed throughout this exercise, so lie down if that feels comfortable for you. Concentrate on your breath and focus on releasing tension in your body. Open up when you feel ready and pull the Cosmic Energy down into your body and aura.

Now create the perfect setting for yourself. It might be a park

*or forest, seashore or lake. Put yourself wherever you know
you feel best. Create your setting so that it lives and breathes
for you. Smell it, taste it, feel it, see it, hear it.*

*When you're ready, place yourself comfortably within it,
preferably on solid earth, not on a body of water. Choose a
natural form of protection around you, whichever you
respond to best. It might be a clear crystal in which you sit.
It can be a glasshouse or a ray of white light from above.
You might want to simply draw a circle around you and
your aura. Choose the protection which best suits you, but
have it be in addition to your usual cloak of protection.*

*When you are comfortable and protected, then create an identical
form of protection opposite you. If you are in a crystal, place a
crystal of the same size near you. If you are in a glasshouse,
make an identical one opposite you. These two protective sources
should be very close to each other without actually touching.
Now place the person with whom you want to cut the ties in the
other protective enclosure. Face each other. (If you are particularly
frightened of the person with whom you need to cut the ties, you
can just put a full-size photo of them in their space.)*

*Take a few deep breaths to focus yourself. Then look at the
energy between the two of you. Study it intently. Where are the
cords which bind you? You may feel these ties or you may see
them as thread or cords connecting you to each other. You
may see that certain chakras are connected to each other.
Sometimes, if the connection is still very tangled, you may see
a mass of tangled, thick rope which crisscrosses back and forth
between you. Some people see the ties as bright beams of light
or dark grey tunnels. You might see steel piping through which
the energy flows back and forth. Whatever you see is real for
you and a suitable image with which you can work.*

*Now you have to consciously cut those ties. What you use is
another personal choice. Some people cut them simply through*

using their mind and watching the ties unravel and fall to the ground. Some mentally take a pair of golden scissors and cut the strings or cords. If it is thick rope or steel, you might need to call upon a golden axe or chain saw. If you see the ties as light, you might want to create a laser beam to sever the connections. Develop your own strategy which works for you.

You must cut all *the ties. This is essential, whoever you are tie-cutting with.* Cut all the ties. *If you are tie-cutting because you feel overly drawn to someone but feel scared about letting them go completely, it is tempting to decide that you will just leave one or two connections. It will not work. Tie-cutting only works when all ties are completely removed. Remember you can never cut unconditional love. Unconditional love is universal and infinite. It will always flow between you. If there are many ties between you, the tie-cutting can last a long time. You may find that ties try to re-create themselves after you have disconnected them. Cut them again.*

It is important that you establish control over the tie-cutting process. It is you who decides to keep the bonds going between you and it is also only you who can help sever them. Even if the other person is still hanging on to you, you can still keep cutting the ties they try to create. If you take control, you will find the ties do not remanifest themselves.

Depending upon your relationship with the person concerned, this can be an uplifting and energising process. It can feel very liberating to release old, stale ties which are doing nothing to further either one of you. It can also be deeply sad and cause pain and tears. Whatever emotion the tie-cutting creates for you, stay with the emotion. Do not shut it off. Let yourself be sad or hurt or whatever emotion is real for you. This is part of your healing process.

When you have finished cutting the ties, you will need to spiritually heal any wounds which may have been created by the cutting process. Sometimes people see the cutting as causing a rip or tear in their aura or a blockage in their chakra, or in the other person's energy field. Some people even see spiritual 'blood' from the cutting. So wherever you have made cuts, you need to spiritually heal. Visualise a bright beam of white light and see it healing over the tender area. You might prefer to use a stream of intense silver light which is often used in spiritual surgery. Place the light upon the area and see it heal and repair any damage. (If you are a visual person and want to create a torch or laser beam for this, do so. Some people just prefer to create the process through thought.)

When that is complete, you then need to get rid of the old ties and cords which are lying around. Again, use your own preferred method for this. Gather them all together and light a fire in which they burn into nothingness. Throw them into a fast-moving stream and watch them swirl away. Are you in a bathing area? Perhaps the threads will wash away through the plughole. Throwing them into the sea is not a good option as the waves may toss them back upon the beach. You might see the sun melt them into the ground or see them sucked up into the universe through a cyclone of energy. Use whatever works for you but don't *hold on to any of them. You should always finish empty and re-energised.*

Now settle back into your protective space. Send the other person on their way with unconditional love but without ties. Let them go. This can be emotional. Let them go and know that it is a healing process for both of you. Then focus on yourself. How are you feeling now? Heal any spiritual wounds with your white or silver beams. Then cleanse thoroughly in your cleansing sanctuary. Wash away any residue emotion. Be gentle with yourself. Sit for a while in your private space and feel yourself gradually become balanced again.

Now close your chakras, one by one, again checking for any wounds at each centre. Heal them again if necessary with

the white or silver beam. Protect each chakra individually.
Now cover yourself with your cloak of protection from head
to toe. Sit quietly for a few minutes and concentrate on your
breathing. Remember where you are and what time of day it
is. Open your eyes when you are ready. Check you are well
grounded before you get up.

This is not an easy exercise. It reinforces just how much we tie and
bind ourselves to others, not necessarily with any positive purpose
or outcome. Letting go spiritually is very hard. We may already have
let go physically. We may be halfway to letting go emotionally and
mentally. Letting go spiritually is a very profound experience which
must be handled delicately and sensitively. Do not worry if you feel
you have to go back over the tie-cutting exercise a number of times
before you can let go. Most people cannot let go in just one session.

There are also physical steps you can take to cut ties. Are you
holding on to items of clothing or objects belonging to this person?
Return them or give them away to charity shops. Do you still have
their photos around? Burn them or give them away. Remember,
however, that you do not want to confuse these actions with cutting
yourself off from those with whom you share a healthy love, respect
and spiritual connection. It is wonderful to have gifts and mementos
from friends and loved ones around you. It is only necessary to get
rid of items if they are creating unhealthy bonds which stifle or
suffocate. Make sure you acknowledge the difference.

The other important aspect with tie-cutting is that we all have
lessons to learn from the ties we form with others. Look at the
people with whom you want to cut ties and first ask yourself what
it is you have to learn from this relationship. You might benefit
from going back over your earlier healing chart and diary. Is this
person just part of a continuous, unwelcome cycle which you have
yet to break in your life? What is your spiritual gift from this
person? Always acknowledge the positive offering that comes with
this experience. This helps you to give the essential unconditional
love with which you can both move on to freedom and holistic
health. It can turn what you might once have seen as a negative
episode in your life, into an enriching and healing experience.

MOVING FORWARD

You have worked your way through a great number of new concepts about what spiritual healing really entails and you have been encouraged to look at new ways of attaining holistic health, both for yourself and others. Not all of what you have read may have been palatable for you and there may still be areas with which you cannot agree. That is excellent! We only learn through questioning and constantly checking what we know to be 'reality'. Accepting everything without question will not actually help you to learn anything.

Keep that questioning mind. Develop it further. Every time you are introduced to a new thought or concept, ask yourself why you doubt it. What is it that does not make sense or feels wrong? Very often it is simply the fact that we have not discussed it before. The more you know about spiritual healing and the more research you do into the matter, the more you realise that we are simply uncovering what has been known for centuries. We are not doing anything new; we are rediscovering what has always been available to us.

In remote areas of the world there are people who live in a truly holistic way, without the help of modern medicine or drugs, and free from pollution, small wars, overcrowding and processed, synthetic foods. They attain ages which we consider extraordinary – well over 100 years old. If they were to be removed from their natural setting to our environment, they would almost certainly quickly become ill, and represent a fast-forwarded version of what has happened to us.

Remember to keep the balance between your physical world and your new spiritual awareness. It is important that we learn to slow down, assess our immediate physical surroundings and work to minimise the negative effects of pollution, overpopulation and deeply unhealthy lifestyles. This attention to our physical surroundings is important. All the spiritual awareness and sensitivity in the universe is not enough unless we also address what is around us. We have been placed on Earth to address the needs of our planet now. Where is the benefit of sitting in deep meditation for an hour each day if we then go out and continue to pollute not just ourselves, but those around us, with insensitive behaviour? Rather, use spiritual advice and guidance to show you how you can best help yourself and others.

Working in the community and working with individuals to improve your own living conditions is a deeply spiritual process. Some of the people who do the most wonderful work today are the unsung heroes of charities affiliated to helping relieve the stress and trauma of everyday living.

Remember, we need to balance all of ourselves before we can know true health. How we try to accomplish this balance can be a constant challenge throughout our life. However, do not confuse spiritual enlightenment with having the perfect excuse to withdraw from society. Constantly strive to balance the emotional, mental, spiritual and physical aspects in you. Whatever you feel you have learned from this book, please go out and share it with others and encourage them to try alternative methods of healing.

This does not mean you should try to impose your will on others. It does not mean you should ever advise people to give up conventional treatment. Suggest they try something small, like deep breathing or a gentle meditation to help them relax, as an addition and complement to traditional methods of healing. If people choose to continue their sole belief in orthodox medicine, let them do so. Do not try to force your opinions on others, but simply adhere to spiritual healing yourself in all its positive aspects so that your own persona can be an inspiration for others. Show people how it works by example, rather than by constant preaching or 'talking at' them. Always respect and listen to other people's opinions.

Another difficult area, once you start to work more deeply with spiritual healing and to feel its undoubted benefits, is how you handle orthodox treatment should it be deemed necessary by your doctor. What do you do if, despite all your work with spiritual healing, your doctor says you must have an operation? Some spiritual healers would say that if you work deeply enough on your own spiritual body, you can heal any condition without having to resort to hospital treatment. They are entitled to their belief system, although they should be wary of trying to impose this thought process on anyone else. Hopefully you will have benefited so much from your spiritual healing that you will not find yourself in a position where a hospital stay is necessary. However, should it occur, consider the following approach.

Use time in hospital and any surgery or traditional treatment as a powerful, additional tool in your own spiritual healing. Accept the orthodox treatment with love and gratitude, embrace the wonders of modern science and give thanks for its physical benefits. Then use alternative healing methods as well.

- *Take homeopathic tablets such as arnica for shock and bruising.*
- *Use the Bach Flower Rescue Remedy.*
- *Sprinkle a soothing essence of lavender or marjoram on a cotton wool ball and keep it by your pillow.*
- *Take a smartphone or iPad with you and listen to your favourite, healing music in hospital.*
- *Place an appropriate crystal under your pillow or on your table.*
- *Wear underwear or pyjamas in your favourite colour.*
- *Prop up pictures of those you love by you.*
- *Ask a friend or relative to bring in healthy food so you can use it as a complement to hospital food, which is often not as nurturing as it might be.*
- *Use any hours of free time as a wonderful opportunity for you to practise different meditations and for you to learn more about the spiritual reasons behind this illness. Ask for spiritual healing from a higher consciousness. You will probably have plenty of time to do this as you recuperate.*

In other words, embrace the gifts that an illness gives you and be open to learning the lessons from it. Whatever orthodox treatment you may be given, use it to help the healing process. If drugs have to be put into your system, then bless them as they enter and ask that they be distributed helpfully and wisely throughout your body. Acknowledge the doctors and nurses for the healing they give you and express your appreciation to them. Let the energies that flow from and around you be open, loving and receptive to all healthy vibrations.

Make sure you also protect yourself from any unhealthy energies at the same time. Of course, hospitals and doctors' surgeries lend themselves to all sorts of discordant vibrations. Know when to close yourself down and remember to protect yourself, particularly as you drift off to sleep. Use your visualisation techniques and imagine a beautiful crystal in a colour which is right for you completely encasing you and the bed on which you lie. Or create a filter screen around you which filters out the negative energies but allows all the positive frequencies to infiltrate and heal you.

Use every known method available to you to assist your healing process, while not resenting or fearing any orthodox treatment you are having. Know that when you leave the hospital, you have undergone a positive experience which has left you wiser, happier, healthier and more loving and appreciative of all that is around you.

Continue to read and to learn about all aspects of spiritual healing. Attend different lectures, courses and workshops on different types of healing. Learn for yourself what works, not what somebody else tells you should work. Be wary of deciding that any one healer has the definitive solution for perfect spiritual healing. Every one of us is constantly learning and striving for further awareness and knowledge. Hopefully, what you know today will only be a small portion of what you know in a year's time. Never believe you know it all, or that you know most of what there is to know, or even that you now know everything you need to know to be an effective spiritual healer. You can never know too much.

It is also recommended that you think extremely carefully before deciding, at any point, to charge for spiritual healing. Many professional healers do charge fees and it is their sole means of income. They believe it is right for them to do so. However, charging money does change the vibrations of spiritual healing. It takes the work into a different realm and can cause great complications with healing energies. This is not to say that it is always wrong. It is simply important for you to realise that when finances become involved, spiritual healing moves on to another level. Do think long and hard before moving into that realm as you may not feel comfortable with the additional pressures and stresses this can create for you and the people you are healing.

Other healing processes

Although this book has attempted to cover in some detail the major forms of spiritual healing that have become well-established practices, you should also be aware that there is a whole host of other spiritually-related healing processes (often labelled as alternative medicine) which you may also want to learn something about in the future. Below is a list of some of these:

Acupuncture involves the insertion of needles into various energy meridians within the body to relieve blockages and increase energy flow (mentioned briefly during our discussions on energies within the human form).

The **Alexander Technique** helps realign the the body (through thought processes and awareness) to allow the maximum flow of healthy energy throughout both the physical and subtle bodies.

The 38 **Bach Flower Remedies** are distillations of the energy (or life force) of different wild flowers in the form of tinctures which are then used to re-balance human energies.

Bioenergetics and Core Energetics form a system which works to release specified, unhealthy energy patterns (called character structures) and thereby improve interactions of energy between people.

Chiropractic and Osteopathy are virtually accepted nowadays as orthodox medical treatment, but tests indicate this form of manipulation of the body (particularly of the spine) positively affects several layers of the human aura as well.

Feng Shui is the Chinese art of living harmoniously within a given space. This is determined by the geographical location involving relationships to water and ley lines, the stars, animals and even neighbours and roads, as well as the physical structure of the space itself.

Homeopathy uses medication obtained from the energy of different herbs which are processed in a precise manner. Detailed diagnosis is necessary for positive results.

Hypnosis is using deep states of relaxation to access further information which then encourages the release of energy blockages. Also used as a means to reprogramme the subconscious negative 'recordings' we have running through our head.

Iridology is the study of the eye to ascertain energy imbalances and also past history of illnesses within the body. This is used primarily as a diagnostic tool.

Kirlian photography refers to electrophotography of the aura (often of the hands) to determine energy imbalances and blockages. Used primarily as a diagnostic tool.

Macrobiotics involves the intake of food which is balanced through yin and yang (feminine and masculine) energies. Also considers the location in which the food is grown and the season and acknowledges the individual's energy needs.

Morphogenetics is the study of invisible fields of organised energy which could also be called group energies or even group consciousness. An example is the famous experiment, known as the Hundredth Monkey Principle, conducted by the eminent biologist Lyall Watson. He discovered that when a group of monkeys on one island were taught a new behaviour, another group of monkeys on a separate island began to exhibit the same behaviour, although there had been no communication between the two groups.

Radionics involves a machine (often called 'the black box') used to broadcast energies into the human aura. The level of frequency used is determined by a diagnosis given from a sample of a patient's hair or blood. Patients need not be physically present in the room for the benefits to be received by them.

Rebirthing uses a deep state of relaxation to regress back to the time of birth and thereby release any trauma and subsequent energy imbalance from that experience.

Shamanism is an ancient practice which utilises different techniques (often involving sound) to access spiritual consciousness.

Transactional Analysis is a diagnostic tool which enables you to assess your relationships with others based on adult, child and parent behavioural patterns. Can be useful to help ascertain energy imbalances.

These are only a small sample of what is out there for you to explore and learn about. You need not spend a lot of money to learn, either. Spend a morning or afternoon in your local library and work your way through the complementary or alternative medicine section. Go into your local health shop and take a good look at all the foods and remedies which are now available. Attend any spiritual or psychic fairs you can and simply wander around them observing people and different energies. Notice what stalls you are drawn to and why. Steer clear of any which make you feel uncomfortable. Explore New Age shops and discover new concepts and healing treatments.

If you can afford it, treat yourself to a healing technique to which you feel drawn. It could be reflexology or aromatherapy or a session with an established spiritual healer. Enrol on a course which will help you further your own healing energies. There are many reputable healing courses on offer nowadays but make sure you meet the teacher before you sign up. Check that you feel happy with the attitude of the teacher and the techniques being taught.

If you want to continue healing others, as well as yourself, remember to keep going back and re-reading the exercises and meditations. You will find them listed under the contents. It is easy to slip into bad habits after even a short period of time. You can forget to close down and protect yourself properly. You may forget to drink plenty of water afterwards or to offer it to the person you are healing. Simple tools can be forgotten if not used regularly. Never underestimate your enormous responsibility towards not just yourself, but the people you are healing. Constantly reassess your own progress and techniques. It is very helpful for you to keep your healing diary up to date. Regularly look back over it and notice your progress, whilst also acknowledging the areas in which you repeatedly feel stuck. You may find you have certain exercises which you enjoy doing and others which you avoid. Do you avoid them because you are also avoiding certain issues in your life that need healing? Keep looking for new ideas and methods through which you can learn and grow.

The spiritual surgery revisited

Now we are going to return to the very first exercise which you came across in the Introduction to this book. Do you remember your spiritual surgery and how it first appeared to you? Let us take a return journey and see how you have progressed. Work through the following exercise when you are ready.

Close your eyes, relax and focus your thoughts. Breathe deeply. Remember your previous visit to the spiritual surgery and what you felt. What did you discover during that time? Can you remember your sense of wonderment at the possibility of what healing medicine was available? Now you want to return and see what else is there for you to discover.

When you're ready, imagine the clean, white door in front of you which is closed. Go up to the white handle, open the door and walk inside.

What do you see? This will be personal, according to your own spiritual growth. The space may seem even bigger and brighter now. You may see quite different medicines and healing tools. Perhaps you are shown some of the healing techniques which you know to be effective. Maybe you see crystals, colours, homeopathic medicines, musical instruments and even other items you may not yet recognise. Are there names written on boxes and items you do not know? Perhaps you will be shown new forms of protection such as shields and filters of different shapes and sizes. Maybe you see protective symbols and animals. You may notice different scents which you have yet to explore. It is for you to discover for yourself.

Spend some time wandering around this wonderful spiritual surgery. What else is there that you now need to study and work with? Keep approaching different 'medicines' and healing tools and see what they are. If you do not know, ask for some help with your exploration. You may even find that a medical spirit or guide manifests itself to help you through this new voyage of discovery. Thank them for being with you and ask them to show you everything possible.

Is there an area in the spiritual surgery to which you feel particularly drawn? What is taking place there? What do you know about it already? What is there for you still to learn?

Realise as you move around that it truly is an infinite space. You could never explore it all in one lifetime. Resolve that you will do what you can during this incarnation.

When the time is right, you will be guided back to the white door. Give thanks for the new forms of healing you have seen and then step outside again. Remember you are back in your chair. Cleanse and close yourself down. Protect yourself. Sit quietly with your eyes closed and reflect upon the new spiritual healing tools. Feel appreciation for everything you have been given. Then bring your attention to your physical body and notice how well-grounded you are. Focus on the grounding energy before you open your eyes and reorient yourself.

Were you shown new and wonderful items you could not even identify? Did you have sensations and emotions which were hard to explain? Perhaps there was a different scent in your nostrils from anything you have ever experienced before. Maybe new spectrums of colour were shown to you. Whatever you experienced, move forward with that knowledge. Use it as an incentive to help you continue along your personal path of spiritual awareness. You may want to return to the spiritual surgery again in the future to guide you towards other methods of healing you have yet to explore.

However you choose to move forward with your spiritual healing, always acknowledge the help, guidance and unconditional love which you receive from that source of higher consciousness, irrespective of any name you choose to call it. Continually improve your relationship with this divine energy. Never feel embarrassed to give thanks and to feel deep appreciation for what you have and for what you are learning. The stronger your relationship becomes with this power, the more effective you will be as a healer, both for yourself and others.

Above all, enjoy every step of the new path you are walking upon and encourage others to likewise embrace their own spiritual awareness.

CLOSING PRAYER

Divine Source of all love and knowledge,
thank you for your protection
and guidance.
I place all my trust in you
and ask that you continue to lead me
along my soul's true path.
I give thanks for the lessons I am learning
and ask that I be shown how to help others
through the realm of true,
unconditional love.
May we as a universe always be blessed
with love, light, health and happiness.

HEALING TOOLS MEMO

This section is to help you make notes about your personal experiences with some of the additional healing tools. It can be interesting and insightful to have a written record of how your thoughts have changed. You can use the prompts in this section as the basis of a diary to increase your awareness of different aspects of healing.

What you choose to write is not about being right or wrong; you will simply record your experiences at various stages of working with pendulums, crystals, colours and sounds.

Re-read your notes occasionally and assess how the healing tools have helped increase your awareness of yourself and others.

PENDULUMS

My First Attempt
The object and type of string/thread I used:

What happened:

Further Attempts
The different pendulums I tried and how they felt:

Which pendulum worked best for me:

Establishing Movements
What means 'neutral'

What means 'yes'

What means 'no

Further Experiences
How I felt about using the pendulum with my chakras and what I learnt:

Other occasions when I used the pendulum and what happened:

What works best for me and my pendulum now
(update this section as you like):

CRYSTALS

First Experiences
The crystals I was drawn to initially (colour, size and shape):

My first crystal and why I chose it:

My first experience of tuning into my crystal:

Further Experiences

The crystals I chose to have around me (list them):

Different ways I experimented with my crystals:

What worked well/didn't work well:

How I felt using crystals with my chakras:

The crystals I choose to have around me now, and why
(update as appropriate):

COLOURS

First Impressions
The colours I was drawn to initially:

The colours I avoided initially:

How the colours may relate to my chakras:

Further Colour Awareness
Colour(s) I chose to concentrate on and why:

What this taught me about myself and others:

Which colours were easy/difficult to create:

How this experience has altered my perception/appreciation of colour:

Colours I feel most comfortable with now (update as you like):

SOUNDS

First Experiences

Sounds I am drawn to:

Sounds I dislike:

Further Experiences

How I felt working with the seven notes of the musical scale:

How my chakras were affected by the musical scale:

How I felt using the vowel sounds together with the musical notes:

How this has now altered my awareness of sounds:

Sounds I now choose to have around me (update as you wish):